Gomułka:
His Poland,
His Communism

Gomułka:
His Poland,
His Communism

Nicholas Bethell

HOLT, RINEHART AND WINSTON
New York · Chicago · San Francisco

The photographs are reproduced by courtesy of
R.S.W. "Prasa," Warsaw.

SBN: 03-082873-2
Printed in the United States of America

CONTENTS

Sixteen pages of black and white photographs follow page 184.

Gomułka:
His Poland,
His Communism

I: GOMUŁKA BEFORE POLAND

When Władysław Gomułka was born in 1905 there was no Poland. The country was divided up between Poland's powerful neighbours—Prussia, Austria-Hungary and tsarist Russia. The Polish language, though not suppressed, was nowhere official. Every Pole who wanted to advance his career had to learn either German or Russian, for these were the languages of power in eastern and central Europe. Poland, although her people were a large national group, was insignificant. In 1667 she had ruled a large empire. 'From sea to sea,' the Poles called it—from the Baltic to the Black Sea. In 1772 she was still a large country with an eastern frontier reaching nearly to Kiev. But in the late eighteenth century three territorial assaults were made on her by her neighbours. Three times she was partitioned. By 1795, the year of the Third Partition, she was entirely consumed.

Gomułka's heritage was a country which for more than a century had been ruled by foreigners. It was a period long enough to give Poles a complex, an obsession about patriotism and about their country's independence. The first line of their national anthem, 'Poland is not yet entirely lost . . .', typifies the mixture of defeatism and defiance with which Poles entered the twentieth century. Most of them had by then developed a hatred of both Russia and Germany.

Gomułka grew up with these normal Polish feelings of intense patriotism and resentment against Poland's eastern and western neighbours. But his upbringing and background were not those of a typical Pole. In the mid-nineteenth century (1831–48) there occurred a Great Emigration from Poland. Some 10,000 of the most talented Poles, including the poet Adam Mickiewicz and the composer Fryderyk Chopin, left their country to work abroad. A tradition was begun. As in Ireland and other foreign-occupied countries, it became

I

normal for the more ambitious elements to leave Poland and seek their fortune abroad. Gomułka's father, Jan, and mother, Kunegunda, did this. They emigrated to the United States where Jan Gomułka worked in the New York slaughterhouses and the Pennsylvania coal mines. They had two daughters: Józefa, two or three years older than Władysław, who lived her life in Detroit and recently died, and Ludwika who was killed tragically in a fire in Krosno in 1965.

The adventure did not succeed: the *émigré* Gomułkas did not like America. Shortly before Władysław was born they returned to their home town of Krosno, between Cracow and Lwów (Lemberg) in the part of Poland ruled by Austria-Hungary. Jan Gomułka worked in the local oil-fields, living at 3 Mostowa Street in the Białobrzegi district of Krosno, and there Władysław Gomułka was born on 6 February, 1905.

No one is yet in a position to write a complete biography of this man. The writer needs access to so many inaccessible sources: the files of the between-the-wars Polish police, the *dwójka* (the *deuxième bureau*) and the *granatowa policja* (the'blue police'), the files of the Communist Party and of the post-war Workers' Party, the files of the Gestapo and the UB (the Polish security police during the Stalinist years). No westerner is allowed to read such information in Poland, let alone to publish it. And the Poles who can refer to these exclusive files are not allowed to write biographies of Gomułka. So the man is, for the moment, partially inscrutable. The full facts about him are locked away in closely guarded drawers. He does not like personal publicity. It seems to him un-Marxist for a socialist leader to be photographed, discussed, dissected and reported in the western style, for a communist to be treated like a film star. He fears the 'cult of personality' as practised by Stalin and, to a lesser extent, by Nikita Khrushchev. Gomułka fought against it and suffered under it. He dislikes it, even if later he found it necessary to adopt some of its manifestations.

But there are abundant published sources. Gomułka has not been able to shun the limelight completely, since his presence has for twenty-five years been so devastatingly felt in Poland. This could not have been achieved without some projection of the personality, without placing some restriction on the man's natural modesty and retiring nature. Whether he likes it or not Gomułka is widely talked about and written about all over eastern Europe. Although the man himself has been simple and withdrawn, his career and political role have been flamboyant. Twice, in 1945 and in 1956, he has reached the top—as head of his country's ruling communist party. Frequently, in 1926, in 1932, in 1936, then again in 1951, he has been at the bottom —abused and imprisoned for his political beliefs. His life, since 1941 at least, has followed the line of a sine-curve. Since 1941 the zeniths and nadirs have followed at almost exact five-year intervals.

This book is a biography of a man who, by his example if not by his actual achievement, changed the course of recent European history. Gomułka is, apart from Marshal Tito, the only European communist leader to have successfully challenged the autocracy of Stalin. He lived, not only to tell the tale, but also to win back political power. His defiance was in many ways greater than that of Tito. Poland was essential to Stalin. It has a 400-mile eastern border with the Soviet Union. It was and is vital to the Soviet Army's east European communications. A man who challenged the extent of Soviet influence in Poland, as Gomułka did in 1948, was challenging the whole basis of Stalin's postwar military and foreign policies. To do this when he was, unlike Tito, effectively in Stalin's power was an act of extreme bravery.

Gomułka was the first to show that a communist government can rule a country, even one with a predominantly non-communist population, in a peaceful and orderly manner without an extensive use of police terror. He was the first to give a communist country freedom of speech (though not freedom of written expression) and certain other important freedoms: foreign travel, no jamming of foreign broadcasts, wide cultural exchange with the West. At the same time he has consolidated the communist rule which in 1956 seemed to be called into question. In a dozen years of rule he has established his personality over the whole shape of Polish politics. His name has become an 'ism'. 'Gomułkaism' was seen in the east Europe of 1951 as a dangerous, traitorous heresy. By 1957 it was, to most east Europeans, an achievement to be envied and emulated. By 1968 it had become an object-lesson for the unwary reforming communist in how hard it is for liberal, progressive ideas to flourish under the influence of the Soviet system. Gomułka became, from the liberal point of view, a fallen angel, the victim of 1968, that tragic year for Poland.

Gomułka's life, which began in the year of the first Russian

Revolution, has been marked by a succession of violence and change. He has lived through seven Polands, each one quite different in its constitution and way of life. Born in the Poland of partition and three-power foreign rule, he spent his childhood during the First World War and saw in 1918 the transition to the Poland of parliamentary democracy and independence. This lasted until 1926, when the military leader Józef Piłsudski carried out a successful *coup d'état* and set up a military dictatorship. This system lasted beyond Piłsudski's death in 1935 until the German invasion of 1939, when Poland was once again occupied, partitioned and ruled by foreigners until the end of the war in 1945. A two-year period of limited parliamentary democracy followed, during which Poland was dominated by communists who still tolerated a genuine, legal opposition. By 1948 there was no legal opposition, instead there was Stalinist autocracy and widespread police terror. In 1954–56 Poland went through an interim period following Stalin's death in which the terror faded away and was replaced by confusion and doubt about the future of Poland. These doubts were resolved in 1956 with the arrival of Gomułka and 'Gomułkaism'. The years of 'Gomułkaism' have been the most stable years for Poland this century. Gomułka has ruled Poland for a dozen years, longer than any other Pole has done for 200 years.

Paradoxically, Gomułka's life, before 1956 so full of violence and sensation, has become sedate and biographically less interesting. He has ruled Poland firmly, seldom cruelly, but without imagination or flexibility. The man who was so boisterous and noisy in his opposition to various governments— Piłsudski-ite, Nazi or Stalinist—lost his flamboyance as soon as he himself began to govern. In the contemporary political scene his years of power have, of course, been the most significant and worthy of study. Historically, though, it may be that Gomułka will be remembered more for his years of opposition, for the lesson he taught other east European countries, perhaps unwillingly, in how to resist Russian absolutism, and for the lesson he taught himself in how to profit from it, and finally to absorb it as part of his foreign policy.

II: EDUCATION
AND AGITATION

Władysław Gomułka received very little formal education. His 1947 short biography claims he completed a primary course at his local school in Krosno, an old eighteenth-century building, still functioning and now called 'School No. 1'.[1] His school report dated 30 June 1917 states that at the age of twelve he had finished only one 'class'. On the other hand, the range of subjects he was studying—Polish, German, history, geography and geometry—indicates that he must have already attended classes, formally or not, for longer. He appears to have been an exemplary pupil. His marks in most subjects (including his two *bêtes noires* of later years, 'religion' and 'German') were excellent. Only in 'drawing' and 'singing' did his standards drop to the more modest mark 'satisfactory'.

The school was operating in wartime Austria-Hungary, although the language of instruction in Galicia, the province where Krosno lay, was Polish. Sadly one cannot now tell what progress Gomułka would have made. In the following year, 1918, came the end of the war, of Austria-Hungary and of Gomułka's schooldays. In 1919, aged fourteen, he went to work as a locksmith's apprentice. It was a three-year course and he had to work ten hours a day.

Gomułka's father was working in the oil industry, in what capacity it is not certain. Some say he was a locksmith, others a free-lance transporter of oil-drums by horse and cart. He was a poor man, but photographs of the family make it clear that they were not destitute, as some modern Polish writers have implied. 'A working man,' wrote Gomułka's biographer in 1947, 'had to work thirteen or more hours every day and could not afford to keep his family even in the most miserable conditions. Capitalists enjoyed the advantage that small children were forced to go out to work, and they were exploited in the most cynical manner.'

5

Władysław Gomułka was brought up as a socialist. His father Jan had cause to feel bitter towards the capitalist system after his abortive attempt to make good in the new world, after returning to Krosno and bringing up his children in poverty. Jan Gomułka took part in socialist political life and his son Władysław, even as a teenage locksmith's apprentice, followed his example. He took part in workers' demonstrations and celebrated the first of May as a workers' holiday.

Qualified as a locksmith, Władysław joined his father in the oil industry and worked in the refineries near Gorlice that formed part of the estate of Count Skrzyński. As yet he showed no sign of becoming a communist. The KPP was formed only when Poland was formed, in 1918, and consisted largely of men who believed in an imminent world revolution. He was too young to have become involved in the KPP's anti-Polish stand during the 1920 war against the Soviet Union. His inclination was more towards the socialist movement. When he was sixteen he joined *Siła* ('Strength'), the youth organisation of the Polish Socialist Party (the PPS).

The PPS was a strange, shapeless party. It covered almost the whole spectrum of Polish politics. Its membership ranged from right-wing military leaders like Józef Piłsudski to out-and-out crypto-communists and sympathisers with the Soviet Union. In 1921 Gomułka attended the second congress of *Siła*, held at Bielsk. He began to read about politics. Almost unschooled and untaught by others, he had to acquire the knack of teaching himself. He consumed the literary outpourings of marxist writers and the left-wing press. His political ideas, partially inherited from his father, crystallised during the early 1920s, the years of economic crisis in Poland.

Gomułka became a marxist. His absorbent, literal mind accepted the correctness of Marx and the basic goodwill of the Soviet Union. True, Soviet Russia had recently been a threat to Poland's new-found independence. But Soviet and Polish communist policies had changed. They no longer challenged Poland's existence. The communists had come to realise that Polish workers and peasants would not support them at all so long as they planned to absorb Poland into the Soviet Union. They dropped this part of their programme. However, communists like Gomułka saw the matter in a more complicated light than the average Polish worker. Independence is a relative term. Poland was still strongly influenced by foreign governments, especially the French, British and American. Foreigners had, after all, arranged for the creation of the Polish state. Much of the capital invested in the new state was foreign capital. Much of the profit from Polish industrial enterprises was being sent abroad to foreign shareholders. A predominantly agricultural country, Poland was forced to import almost all the manufactured goods she consumed. These she paid for by exporting her agricultural produce, a cheap commodity.

To many thinking, politically-conscious Poles, socialism was only common sense. Poland was, in a sense, being 'exploited'. In the 1920s rich men and rich governments had little of the present 'enlightened' approach towards young, newly-independent, developing countries. Anyone who gave 'aid' required the due return on his investment. Altruistic capitalism was a contradiction in terms. Differences between rich and poor, countries as well as individuals, were immense, greater than they are now. Indeed, the surprising thing about the Polish situation was that socialism was so weak, that the shapeless, artificially-created government was able to gather such support. But for the huge, threatening, socialist country to Poland's east, it would scarcely have been able to do so.

Socialism and communism were making slow progress in Poland, a newly-independent country, conscious of its new national identity and still wary of its two imperialist neighbours who had ruled Poland so recently. After all, it was in Germany and Russia that socialism was born and grew up.

One can imagine the dilemma and the torn feelings of Władysław Gomułka, a fifteen-year-old boy, when war broke out between Poland, the country he loved with normal Polish patriotic fervour, and Soviet Russia, the country he had grown to admire above all others for the brilliance and success of its socialist ideas. To the many non-Polish members of the Communist Party of Poland the issue was plain. The Soviet Union was *the* country. Loyalty to her must come above loyalty to Poland, a bourgeois and therefore transitional entity which had not existed two years before, and which might disappear any minute.

The KPP propaganda of the time is typified by a leaflet published in June 1920: 'Soldiers of the Polish army!' it called, 'Revolution in Poland will conquer only when you, Polish soldiers, stop obeying your traitorous leaders, when instead of fighting your brothers, the workers and peasants of Russia and the Ukraine, you turn your arms against your officers, the bourgeoisie and the landowners.' 'He who fights against Soviet Russia,' claimed the leaflet, 'fights against the working class of the whole world and is an enemy of the people.'[2]

Such sentiments were not well received by the Polish population at large; especially in August 1920, when the Red Army was lining the Vistula ready to attack the Polish capital and destroy the Polish army. True, the Poles did manage to turn the tables, win the war and sign an advantageous peace treaty with the Soviet Union. But by then there was good reason in most of their minds to hate the communists in their midst, to declare them traitors to their country and to declare the Communist Party illegal.

This short war illustrates the basic dilemma of Gomułka's political life. As a socialist he admired the Soviet Union. As a patriot he loved Poland. Were these two feelings incompatible? Was it possible to be a Pole, a communist and a patriot all at the same time? Most Poles thought not. Gomulka thought yes. He tried to come to terms with his dilemma. Only half a century later did he succeed in finding a satisfactory solution, and even then it was a satisfaction shared by few of his fellow-countrymen.

Gomułka's activity of the 1920s and 1930s is sparsely documented. Gomułka has written no memoirs, neither have his close friends nor members of his family. One cannot know for certain why Gomułka joined the Socialist Party (the PPS) rather than the communists. Clearly the KPP's anti-nationalism, obsession with 'world revolution' and support for Russia in the 1920 war played a part in his decision. But whatever doubts he may have had about Soviet foreign policy, he wavered not one inch in his support of communist ideology. He joined the marxist left-wing of the PPS, and in 1924 he was expelled from *Siła*, the PPS youth organisation, for his outspoken criticism of the rightist leadership of the Party. He called them 'reactionaries' and 'traitors to the working class'.[3] Clearly he was a communist already in all but name. The fact that he had not yet joined the KPP was a measure of the extent to which it was discredited. Gomułka went into trade-union work, organising the left wing of the Chemical Workers' Trade Union (the Związek Zawodowy Robotników Przemysłu Chemicznego).

About this time too he began his career as a political writer.

He contributed to *Trybuna Robotnicza*, the journal of the Union of Town and Country Proletariat (a communist-front organisation) and later to *Samopomoc Chłopska* ('Peasants' Self-help').[4]

1926 was the year in which Gomułka was twenty-one, in which he joined the Communist Party (the KPP) and in which he was arrested for the first time. His 1947 short biography claims that the Polish police took an interest in him from the start, but that until 1926 they confined themselves to searching his flat and observing his activities. Then on 1 May, a few days before Józef Piłsudski's *coup d'état*, he was arrested.* His biographer writes: 'In the days preceding the Piłsudski coup it was thought wise to render harmless such a keen agitator as Gomułka.' His crime was 'distributing a legal First of May leftist publication', the journal *Samopomoc Chłopska*. But on 12 May the coup took place. There were two or three days of desultory fighting before Wincenty Witos, the Peasant Party leader who had been democratically elected Premier, was pushed aside. (Witos was to emerge only nineteen years later in 1945. The last democratic Premier of Poland, it was inevitable that Stalin, Churchill and Truman should call upon him in their half-hearted, half-genuine moves to restore Polish democracy. And it was in character that he should have died later that year after a brief glimpse of the democracy post-1945 Poland was to have.)

In the days that followed Piłsudski's *coup d'état* there was confusion in Poland. In the words of Charles Malamuth, a modern historian and writer about eastern Europe:

'The communists demanded that the demonstration be routed past the courthouse and adjoining jail where young Gomułka was under arrest, calling for his immediate liberation. But the strike committee, nominated by PPS leaders, ignored that demand. After a hearing at the Krosno court, he was either very lightly punished or released without serving any sentence (the record on this point is moot), for shortly after he went to Warsaw.'[5]

Gomułka's 1947 biographer states more precisely that he

* This is the date given in Polish sources. Jerzy Mond in his article on Gomułka in the Paris monthly *Kultura* (September 1963) says the date of Gomułka's arrest was 12 June.

was held in prison for a few months, after which 'proceedings against him were discontinued'. He thus missed the internal dispute among communists about the KPP's 'May Error' in supporting the Piłsudski coup. By the end of 1926 he was busily engaged in a new activity—organising strikes. It was something he did very well. His first successful strike was in the oil-fields of Borysław. Then in 1927 he moved to the Warsaw area to live in Marymont, outside the city.[6] He was secretary for the Warsaw area of the Chemical Workers' Trade Union. According to Malamuth:

'A police report of August 1927 identifies him as having delivered a speech in that capacity, urging the workers to celebrate the 10th anniversary of the "Great October Revolution" and to press for establishment of cordial relations between Poland and the Soviet Union. In the same speech he was reported to have castigated the Piłsudski government as reactionary.'

In January 1928 he moved back to the Cracow area. He was secretary of the Chemical Union's office in Dąbrowa Górnicza and a member of the KPP local committee in Zawiercie. The Chemical Union was known as being left-wing-dominated, and as such it fell foul of the Trade Unions' Central Commission (the KCZZ) which was controlled by the Socialist Party. Since the Piłsudski coup the trade union movement had been drawn away from communism and the far left, and in 1928 the KCZZ had the Chemical Union expelled from the Union of Professional Associations.[7] Gomułka was then the Union's leading activist, its membership being between four and five thousand. He reorganised it under another name and became its secretary-general.

By now an acknowledged communist and a member of the KPP, Gomułka seems also to have taken part in the work of a left-wing Socialist Party group, the revived PPS-Lewica. At their first National Congress in July 1929, he was elected a member of a fifteen-man commission to work on the Party's programme.[8] But shortly after the congress the leadership of the PPS-Lewica changed and the commission never came into operation. According to contemporary police records, he was on 21 July elected also a member of the Party's Central Committee.[9]

These were years of industrial unrest and frequent strikes, many of which Gomułka helped to organise. His biographer notes that his was not the life of a normal active politician: 'He spoke not from the parliamentary tribune but at workers' gatherings or at illegal mass meetings.' As such, he did not make particularly fast progress within the hierarchy of the intellectual dominated KPP. As an agitator he took more risks than the KPP leaders, whose efforts were geared more towards propaganda and underground journalism. His was a highly controversial occupation. While some Poles might see him as a dedicated champion of proletarian justice and workers' interest, others regarded him simply as a 'wrecker', an ambitious political figure capitalising on Poland's financial difficulties to further his own career, thereby making worse what was already bad. There was a great hatred and fear of communism in between-the-wars Poland, not only among the ruling classes but also among most of the peasants and many of the workers. Gomułka's struggle was an uphill one. The KPP had only about 30,000 members and few political prospects. It was assumed that the only force that could bring communism to Poland was the military might of the Soviet Union.

In 1931 Gomułka was a member of the Central Trade-Union Office of the KPP's Central Committee.[10] That January he also played a leading part in founding the Trade Union Left (Lewica Związkowa), a revolutionary organisation that could be set against the main trade unions. He became secretary of its National Committee. The Trade Union Left was a small organisation (in 1933 its membership was about 51,000), but it was the main communist-controlled trade-union group. One might expect that Gomułka, as its secretary, would have been an important man in the Communist Party of Poland (the KPP). The fact that he was not may well be a serious reflection on the way the KPP was conceived, constructed and governed. To judge from his later remarks about the KPP and its leaders, Gomułka took to heart and resented their intellectual, non-working-class attitudes, their ideological bickering and continual scribbling and talking. Reading about the pre-war Polish communists, one feels they must have spent their energy on conferences, books, journals and pamphlets. Gomułka saw the task and duty of a communist in a different light. He spent his time with the workers. He had little time, either then or when he was ruler of Poland, for the intellectual communist whose life and style of living has nothing in common with those of the ordinary working man.

Gomułka was one of the exponents of the 'occupation strike'. This weapon was first used by Polish workers at the end of the 1920s. Strikers would occupy the place of their work and remain there until ejected. It was a clever device, preventing the management from using the 'lockout' or sending unemployed men into the factories as strike-breakers. Between the wars this type of strike was known throughout the world as the 'Polish strike'. It had seldom been used elsewhere. (Only in the 1960s did the 'occupation strike' gain a new lease of life when students began occupying their place of study. The 'occupation strike' became the 'sit in'. Early in 1968 Gomułka had the misfortune to see this device used against him by students of the University of Warsaw. But at least he knew how the 'occupation strike' can be countered. Police were sent into the buildings to disperse the strikers by force.)

As leader of the Trade Union Left and a constant strike organiser, Gomułka was becoming more and more of a thorn in the *sanacja* flesh. In 1932 he was living in Łódź, a large industrial city south of Warsaw, in one of an ugly row of houses in Eighth of March Street. His plan was to organise a general strike. One was planned for 17 June, but it was not a success. Then on 28 August twenty-five communists and Trade Union Leftists met at a place called the 'Little Windmill' near Łódź. Gomułka was the ringleader. It was meant to be a secret conference, but some of the delegates were followed to the 'Little Windmill' by police agents. The police burst in on the meeting, attacking and arresting. Eleven of them they caught on the spot. Gomułka fled, pursued by a police agent who shot him in the leg. According to Hansjakob Stehle:

'Gomułka had arranged a meeting with his comrades in the open air outside the town. One comrade, posted in a tree as lookout, failed to notice the police, who were acting on a tip-off, in time. Gomułka was taken to the Catholic hospital of St Joseph in Łódź in a farm cart.'[11]

It was a serious wound which still gives Gomułka pain. It left him with one leg a centimetre shorter than the other, to correct which he now wears one built-up shoe. Gomułka received the longest sentence of all. He and Józef Krawiec were sent to prison for four years. The others were imprisoned for between one and three years. After two years he was released from prison for compassionate reasons. His leg wound had not entirely healed and he suffered from some infection of the lungs.

The next two years of Gomułka's life are a mystery. According to his entry in the *Great Soviet Encyclopedia* (hastily inserted in a supplementary volume after his 1956 rehabilitation), he spent the years 1934–35 at the International Lenin School near Moscow.[12] Strangely, this item is not mentioned in his 1947 Polish biography. The question is, was it merely politically inconvenient to mention his Moscow training in Poland's difficult transitional year of 1947? Or did the Moscow training never in fact happen? Hansjakob Stehle writes, 'the present writer learned from a reliable source that Gomułka had no training in Moscow'.* If this is the case, one wonders where Gomułka learnt his Russian, which is accented but excellent.

At the end of 1935 Gomułka was back in Silesia. He lived in Swiętochowice in the house of one Pawel Dyląg, his work being in a district of the town called Lipiny. He was a member of the KPP Regional Committee there. With the Committee's secretary, Mieczysław Figuła, he helped prepare the 'occupation' and hunger strike among the miners of Chropaczowa which took place on 23 March 1936. It was his last piece of pre-war militancy. The 'blue police' were by now really gunning for the militant communists. At the end of March they arrested Gomułka, Figuła and seven other revolutionary leaders. A modern Polish historian describes the events that followed:

'In the Katowice prison Mieczysław Figuła managed to keep in contact with Władysław Gomułka, who was in solitary confinement. In spite of the difficulty involved in contacting his comrades, Gomułka kept their spirits up and issued them with instructions. The prosecutor's office was making energetic preparations for the trial. On 29 September 1936, as reported in the press of the time, an important criminal trial of communists began. The judges were carefully chosen. Sixteen suitably prepared witnesses were heard, most of them police officials and informers. A

* The *Osteuropa Handbuch Polen*, published in Cologne, 1959, claims Gomułka spent the years 1934–36 in the Soviet Union and attended 'Komintern Hochschule' there.

sensational event took place during the hearing. One of the accused, Franciszek Golenia, profited from the confusion and made his escape.'[13]

This time Gomułka received an exemplary sentence, seven years' imprisonment. His chief in the local communist committee, Figuła, got only four years. This strange discrepancy indicates either that Gomułka's position in the movement was higher than it appeared, or that the *sanacja* police regarded him as a particularly dangerous man. Probably both. There were many trials of communist 'subversives' in Silesia around this time, and Gomułka's sentence was one of the longest awarded. In January 1937 the Polish Court of Appeal reconsidered the sentences and reduced many of them. For example, Figuła's four years were reduced to three. But Gomułka's seven years stayed, keeping him in prison until the outbreak of war on 1 September 1939.

The first one and a half years of his sentence Gomułka spent in solitary confinement. He was moved from prison to prison, ending up in Sieradz, west of Łódź. According to *Time* magazine, 'he shared a cell with six other communists. He did not speak to them for eighteen months because he differed with them on minor ideological grounds.'[14] It seems an unlikely story. Gomułka was a fervent communist, but not a dogmatist. More probably his lack of conversation, if such there was, was caused by his constant reading and study. His years in prison were important and productive. They were his university. He had never been much of a talker, only an orator. His three and a half years of silence were a preliminary to action. War and enemy occupation were to provide him with action in plenty.

III: THE COMMUNIST PARTY AND POLAND

This chapter will not attempt to summarise the twenty-year existence of the Polish Communist Party (the KPP). It will try rather to give a hind-sight, Gomułka's-eye impression of it. What was his view of the Party he joined in 1926? It can be clearly enough judged from his speeches. Generally it was a favourable view. As a patriotic Pole he believed that socialism was the answer to the vast problems of newly created Poland. He believed in the principles Russians had fought for in the October 1917 revolution and the Civil War (1917–22) and regarded the Soviet Union as Poland's natural ally, geographically as well as politically. But he saw no reason why a socialist Poland should be governed exactly according to the Soviet model. Polish socialism and Russian socialism should, he thought, be slightly different. It was on this point that the views of Gomułka and the KPP diverged.

The 1920s were the golden years of marxism-leninism, the ideology which had swept over Russia and was now spreading its influence across Europe. But the Party Gomułka joined was not all that he might have hoped. It was not a Party of Polish workers and peasants—far from it. It contained very many intellectuals. In February 1932 fifty-nine per cent of its members were intellectual, thirty-one per cent were peasants or agricultural workers and only ten per cent workers.[1] Secondly, the national composition of the Party was not entirely Polish. Many of its members (some estimate as many as sixty per cent) were Jews.* And in between-the-wars Poland hardly any Jews were assimilated into the Polish state. They possessed Polish nationality, but it was a nationality which before 1918 had not even existed and which they did not feel was theirs. Many of

---

* The proportion of Jews in the KPP is, however, difficult to assess exactly. Andrzej Werblan in *Miesięcznik Literacki* (June 1968) gives it as twenty-two to twenty-six per cent.

them had lived quite happily under the rule of the partitioning powers, Russia, Prussia and Austria-Hungary, who put them on an equal status with the Poles they governed. Many Jews preferred the rule of these powers to an independent Poland, its government influenced by a powerful Roman Catholic Church. In Poland they formed a ten per cent minority and were subject to the irritations and restrictions imposed upon them by popular anti-semitism and Church intolerance. It was they whose hearts warmed to the new movement. It was international and therefore all the more attractive to Jews. But most Poles took a more prosaic view. To them communism was not international but Russian. Their heads full of fresh unpleasant memories of the neighbouring foreign powers that had ruled them for so long, they still had a tendency to reject Russian ideas as alien, even as 'barbaric'. They still felt superior to the Russians in culture and general civilisation. Many Poles saw communism as an excuse for a new imperialism and they were suspicious of it. Intellectuals found it easier then others to rise above such natural prejudices. They were impressed by the great intellectual achievements of the early Soviet years, joined the KPP and dominated its leadership.

The problem that bedevilled the KPP and stopped it becoming as influential as other European communist parties was its attitude to the Polish state and the independence of Poland. The party was formed on 16 December 1918 in Warsaw at the moment of independent Poland's rebirth after years of foreign rule. It was an amalgamation of the Social-Democratic Party of the Kingdoms of Poland and Lithuania (the SDKPiL) and the left wing of the Polish Socialist Party (the PPS-Lewica). The SDKPiL had operated mainly in the areas ruled by tsarist Russia, and the whole party was Russian-orientated. Its leading light, though, was Róża Luxemburg, who also co-founded the German Communist Party. Her angry correspondence with Lenin on the nationality question was a harbinger of much future Russian-Polish ideological dispute.

At its Party Congress in 1905 the SDKPiL had passed a resolution to the effect that 'the independence of Poland, which is what the PPS social imperialists are fighting for, would be harmful to the international proletariat and the international social revolution'. Independence aspirations were dismissed by them as 'dreams of the Polish nobility'.[2] In 1917, in the months of growing Bolshevik power, it was the *Russians*, Lenin and

Stalin, who were in favour of allowing Poland, as they later allowed Finland, to leave the new socialist state. One of Stalin's first diplomatic acts was to travel to Helsinki to negotiate Finnish independence. The Polish socialists, among them the notorious Cheka leader Feliks Dzierżyński, opposed this view. They wanted Poland to join the new Soviet Republic. Lenin overruled them. Once he had renounced the three-power partition of 1795, the road was prepared for the new state, and made clear by the collapse of Germany and Austria-Hungary. Polish communists opposed Polish independence even after its achievement. In 1918 they condemned 'all illusions connected with creating an independent Polish state'. It was the view of Róża Luxemburg, later branded by Stalin as the heresy 'luxemburgism', that self-determination is impossible under capitalism and unnecessary under socialism.

The new party was known as the Communist Workers' Party of Poland, the KPRP. (In February 1925 the word 'Workers'' was dropped.) The basis of its opposition to the new Polish state was a genuine belief, held by many communists and non-communists in the months that followed October 1917, that world revolution was at hand. The KPRP particularly opposed the formation, with French help, of the Polish Army on the understandable ground that it was meant more as a bulwark against communism than as a national defence force. They took no part in the legal and political life of Poland. They boycotted the January 1919 elections to the Polish parliament (the Sejm), and devoted their energy to agitation and subversion. They thought they had only to wait and the tide of world history would sweep from the East across all Europe. Like the apostles, they believed in an imminent second coming.

The over-optimism of the early KPRP is now admitted and deplored among modern Polish communists. On 6 December 1945 Władysław Gomułka announced at the first Congress of the Polish Workers' Party (the KPP's successor) that 'the Communist Party of Poland was weighed down with the past mistakes of the SDKPiL movement on the nationality question'. (The following sentence of his speech is cut from the published text.) In 1965 Tadeusz Daniszewski, a leading Polish communist historian, wrote in an article on the KPP for the new Polish *Great Universal Encyclopedia*:

'The basis of the KPP's programme and tactics at this time

was above all the conviction that revolution was near in Germany and the whole of Europe. . . .

'The KPP leaders had not yet realised that the most burning issue that inspired the struggles of the Polish working masses was the unification of all Polish lands in an independent Polish state, and the carrying out of democratic social reforms, especially agricultural reforms.'

The results of these un-Polish policies were brought to a head by the 1920 war against the Soviet Union. The frontiers of eastern Europe were in a state of chaos, caused by the Russian Revolution, the end of the World War, and the complete national reorganisation of the area, being implemented with difficulty and a certain incompetence by the victorious Allies. While they were in agreement that an independent Poland was morally justifiable and politically useful, the Allies were in doubt as to the exact meaning of the term 'Poland'. Situated in the midst of a flat, continental plain, with no natural frontiers, Poland had many times changed its shape and size. In 1918 the Allies tried to construct a Poland out of the territories populated by Poles. This could not be done exactly. There were frequent Polish-populated enclaves in otherwise German areas, and vice versa. Another problem was that the new state would have only a small length of coastline, some thirty miles of 'Polish corridor' with no important harbour. The allies therefore created a strange, unnatural 'free state' around the German-populated city of Danzig (Gdańsk). This was to be a tiny self-governing state, but within the Polish customs area and therefore available to Poland for trade purposes. In the east a line along the River Bug was proposed by the British Foreign Secretary, Lord Curzon, as the frontier with Russia. (It was not implemented, but was resurrected twenty-five years later by the Russians and made the basis of much East-West argument.)

Many Poles were dissatisfied with the establishment of such a 'puny' Poland. They had been thinking in terms, if not of the old empire 'from sea to sea', at least of a Poland within the pre-partition frontiers of 1772, which included the cities Lwów, Wilno, Minsk and a large part of western Byelorussia and the Ukraine.

With this in mind Józef Piłsudski, the military leader who was the power behind the liberal-democratic throne, set about plans to follow in the footsteps of his seventeenth- and eighteenth-century predecessors and increase Poland's territory at Russian expense. He watched with some satisfaction the birth-pangs of that other new state, the Soviet Union. The Russian Civil War had been straining the Red Army's resources to the utmost. The anti-Russian and anti-communist revolt of Simon Petlura in the Ukraine gave Piłsudski his opportunity. He made an anti-Soviet pact with Petlura, and a plan for a Polish-Ukrainian union after victory had been obtained. On 7 May 1920 Polish-Ukrainian armies invaded the Soviet Union and occupied Kiev.

A month later the Soviet forces turned the tables. Under two well-known Soviet marshals, Tukhachevsky and Budienny, reinforcements moved speedily from the Caucasus to the western front, broke the Polish-Ukrainian line and advanced quickly westward. By the middle of August the Red Army was lining the Vistula and preparing for an assault upon Warsaw.

Throughout the summer of 1920 the Polish Communist Party supported the Soviet offensive against their country by every possible means. They saw the Red Army as their ally, the military arm of the *world* proletariat. In this they were completely at odds with the vast majority of Poles, who saw the Red Army merely as the army of alien Russia. In August it seemed that the communists' non-Polish policies had won the day. The Red Army was in full cry and seemed likely to over-run not only Poland but also Germany and most of Europe. In Hungary a socialist revolution had already gained power, although briefly, under Bela Kun (1919). In Germany communist influence and potential was at its height. World revolution, guided by Trotsky's ideas and by Trotsky's Red Army, seemed a real possiblity.

In mid-July the communists set up a provisional government for the future communist Poland. This Revolutionary Committee, known as the 'Revkom', sat in Białystok, the first large Polish city to be captured by the Reds. Its leader was Julian Marchlewski, and among its prominent members were Feliks Dzierżyński, Feliks Kon, Józef Unschlicht and Julian Leszczyński (KPP leader several times during the 1920s and 1930s). Other prominent 'Revkom' members included Marceli Nowotko, the first Secretary of the revived communist party, the PPR, during 1942, and Bolesław Bierut, PPR Secretary-General 1948–56.

Among the western powers the rapid Red advance caused some panic. An Anglo-French military mission was sent to Warsaw, and in July-August it tried to arrange an armistice. Plans to send arms to Poland were resisted by many influential forces. The Danzig dock workers refused to unload the shipments, and in England there was a strong 'Hands off Russia' movement supported by, among others, the union leader Ernest Bevin.

It was then that Piłsudski launched the counter-attack later known as 'the miracle on the Vistula'. His victory has also been called 'the eighteenth most decisive battle in the world's history', the theory being that if he had not won the Red Army might have moved across Poland, across Germany and beyond. The counter-attack was a huge success. Within a month the Poles had captured back all the territory they had lost. The Soviets, having won the Civil War, were prepared to swallow the loss of the Polish war and come to terms, which they did by signing the Treaty of Riga on 12 October 1920. Poland thus gained large areas of the Ukraine and Byelorussia, together with the problem that came with a mixed population which except in certain cities was largely non-Polish. These Ukrainians and Byelorussians numbered nearly twenty per cent of the population of the Polish state.*

After this war the Polish communists found they had lost what little influence they previously had, being generally regarded as agents of the Soviet Union and as traitors to Poland. They had set up a pro-Soviet 'government', had tried to organise strikes and to persuade Polish soldiers to desert. True, it was Poland who started the war, but this did not, in the eyes of most Poles, excuse the communist attitude.

The years 1920–21 marked a series of defeats for world communism as well as for Polish communism. There were the Red Army's defeat on the Vistula, the collapse of the Bela Kun régime in Hungary, the failure of the communist coup in Germany (March 1921) and the introduction of Lenin's New Economic Policy (NEP) to restore order to the Soviet economy.

* At this time according to Dziewanowski (*The Communist Party of Poland*) about thirty per cent of the population of Poland were non-Poles. There were about 5,000,000 Ukrainians, 3,000,000 Jews, 1,500,000 Byelorussians and 1,000,000 Germans. According to Lucjan Blit (in *Gomułka's Poland*) the proportion of non-Poles was forty per cent.

Communism was proceeding, in Lenin's words, by two steps forward followed by one step backward. The years 1920–21 were the backward ones. Even the Polish Communist Party felt obliged to make concessions. Discredited as they were, their organisation illegal and in disarray, they did what communist parties usually do when they find themselves in a state of weakness, they made concessions. They decided to play a more practical and sober political game. They recognised the independence of Poland and called for a united front of all 'democratic' parties to fight imperialism. This was a tactic designed mainly to split and attract supporters of the large socialist party, the PPS. 'We will go part of the way together,' Karol Radek had said of the socialists. Unable to fight the November 1922 elections under their own name, they used the cover name 'Union of Town and Country Proletariat' and polled 132,000 votes. They won two deputies to the Sejm (parliament): Stefan Królikowski and Stanisław Lańcucki.

The leaders of this new-style Party were known in politics by pseudonyms—Adolf Warski, Wera Kostrzewa and Henryk Walecki. They were known as 'the three Ws'. In their propaganda they claimed the KPRP was the only party that stood for the 'real' independence of Poland, that Poland was not yet really independent since much of the country's wealth and most of its industry was owned by foreigners, and since Polish foreign policy was strongly influenced by the French, British and Americans. Of course there was some truth in this, and the communists gained some support as a result. A potentially popular policy, too, was their intention to confiscate the large estates, without compensation to the owners, and distribute the land to the peasants. Less well received was their demand that the lands Poland had just won in battle, western Ukraine and western Byelorussia, should be returned to the Soviet Union. The KPP kept these areas administratively separate from themselves, and separate communist parties were formed for them in the autumn of 1923.

In April 1923 the Party tried to achieve a union with the socialist party (the PPS) and its Central Commission of Trade Unions (KCZZ). Their offer was turned down. In a letter to the communist Sejm deputy Królikowski a prominent PPS politician explained the reasons why: '. . . with you, gentlemen, one can never tell where the ideologist ends and where the Russian agent begins.'

'Not many years ago, as the SDKPiL, you frantically opposed our efforts to achieve independence. After Poland won independence, you still opposed it. You lead Cossack regiments against your own country. . . .'[3]

After the death of Lenin (24 January 1924) the Polish party's situation was complicated further by the struggle for power in the Soviet Union between Stalin and Trotsky. Many of the leading members of the KPRP had supported Trotsky. (It was he who as People's Commissar for War in 1920 had come near to bringing communism to Poland, and had provided the Polish communists in Białystok with a brief taste of power.) Such men were internationalists who had little sympathy with Stalin's primary aim of 'socialism in one country'. The Polish party had been a co-organiser of the Comintern in 1919, and had placed great hopes upon it. Up to Lenin's death the Comintern had been dominated by Trotskyists. This is why one of Stalin's first tasks was to reduce the importance both of Trotsky and of his Comintern. The Polish party leadership, the 'three Ws', was to be his next target.

Under Stalin's instigation, a rival group began to challenge the 'three Ws' for the KPRP leadership. Known originally as the 'Minority' faction, its leaders were Julian Leszczyński, L. Domski, J. Heryng, A. Lampe and S. Amsterdam. Backed by Stalin and his supporters, they attacked the 'three Ws' at the Fifth Comintern Congress in July 1924 in Moscow for taking a conciliatory attitude to the bourgeois forces in Poland, i.e. for doing exactly what the Soviet leaders had been doing in their own country. A 'Polish Commission' was set up to investigate charges of 'right-wing opportunism' in the Party leadership. Its members were Stalin, Molotov, Dzierżyński, Józef Unschlicht, Dmitri Manuilsky (later Comintern secretary) and the German communist leader Ernst Thälmann. The 'three Ws' were subjected during three days of discussion to a stream of abuse similar to that suffered, twenty-five years later, by Gomułka. The party leaders were reformists, not revolutionaries, claimed Leszczyński, and reformism was *ipso facto* anti-Party. For instance, the Sejm deputy Królikowski had proposed a motion to reduce the period of military service. Would the cause of revolution be advanced by such politicising? The members of the 'Polish Commission' thought not. On the contrary such small improvements in the working man's lot would be a hindrance to revolution, since they would make him less discontented and desperate for change.

Luckily for the Poles in 1924 Stalin was not yet in full control of the Soviet administration and his disposition to cruelty and repression had not taken effect. Communists were used to argument and abuse from comrades who disagreed with their particular line, but not yet to terror. Until then terror had been employed mainly against anti-communists, not by communists against each other. The Polish leadership therefore resisted Stalin's accusations quite openly and daringly: 'One thing we know for sure: for our Party, for the whole Comintern, for the whole revolutionary world proletariat, the name of comrade Trotsky is irrevocably linked with the victorious October revolution, with the Red Army and with communism.'[4] Stalin can hardly have been pleased either with the statement of Wera Kostrzewa, which he may well have interpreted as a direct insult: 'Trotsky is the only man in Russia today who could become an object of mass veneration. Now that Lenin is dead, there is a need to find such a man. It arises from Russian tradition and the spirit of the time.'[5]

The 'Polish Commission' took a severe attitude to such defiance. The leadership was dismissed and replaced by Leszczyński, Domski and other left-wingers. It was the first example of direct Soviet interference in the running of the Polish Communist Party. It was not to be the last.

The Comintern also took it upon itself to comment on the frontiers of the Polish state, demanding the return to the Soviet Union of Poland's new eastern territories. The KPP had already accepted this, so it was not a point at issue. But trouble came at the Third KPP Congress, held a few months later in March 1925, in Minsk. Tadeusz Żarski, a supporter of the 'rightist', 'Majority' three Ws, revealed that the Comintern leader Dmitri Manuilsky had asked the KPP to agitate for the surrender of Polish territory in the west, Upper Silesia and Pomerania, not this time to the Soviet Union but to Germany.

At this time it was clearly Soviet policy to try to weaken the Polish state, to reduce its size and importance. If the Soviets had had their way and Poland had given up all they thought she should give up, Poland would have been deprived of well over half her territory: western Ukraine and western Byelorussia, Wilno and the Lithuanian territories, Polish Silesia and

Polish Pomerania. Poland would have become a small, land-locked country. It is not hard to see why the Soviet-dominated Comintern tried to force such an 'unpatriotic' line upon the Polish communists, and why the line later came to be accepted. The KPP was weak. It had little chance, especially after the Polish-Soviet war, of obtaining power either by politics or by popular revolution. Polish communists had supported the Soviet Union against Poland in the 1920 war, and only belatedly and with reluctance accepted Polish independence. It might not, the Soviets thought, be too difficult to persuade them to renounce much of the territory of a country which, after all, had not even existed a few years previously and which might in a few years' time cease to exist once again.

A more important factor, from the Soviet point of view, was that if the Polish communists could be persuaded to renounce those areas which had significant German populations, it would greatly strengthen the hand of the Communist Party of Germany. The German party was an entirely different matter. It was strong and, in 1925, had a good chance of winning power. Germany, the land of Marx, was seen by revolutionary marxists as the key to Europe. Once Germany was won over, Poland would surely drop like a ripe plum. The Soviet Union therefore considered its interest lay in supporting Germany at Poland's expense.

For the moment the KPP resisted this Comintern pressure on the German issue. But the Party was still in a parlous state. Throughought 1925 the struggle for power continued, resulting in an uneasy right-left coalition led by Leszczyński and Warski. Then in May 1926 a further event blackened the KPP in the eyes of Stalin and Russia.

During the eight years 1918–26 Poland was governed by parliamentary democracy. This was the first and, unless one counts the abortive attempt of the years 1945–47, the only time that such a system has governed Poland. Parliamentary democracy did not work. It suffered from all the faults of the Fourth Republic in post-Second World War France—a multiplicity of political parties, constantly changing administrations, confusion. The constant need for political compromise caused the election of weak leaders who were not able to deal with the immense problems of the new Poland. Successive prime ministers were not able to reconcile the Poles' genuine love of freedom with their traditional chauvinism and suspicion of foreign neighbours and national minorities, their newly-independent patriotic fervour with their weakness as an administrative unit. The style of each prime minister was further cramped by the thought of Józef Piłsudski, Marshal of Poland, officially without power but ready to seize it when absolutely necessary, or to accept it when, like Cincinnatus or de Gaulle, it should be offered him by the people. He was not of the usual run of military dictators. Before the First World War he had been a leading member of the socialist party (the PPS). Much of his support had always come from the left wing. But he was of course anti-communist, a believer in strong government and intolerant of political oppositions.

In May 1926 Piłsudski announced himself disillusioned with the Polish politicians and proceeded to take over the country by a military coup. During the three days of fighting (12–14 May) the Communist Party supported Piłsudski. They put out a leaflet containing the words: 'The place of the worker and peasant is in the ranks of the revolutionary forces of Marshal Piłsudski.' This was a brief but disastrous change of line from that of the KPP conference in Minsk a year earlier, where Domski had denounced Piłsudski and his PPS supporters as 'social fascists'. The new 'coalition' KPP leadership had taken a different view. Early in 1926 in a newspaper article Warski remarked upon Piłsudski's great popularity among Poles, even among workers and peasants.[6] Perhaps he saw Piłsudski as a Kerensky who could provide Poland with a 'February Revolution' and so help the communist cause *malgré lui*. Anyway, the communists supported the coup of the man they were later to brand as a fascist.

By the end of May the KPP had changed its mind. It now realised that Piłsudski's coup would probably strengthen Poland. They launched journalistic attacks on the new régime. But it was too late. They had now burnt their boats both with Piłsudski and with Stalin. Their earlier standpoint had been noted in Moscow with displeasure and was thought to add weight to the Comintern's already strong feelings against the Polish party. It was soon clear that Piłsudski, far from being a 'socialist' or even a 'bourgeois', was to be cast in the role of 'fascist'. An indictment of the KPP's mistake was read by Stalin in Tbilisi (Tiflis) on 8 June:

'. . . the Polish Communist Party is very weak, and it has

made itself even weaker in the present crisis through its mistaken attitude to Piłsudski's army. Because of this it was unable to stand at the head of the revolutionarily-inclined masses.

'I must confess that in this matter our Polish comrades have made a grave error.'[7]

This tactical slip on the part of the KPP, which became known as the 'May error' was not forgotten for thirty years. It was constantly used by Stalinists and dogmatic Marxists as a stick with which to beat the Polish party. It was seen as epitomising all their destructive weaknesses. In 1938, after the Party's dissolution, a Soviet encyclopedia declared:

'In May 1926 during the Piłsudski coup the KPP politic-ally supported it, under the influence of fascist agents who had penetrated the leadership, masking the fascist charac-ter of the coup and passing it off as a democratic move-ment of the petty bourgeoisie. This position was held by leaders of both of the then factions—the "majority" and the "minority" factions.'

After the coup the situation in the KPP deteriorated further. Their party programme still had much to commend it. There was a clear case for land reform in between-the-wars Poland. Promises had been made by successive prime ministers that something would be done about this. But little ever happened. The KPP at least promised action and received some support on this account. In the Polish general election of March 1928, the last free election held in pre-war Poland, the communists won 7·9 per cent of the votes, twice as many as in 1922. But this support dwindled when peasants saw what was happening in the Soviet Union. In 1929 Stalin began the forcible collec-tivisation of the Russian countryside. It became clear that this was the real communist platform. Land reform was only a standby measure.

In the early 1930s the Comintern again pressed the matter of the frontiers with Germany. Since 1926 the leadership of the KPP had been in constant dispute. Their conferences, generally held in the Soviet Union, would be full of mutual abuse from 'rightist' and 'leftist', with the issue finally decided by Soviet pressure. In 1932 the 'leftist' KPP leadership of Leszczyński and Heryng gave in to the Soviet and German demands. A KPP propaganda brochure published in July 1932 contained the resolution:

'With regard to Danzig, the KPP opposes the yoke imposed upon it by Poland and the League of Nations . . . and recognises the right of the Danzig population to unite once again with Germany from which it is now forcibly separated.'[8]

Six months later the KPP journal *Nowy Przegląd* reported a resolution passed on 29 January 1933 by the 'Polish-German Workers' Committee' in Gliwice, eastern Germany, where the journal was printed:

'After eleven years of Polish occupation of Upper Silesia . . . the KPP declares that the victorious Polish proletariat . . . will annul all the rulings contained in the Treaty of Versailles with regard to Upper Silesia and the Pomeranian corridor, and will ensure the populations of these lands the right to self-determination even as far as secession from Poland.'[9]

It is fair to say that the KPP held these views only for a short time. A few days after this resolution was passed, Hitler came to power in Germany and started severe repressions against German communists. The chance of the German party achieving power grew less, and Polish communists no longer felt obliged to appease German nationalism. Moreover, it became clear that the new threat—Hitlerism—was an even greater danger to communism, especially to Polish communism, than 'bourgeois democracy'. 'We communists respect the independence of Poland', the KPP announced in 1935 in a resolution at its sixth Plenum.

'We communists are the inheritors of the best traditions of the Polish nation's struggle for democracy and independence. . . . We communists are deeply attached to our homeland. . . . We shall not allow our country to become a bridgehead or a stamping ground for the Hitlerite generals.'[10]

Although a more reasonable programme had now been adopted, the KPP was weaker than ever. Its popularity, influence and freedom of movement had all suffered from the stern anti-communist policies of Piłsudski-ite (nicknamed *sanacja*) Poland and Hitlerite Germany. The police force of the Polish dictatorship, known as the *deuxième bureau* (or in Polish *dwójka*), did not have the same tolerant attitude to the KPP as the earlier democratic governments. Communists were frequently arrested, charged with subversive activity and imprisoned. In 1934 a detention camp was set up in Bereza Kartuska near Brześc nad Bugiem (Brest Litovsk). Several thousand political prisoners, from the 'Centre-Left' (the coalition of anti-Piłsudski peasant and socialist parties) as well as from the communists, were confined there in conditions of hardship.

The relations between the KPP and Stalinist Russia were hardly happier. In spite of numerous changes in leadership, the Party still contained many supporters of the Trotskyist line. In 1932 a group of prominent Trotskyists, including Isaac Deutscher, was expelled from the Party and emigrated. This group came to be associated with demands for a united anti-*sanacja* front—a course of action which would, according to modern Polish communist historians, have been a more realistic policy. For instance, in the 1960s Tadeusz Daniszewski writes with disapproval of the KPP 1932 programme:

'This programme did not consider the differences existing between the ruling *sanacja* and the Socialist Party, the Bund* and the Peasant Party. It did not consider the possibility of broader cooperation with these parties in the battle with the *sanacja*.'[11]

By the time this policy changed, after the rise to power of Hitler, the anti-*sanacja* parties were no longer interested in cooperation with the KPP. They imposed conditions on it: a break with the Comintern, an end to persecution and to 'dog eat dog' purges inside the Party. This second condition gained increased importance by the mid-1930s, when Stalin had come to realise that the simplest way of dealing with political trouble-makers was to kill them. One of the first to suffer from Stalin's brutality was Jerzy Sochacki, from 1926 to 1928 a

* The Bund was a political organisation of Jewish socialists.

communist deputy to the Sejm, who died in 1933. In 1935 Tadeusz Żarski (who had opposed the Comintern on the question of the frontier with Germany) was executed in Russia as a Trotskyist, and by 1937 the trickle of trials and executions had become a Great Purge. Some KPP leaders—the lucky ones —were in Polish prisons, or detention camps. Władysław Gomułka was one of these. The others were summoned to Moscow, assembled together, and liquidated. At least twelve of the members of the KPP Central Committee were either executed or died in prison. Julian Leszczyński was accused of being in the pay of the Polish police and of having been allowed by them to escape from a Warsaw courtroom in 1925. Warski, Walecki and Wera Kostrzewa were accused of being *sanacja* agents. Several hundred Polish communists of lesser importance also disappeared.

The KPP, after its spirited defence of Trotsky at the 1924 Comintern Congress, had become a Trotskyite symbol, even in a few cases a refuge for Trotskyites from outside Poland. It is hard to explain the extent of Stalin's distrust and hatred of the Polish party. Before the Revolution Stalin had spent some time in Poland. He is said to have been shocked and dismayed by the Poles' dislike not only of tsarism, but also of Russia. It was a dislike which Stalin was to vent upon the Poles in retribution and with great cruelty. Perverse to the last, as it is perhaps in the nature of Poles to be, they never really accepted the Stalinist line. As internationalists they had flocked to fight for communism in the Spanish Civil War, where their 'internationalist' slogan 'For your freedom and ours' typified the whole situation as they saw it. They detested the provincial 'Freedom in one country' slogan which Stalin found more expedient. And they resented being treated as the poor relation of European communism, the bridge between Russia and *Germany*, a country which Stalin respected and saw as the key to Europe.

Stalin regarded the KPP as a threat, a gathering of intelligent, talented communists living in a country dangerously close to the borders of the Soviet Union and a short distance from its main cities, weak perhaps, but quite capable of keeping Trotskyism alive, and therefore preserving the seed of disunity. The word Trotskyism had become a label to be attached to any defiance of Stalin's will. To destroy it inside the Soviet Union was not enough. An international ideology had international heresies. To drive such heresies abroad was not enough. This is why, even in Mexico City in 1940, Trotsky was still a danger, and why it was necessary to drive an ice-pick through his skull. Stalin's persecution of the Poles is recognised and condemned by modern communists. Tadeusz Daniszewski writes: 'In 1938 on the basis of slanderous accusations of having penetrated KPP organisations as agents-provocateurs . . . many KPP leaders who were then in the USSR in emigration fell victim to repressions connected with the so-called "personality cult".'[12]

In the summer of 1938 Stalin decided to destroy not only individual Polish communists but also their Party. He, or rather his Comintern, dissolved the KPP on the ground that it was so infiltrated by enemies that it could not continue. In the words of the Comintern leader Dmitri Manuilsky:

> 'In order to split the communist movement, Fascist and Trotskyist spies tried to form artificial groups and factions in some communist parties and stir up sectarian strife. . . . [The party] most contaminated by hostile elements was the Communist Party of Poland, where agents of Polish fascism managed to gain positions of leadership. These scoundrels tried to get to the Party to support Piłsudki's 1926 coup. . . .'

The *Shorter Soviet Encyclopedia*, published in 1938, announced that:

> 'Right from the beginning of its existence the fascists tried to disorganise and confuse the KPP. They infiltrated agents and members of the subversive Polish Military Organisation (the POW). . . .'

During the show trials of 1938–39 the very word 'Polish' became one of abuse, almost synonymous with words like 'fascist' or 'Trotskyist'. For the next seventeen years loyal Polish communists were made to look back on their party, the KPP, with mixed feelings, as a former enthusiastic member of the world movement, but also as a party infiltrated and largely led by traitors and spies. For the rest of 1938 and 1939 Polish communists, their party cut away from under them, confined their political activity to trade union work. According to Manuilsky, writing in 1939, 'they have investigated their leading workers and removed those whose political honesty was in question. They have dissolved illegal organisations which were particularly contaminated, and have begun to form new ones in their place.' But the Comintern resolution specifically forbade them to form another communist party. They would have to wait for permission before doing that, and before the question was able to arise a year had passed and Poland was at war.

IV: THE 'IMPERIALIST' WAR

When the German armies invaded Poland on 1 September 1939 Gomułka was still serving his seven-year term in the prison of Sieradz. He was the 'community leader' of 400 communists there.[1] Most of the other important communists were then in prison at Rawicz, near Poznań on the German border. The inmates of Rawicz included the future leaders Marceli Nowotko and Paweł Finder.

The Polish armies fought bravely against the invaders but they were no match for them. Against the Germans' 2,400 tanks they had only 180 of inferior manufacture. They had only 420 aeroplanes against the Germans' 2,000.[2] The Polish Army had been largely trained according to the experience of the Polish-Soviet war of 1920. The German army had had more recent practice in the Spanish Civil War. Accounts of Polish warriors on horseback charging German tanks are often dismissed as legend. But this did take place. There were many Polish commanders, even in 1939, who thought that tanks were a passing phase, that they would never supersede cavalry.

Although Great Britain and France declared war on Germany two days after the invasion, they did little to help the Poles. British proposals to bomb Germany during the first days of the war were rejected on the simple ground that Germany might perhaps bomb Britain back. The British and French forces seemed stunned by the speed of the Polish collapse, and by the success of Hitler's *blitzkrieg*. The French sat tight behind the Maginot Line, while the British thought about preparing an expeditionary force. By 7 September the Germans were outside Warsaw.

In the general panic the Polish prisons were left unattended and the prisoners were able to escape. Some of them made their way to military units, volunteered to join up and were accepted. They fought in the regular forces. Some communists, even when Poland was on the point of collapse, were refused the right to join the army. To some Poles the 'Red menace' was still a greater evil than Nazism. Władysław Gomułka, suddenly released from Sieradz, reached Warsaw where there was to be a last-ditch defence. The first act was to secure the release of their comrades from Warsaw prisons. Among these were Edward Ochab and Małgorzata Fornalska. They did not join the Polish Army, by then already on the point of collapse, but built barricades and prepared to defend the city. Although a tiny number compared to the regular forces defending Warsaw, they did help their capital city to survive three weeks. The final capitulation took place on 27 September.

On 17 September an event occurred that did lasting damage to Polish-Russian relations. The Soviet government, having tried and failed during 1938 and much of 1939 to come to an agreement with Great Britain, France and Poland to resist further Nazi aggression, had signed on 23 August a pact with Germany. On the face of it, it was a simple non-aggression pact. The Soviet Union, the natural enemy of Nazi Germany, decided her interest now lay in coming to terms with her. The pact was presented to the world as an act of self-defence and essential self-interest. Even today the pact is viewed by Soviet historians as a necessary evil, an unavoidable compromise with the class enemy which provided a temporary breathing-space for the Soviet Union to build up her forces.

This is part of the truth, but only part of it. The Soviet Union had the right to protect herself, of course, by all possible means. She had tried for an alliance with the western powers and failed. The Nazi-Soviet pact was a last resort. What *was* disgraceful about the pact was the definite provision made in it for the Soviet Union to expand her borders and absorb territory from her small western neighbours, Poland and the Baltic States. In the 'Secret Additional Protocol' to the pact, discovered only after the capture of German archives, we read the following paragraphs:

'In the event of territorial or political changes taking place on the lands belonging to the Polish state, the boundary between the German and Soviet sphere of interest will run approximately along the line of the rivers Narew, Vistula and San.

'The question of whether or not it is in the interest of both sides to maintain an independent Polish state, and within what boundaries, can only be finally resolved in the light of further political events.'[3]

In other words the 'Secret Protocol' was a plan to partition Poland. During the first fortnight of September 1939 Germany kept the Soviet Union fully informed on the progress of her army across Poland. On 9 September the Foreign Minister Molotov congratulated the German Ambassador Schulenburg (three weeks prematurely) on the capture of Warsaw. He informed him of the date planned for the Red Army to cross the Polish frontier. During the next few days the tone of the Polish Soviet press became more and more anti-Polish. Polish aircraft were accused of violating Soviet air space. Polish troops were said to have committed acts of violence against the Ukrainian, Byelorussian and Lithuanian minorities. Finally in Moscow at 3 a.m. on the morning of 17 September the Polish Ambassador Grzybowski was summoned by Molotov and presented with a note announcing the Soviet intention of invading eastern Poland 'in order to protect the lives and property of the inhabitants of western Ukraine and western Byelorussia'. 'The Polish government has collapsed,' the note read, 'and shows no sign of life. This means that the Polish state and its government have in fact ceased to exist.'[4] An hour later the Red Army crossed the Polish frontier. 'The Polish landlords (*polskiye pany*) have involved themselves in an adventuristic war,' wrote Khrushchev, then First Secretary of the Ukraine.

In many places the Russian troops were welcomed by Poles who thought the Soviet Union was coming to their aid against Germany. This impression was soon dispelled. Very little resistance to the Red Army's advance was put up by the Polish army, confused as it was and very close to total defeat. Soviet forces moved quickly across western Ukraine and western Byelorussia, taking up positions along the line of the River Bug (east of the Vistula, the line originally agreed).

During the evening of 17 September[5] the leaders of the Polish government, which some days previously had evacuated itself and the diplomatic corps to Krzemieniec in south-eastern Poland, crossed into Romania and asked for asylum in accordance with a prearranged Polish-Romanian agreement. The Romanians, frightened of the repercussions from Germany if they revealed even the slightest breach of neutrality, required the Poles to sign an undertaking to refrain from any further political activity. When they refused, the Romanians interned them.

On 18 September a joint Soviet-German *communiqué* announced that their military operations in Poland were 'in no way contrary to the spirit or the letter of the non-aggression pact concluded between Germany and the Soviet Union'. The aim of the operations was 'to restore peace and good order, which has been shattered because of the collapse of the Polish state, and to help the people of Poland to build new conditions for the existence of their state'.

Neither the Germans nor the Russians lived up to this declaration. By the beginning of October the last Polish point of resistance had been overcome and the campaign was over. The German and Soviet armies established themselves behind a demarcation line some distance to the east of the one agreed during August. In the Soviet-occupied areas there was an influx of Soviet administrators, Khrushchev prominent among them. Plans were put under way for the occupied areas to be absorbed into the Soviet Union. Elections of a sort were held, after which the lands were admitted into their respective Ukrainian and Byelorussian republics on 2 November.

The German-occupied part of Poland was administratively divided in two. Pomerania, Danzig, Silesia and all other areas where there had been any German population at all were absorbed into the German Reich. The rest, a circular land-locked area that included Warsaw and Cracow, the new capital, became a German colony with a German military administration called the 'Government General', ruled by Hans Frank, an extremely brutal man.

This succession of violent events caused confusion among Polish communists. Many of their number killed in the Stalinist purges, their party dissolved, their country battered by war and occupied by foreign armies, they themselves only freshly out of prison—it is a wonder that any of them were able to think logically or act with circumspection. Most of them did the natural thing and travelled east into Soviet-occupied territory. Władysław Gomułka was one of these. He went to Lwów (Lvov), the main city of the Western Ukraine, where he worked as head of a department in a factory that made textbooks. Lwów and Białystok became the two main centres for Polish communists. Białystok was known locally as 'the capital of Poland'.

Probably the Polish communists, naturally optimistic as well as deprived by their imprisonment of news of recent events, did not realise the full horror of what had been going on in Russia during the purges. Even so, they can hardly have hoped to be greeted with open arms as they fled from the Hitlerite hordes into Russia. The Polish and Soviet parties had been at dispute for too long for that. Communist or not, all the Poles who suddenly found themselves under Soviet administration were treated by the authorities as potential enemies. In the words of a modern Polish historian, writing in a Warsaw ideological journal in 1957:

'The position of Polish communists in these areas was not an easy one. The Polish Communist Party had only just been dissolved and the Soviet authorities did not behave towards them with complete trust. A role was played also by what we now call the "Beria terror" or the "Yezhov terror". In the beginning only those comrades were trusted who had spent years in *sanacja* prisons. They were given jobs in local administration and allowed to introduce their friends.

'At first too there were certain irregularities in the behaviour of the Soviet authorities of western Ukraine and western Byelorussia. . . .'[6]

This last sentence is a gross understatement. Until the files of the NKVD are thrown open to public scrutiny it will not be known exactly how many Poles were arrested and imprisoned in the horrible conditions of Soviet 'corrective labour' during 1939–41. The more cautious western historians estimate the figure as 'hundreds of thousands'. The most often quoted figure is 1,500,000.[7] After destalinisation this truth was admitted in a watered-down version by both Polish and Soviet authorities. This is how a modern Polish history describes the terror:

'The Soviet authorities were making use of repressive measures against the forces of Polish reaction in these areas. As a result of distortions of justice, and sometimes simply of misunderstandings, these repressions also sometimes fell upon Polish anti-fascists and communists. During the first months of 1940 the security organs began to deport unreliable elements deep into the Soviet Union. Because of these injustices, certain members of the progressive wing of the Polish *émigré* community became disorientated and disappointed. Some of them even underwent a crisis in their relationship with the Soviet Union. Some moved themselves deep into the Soviet Union of their own free will, *while others tried to move to the territories occupied by the Nazis* [author's italics].'[8]

Poles were being arrested by whole categories.[9] Members of the 'ruling classes' were deported *en bloc*: politicians, administrators, merchants and officers in any of the services. Also arrested were men of more humble rank who could be classed as their 'servants'; policemen, postmen, clerks and employees of foreign embassies or government departments. Especially suspect were Trotskyists and men with any form of political background, even, or perhaps particularly, a communist background. Luckily for Gomułka, he had spent three years before the invasion in a *sanacja* prison and so was assumed to be 'clean'. His job in the book factory was a humble one, but it was better than corrective labour. He was later allowed to contribute to the Polish-language newspaper *Czerwony Sztandar* (Red Banner), published in Lwów. Another Polish newspaper *Sztandar Wolności* (Freedom Banner) was started in Mińsk in 1940. The title of this new journal indicates, perhaps, the subtle change in the Kremlin's attitude to Poland that occurred during 1940.

In the German-occupied areas the communists, their number again and again reduced by the disasters their country and their movement was enduring were in a state of embitterment and confusion. Modern Soviet communists are none too proud of the Nazi-Soviet pact. They claim the Russian Government signed it unwillingly. Still, they certainly flung their energies with some vigour into the distasteful task of being Nazi Germany's ally. By no standard did they remain neutral in the conflict. They supported Germany against France and Great Britain. A leading article in *Pravda* (30 September 1939) named Germany and the Soviet Union as peacemakers, and England and France, their government and ruling classes, as responsible for the continuation of the war. Trade between Germany and

37

Russia, especially in war materials, developed widely. The Comintern leader Georgy Dimitrov, in an article called 'The War and the Working Class of the Capitalist Countries',[10] explained the Soviet Union's international view of the war: that it was an unjust war, an imperialist war in which the working classes (in France and Great Britain at least) should refrain from taking part. Workers were called upon to disobey the orders of their officers, to overthrow their political leaders, to turn the war from an imperialist war into a class war. This was to build castles in the air, as modern Polish historians realise and confess:

'They [the Comintern] did not sufficiently realise the necessity of defending the nations threatened by fascism. Their struggle was a just element in the war right from the beginning. In this sense the Comintern line was a step backward compared to the line expressed at the beginning of 1939. By not expressing a clear view about the character of the Polish-German war of September 1939, the Comintern gave the impression that the Polish people's struggle to defend itself against the Nazi invader was an unjust struggle.'[11]

Many Polish communists who returned disillusioned from Russia to German-occupied territory brought with them copies of Georgy Dimitrov's article and other similar literature. This added to the confusion.

Dimitrov's article, wrote Marian Malinowski in 1957, 'became the axis around which revolved the ideological discussions of Polish communists'. The communists in occupied Poland were still split between orthodox marxism-leninism and Trotskyist internationalism. They formed clubs. Two of them, 'Hammer and Sickle' and 'The Association of Friends of the USSR', took a 'simplified' view of the future of Poland: it was to become a Soviet republic, just as western Ukraine and western Byelorussia did in September 1939, and the Baltic states of Estonia, Latvia and Lithuania did in June 1940. This view was opposed by another, more realistic communist group called 'The Union for the Liberation Struggle' (*Związek Walki Wyzwoleńczej*), in which Marian Spychalski (who later became Minister of Defence) and Jerzy Albrecht were prominent members.

The communists faced yet another difficulty. The Comintern dissolution order of mid-1938 contained a clause forbidding the Poles from forming another communist party without direct approval from the Comintern. This was ostensibly to prevent the so-called fascist 'infiltrators', who had penetrated the KPP and were dissolved with it, from forming a new party as a provocation. In fact it was probably simply another way for the Soviet party to maintain their hold over the recalcitrant Poles. But after the 'September catastrophe' this Comintern order became quite ridiculous. The communists under German rule were cut off from communication with the Comintern. It was impossible to consult the Comintern on anything. They had to obey the last orders they had received. This meant that, strictly speaking, they should not form themselves into any administrative units, they should not take any joint political action, they should hardly do anything at all.

By coincidence this, for the moment, suited the Soviet book. It was generally their policy for the Polish communists to do nothing. The Russian régime was adapting itself to the new conditions offered by their pact with Germany. They were not unhappy with the situation: security (in theory at least) on their western border, their two enemies the fascists (Germany) and the imperialists (Great Britain and France) in the process of destroying one another. The last thing they wanted was an 'adventure' launched by their comrades in German-occupied Poland that might put in jeopardy the whole non-aggression pact. In fact there is evidence that the German and Soviet delegates who signed the 28 September 1939 treaty on frontiers, arranged at the same time for joint action to combat Polish resistance to their occupation régimes. It is said that an NKVD (Soviet Security Police) commission came to Cracow in March 1940 and held talks with its German equivalent.[12] A memorable occasion it must have been. Fortunately the Gestapo and the NKVD were not able to take their collaboration very far. The mind boggles at what these two organisations might have been able to achieve if they had been able to spend more than a few months in alliance.

The communists' confusion was leading them into strange excesses. A communist splinter group called the *barykadowcy* (which developed out of a Socialist Party group called 'Freedom Barricade') came out with a novel solution to the prob-

lems of Poland. By their reckoning, socialist power would come
not from the east, but from the west. The German and British
working classes would revolt against their leaders and carry the
standard of world revolution across Europe to Poland. Poland
would then become a member of the United States of Socialist
Europe. No wonder this period (from September 1939 to June
1941, when Germany invaded the Soviet Union) is not one
that is covered in any great detail by modern Polish historians.
It is too full of painful and confusing memories. The excesses
of Stalin, his mass deportations and murders, were combined
with a cynical disregard of communist principle in favour of
national self-interest. Poland, the country whose communist
party he had treated so cruelly before the Second World War,
became his first victim during the war, at least during the first
two years of it. Both then and after the war Russian and Polish
communists tried to justify the invasion of eastern Poland by the
Red Army. They pointed out that much of the population of
these eastern areas was non-Polish, and that the Soviets were
doing no more than 'protecting' or even 'liberating' their own
people. Later, after the Germans attacked Russia, the Soviets
claimed their attack on Poland was a piece of far-sighted
strategic planning, all part of a scheme to narrow the western
frontier with Germany and provide room for manœuvre in the
inevitable future war. But hardly any Poles accepted these
explanations. The Russian attack itself they might have been
able to forgive. What they could not forgive was the cruelty of
the occupying Red Army and the NKVD towards the very
people they claimed to be 'liberating'. To the Polish way of
thinking, either the Red Army were 'liberators', or else they
were a hostile occupying army. They could not be both. The
criterion was their behaviour during the twenty-one months
after September 1939. This behaviour was, by any standard,
appalling. The Russians were therefore judged to have showed
themselves a hostile force, an enemy of the Poles. To all Poles,
apart from the most loyal communists, they were 'public
enemy number two'. And they were labelled as such by
Władysław Sikorski in November 1939, shortly after his
appointment as Premier-in-exile.* The aims of his new government, he announced in France, were 'to conquer the Germans
and to prevent the bolshevisation of Europe'.[13] These were the

* 1881–1943. Premier of Poland 1922–23 and a well-known
opponent of Piłsudski during the years that followed.

priorities. The Germans and the Bolsheviks were now tarred with the same brush, not only by the right-wing *sanacja* groups but also by the 'liberal' supporters of Sikorski. All this explains why in June 1941 the Poles found it so hard to forgive. They knew it was in their interest to forget what the Russians had done to them, but they could not immediately turn enemy into friend. Many of them tried. A few succeeded. Some never tried. For them the Russians were the eternal enemy, untrustworthy and imperialistic. It was this issue—the attitude towards the Soviet Union—that split the Polish nation most horribly.

During the second half of 1940 Polish communists were able to make their move towards their reorganisation as a political party. Certain events—the Soviet Union's absorption of the Baltic states during June, the German seizure of the Romanian oilfields (7 October), Molotov's unsuccessful visit to Berlin (12–14 November)—were putting the Nazi-Soviet pact under strain. The Polish communists in Białystok and Lwów had several times, obeying the 1938 Comintern order dissolving the KPP, approached the Comintern asking to be allowed to form a new communist party. The Comintern, not wishing to rock the boat of German-Soviet alliance, had rejected the requests. But now they changed their minds. It was decided that the nucleus of a Polish party should be got together, just in case it might become necessary. A representative was sent by Georgy Dimitrov, the Comintern leader, to Lwów and Białystok to recruit an 'Initiative Group'. Eventually a number of them were taken to Moscow for training. Among their leaders were Marceli Nowotko, Paweł Finder, Jan Turlejski, Anastazy Kowalczyk and Bolesław Mołojec. During 1940–41, as Soviet-German relations deteriorated, these men began to acquire some importance. They were now a card in Stalin's hand, the nucleus of a future communist party. At the moment there was little that could be done with them, but Stalin believed in contingency planning. Even he, though, can hardly have guessed what a powerful body this handful of men was to grow into. For in 1941 Polish communists had nothing. They had no country and no party, not even an illegal party in exile. They were officially damned by their ally the Soviet Union as well as by their enemies. As for Poland itself, the events of the previous two years had seemingly blackened the communists' reputation for ever. For the second time in twenty years Polish communists had supported the Soviet Union in a Polish-Soviet armed conflict. They had opposed Poland's original independence in 1918. They had supported the Soviet Union in the 1920 war and in demands for Poland's eastern territories. They had supported Germany in the early 1930s in her demands for Danzig, Upper Silesia and the Pomeranian corridor, and Lithuania in her demands for the city of Wilno. Finally, they were blamed for the Soviet attack on Poland of 17 September 1939 and the subsequent Soviet absorption of forty-seven per cent of Poland's territory. For these reasons communists were distrusted by the majority of Poles.

The German army attacked the Soviet Union on 22 June 1941. Immediately, with a speed that was almost embarrassing, Soviet foreign policy was transformed. The 'imperialist' war became the 'Great Patriotic War'. The British and French 'warmongers' became gallant allies in the battle against fascism. Within three weeks (12 July) an Anglo-Soviet mutual assistance agreement was signed. The Soviet Union at once began to negotiate with the Polish government-in-exile, which after the fall of France had established itself in London. The Polish 'London Government' was no powerless refugee group. Many thousands of Poles who owed allegiance to it were already fighting the Germans as part of the British armed forces. In Poland an underground force known as the Home Army (the *Armia Krajowa* or AK) was operating and receiving its orders by radio from the London Government. Of more direct concern to the Soviets were the hundreds of thousands of Poles in Soviet labour camps. What was to be done with them? By coming to terms with the 'bourgeois' London Government, the Kremlin would be able to solve a problem of internal administration as well as to gain a powerful ally.

General Władysław Sikorski, Premier of the London Government, was still not in a strong bargaining position. Many Poles hated the Russians so much they were against his even talking to them. Were the Russians suddenly absolved from their crimes and turned into friends, simply because the Germans had attacked them? Whatever doubts Sikorski may have had, he clearly saw it as his duty to negotiate, if only for the sake of his countrymen who were still the Russians' prisoners. On 30 July 1941 an agreement was signed by Sikorski and by Ivan Maisky, the Soviet Ambassador in London. It provided an 'amnesty'—a word that really stuck in the throat—

for the Polish prisoners in Russia. Many Poles saw Sikorski as a traitor who had lowered the national pride by agreeing to such an insult. The former prisoners in Russia were to be formed into a Polish army that would fight shoulder to shoulder with the Red Army against the Germans. This would be commanded by Władysław Anders, a colonel in the prewar Polish Army, who for this purpose was moved from a cell in the Lubjanka prison in Moscow to a luxury flat full of champagne, caviare and gifts for such an honoured guest.[14]

After June 1941 the Russians no longer needed to inhibit communist activity in German-occupied territory. But now there was the Sikorski-Maisky agreement, a new complication. Again the Polish communists found themselves in the position of not being allowed to 'rock the boat'. The agreement with 'bourgeois' Poland was important to the Soviet Union, then suffering terrible blows from the German *Blitzkrieg*. The Polish communists were expected for the moment to play second fiddle to the Polish 'bourgeois' ally. They were being kept in reserve as one of Stalin's contingency plans. The first months after the German attack the 'Initiative Group' in Russia spent in training and discussion. They were preparing for a parachute drop on Poland and had to settle the basic rules under which they would operate. One important matter was the name of the future party. The obvious name 'The Communist Party of Poland', was out of the question. The Party under this name had been dissolved and had not been rehabilitated. Polish communists in Poland were still suspected of Trotskyism, quite unjustly since the reality of the occupation did not allow for such luxuries. Nationalism had come into vogue, even among communists, and Trotsky had died on 22 August 1940. But still the label stuck. Stalin would not have another 'Communist Party' in Poland. Also the Soviet Union, in its new frame of mind, had to take into consideration the views of the London Government and the Polish people. Among most of them the Polish Communist Party was thoroughly discredited. It was regarded purely as a Soviet agency which had assisted Hitler to conquer their country. The new Polish communists needed a new name to go with their new image as a patriotic party firmly committed to an independent Polish state. They would win popularity by appealing to the Polish *raison d'état*, by stressing the need for friendship and military alliance both during and after the war with the Soviet

Union. The other features of their political platform, such as land reform and the nationalisation of the major industries, were not emphasised in the new manifesto.

With these thoughts in mind the Polish communists, as they prepared during the autumn of 1941 for the foundation of the political party which now rules Poland, decided not to use the word 'communist', indeed to ban it from their writings and propaganda. In the mind of almost every Pole it was a bad word, and it had to go. Their choice fell instead on the name 'Polish Workers and Peasants' Party' (Polska Partia Robotniczo-Chłopska), but even this sounded too 'red' for the mood of the moment. The name finally adopted was 'Polish Workers' Party' (Polska Partia Robotnicza), which was suggested by Georgy Dimitrov personally. The communist party was thereafter known by its intitials as the 'PPR'.

By the middle of September 1941, the first part of this 'Initiative Group' was ready to go to Poland. The group, about a dozen of them, flew first to Viazma, about 120 miles west of Moscow. The Germans were nearly upon Viazma, having advanced about 500 miles into Russia in the two months since the start of the war. They had to take off as far west as possible, since the round trip to Warsaw and back was about 1,500 miles and a strain on the aeroplane's fuel capacity. But the aeroplane crashed shortly after take-off. Five of them were injured and one, Jan Turlejski, died on the way to hospital. By the time they had recovered from this false start, battle was raging around Viazma, and the party had to be evacuated to Moscow. A month later, in mid-October, Moscow itself was in danger. Thousands of her citizens were fleeing eastwards. The Soviet government and administration was evacuated to Kuibyshev, 600 miles south-east of the capital. The Polish communist leaders went with them.

After a few weeks the Moscow panic subsided and the party were able to return to Pushkino, north of Moscow, where a Comintern school had been in operation for some years. Here they met the second group of Polish communists that had been undergoing training. It was led by Aleksander Kowalski, Malgorzata Fornalska and Janek Krasicki. After a few days in Moscow and a final meeting with Dimitrov, the first group was parachuted successfully onto Wiązownia, a village fifteen miles from Warsaw on the Lublin road. A week later the others were dropped on to various towns around Poland.

Władysław Gomułka was not at this time one of the leaders of Polish communism. During his time in Lwów he filled a modest job. He was a junior factory administrator. He was not one of the communists selected for the 'Initiative Group' or for training at the Comintern's expense. Shortly after the German attack he had made his way west, across the line of battle, to his native province of Rzeszów, in the foothills of the Carpathian mountains. By the time the 'Initiative Group' had arrived in Poland in the last days of 1941, Gomułka was already established in south-east Poland as a resistance leader. It was not until the summer of 1942 that he came to Warsaw to take up his first important political post, the leadership of the PPR's Warsaw organisation. In December 1942, he joined Małgorzata Fornalska, Józef Wieczorek and Aleksander Kowalski as a member of the Central Committee.

The Initiative Group set about the foundation of the new party.[15] Armed with the approval of the Kremlin and the Comintern, they were able to claim the allegiance of most of the communists in German-occupied Poland. The leadership of the Party went to three men, a *troyka*: Marceli Nowotko, Secretary of the Party, Paweł Finder, his deputy, and Bolesław Mołojec. On 10 January 1942 PPR published its first document —an appeal with the significant title 'To Workers, Peasants and Intellectuals. To all Polish patriots'. This first declaration consisted mainly of a patriotic appeal to all Poles to fight the Nazi invader. Of course, the PPR supported the Soviet pact with Premier Sikorski. It had to. But it criticised Sikorski for putting difficulties in the way of an understanding with the Soviet Union. The need to be friendly with Russia, announced the PPR, was dictated purely by Polish patriotism and *raison d'état*. The Party was careful to gloss over its link with communism. It declared that, although founded with the Comintern's blessing, the PPR was not a member of the Comintern.

This announcement caused dismay among some communists who did not understand the Soviet need at the time for an antifascist 'national front' party, ready to collaborate with 'bourgeois' groups. To them it seemed suspicious that a communist party should form itself and not use the name 'communist', and that it should announce shamelessly that it was not a member of the international communist movement. Unable to communicate with Moscow to check the PPR's *bona fides*, they suspected a provocation. Their doubts were only gradually dispelled.

But the majority of Poles, non-communist or even anti-communist, were not at all deceived by the PPR's patriotic protestations. It was enough for them that nearly all the leading PPR members were formerly in the prewar Party, the KPP. Poles in Poland were at first even less inclined to patch up differences with Russia than were Poles in emigration. They were not prepared to fight in alliance with Russia, the lesser enemy, in order to defeat the greater enemy. Many of them took a perverse delight in the German victories of the second half of 1941. It was agreeable to see the Russians who had 'stabbed them in the back' in September 1939, suffering the same misfortunes as themselves. Practically speaking, of course, it is hard to see how Hitler's successes could fail to harm the Polish interest. As the German army moved east, Poland, instead of being an outpost, was becoming the heart of the Nazi empire and essential to German communications. The day of liberation was being put further and further into the future. But this Poles did not seem to mind. Stalin's armies were retreating and surrendering, often putting up even less resistance than the Polish armies had two years earlier.

'Let us not worry about the German victories!' read a headline in *Information Bulletin*, the underground journal of Sikorski's Home Army (the AK). 'Our enemies are destroying each other before our eyes,' wrote the AK journalist in Poland, only a week before the Sikorski-Maisky agreement was signed. Presumably, the hope then was that the Germans would overreach themselves in the east, leaving their western flank open for Britain and her allies (who at that time were very few) to sweep across Europe, through Germany and Poland. Such naïve lack of realism is not as grotesque as it sounds. The Poles were cut off from much of the world's news. Starved of fact, as well as of food and freedom, they were living on their hopes. In 1941 it was towards Britain that most Poles were turning their gaze. The British had let them down once already, by not helping them in September 1939. Surely they would now make up for it by fighting to liberate Poland? Was not Poland Britain's most loyal ally in the war against Germany?

The London Government and its Delegation in Poland were becoming optimistic. Since the German attack on Russia their political position was improving immeasurably. From being a group of almost friendless *émigrés*, 'wanted bandits' of the German régime or 'socially unreliable elements' of the Soviet régime, they had suddenly become a force to be reckoned with, a participant in the world political scene. In Russia Sikorski himself, from being a source of crude cartoon humour, was being hailed as a glorious ally. The 30 July 1941 agreement he negotiated with Maisky, apart from the insulting reference to the 'amnesty', was really quite favourable to the Poles. The hundreds of thousands of Poles in Russia were able to set up their own local administration, schools, places of worship, even a *deuxième bureau* (*dwójka*) which, among other things, conducted intelligence operations on behalf of the British and Americans and security clearances on Poles suspected of communist sympathy. The question of the future Polish-Soviet frontier was still at issue, but there had as yet been no challenge to the 1939 frontier which was favourable to Poland. On 14 November 1941 Stalin told the new Polish ambassador in Moscow, Stanisław Kot, that he was in favour 'of rebuilding an independent Polish State, irrespective of its internal political system'.[16] He was treating the Poles with unaccustomed deference, to which they were replying with hostility. On 30 June 1941 *Rzeczpospolita Polska*, the London Government newspaper, had called the German-Soviet struggle 'a great step forward'. 'The whole Polish people,' the article went on, 'watches with deep and great joy the bloody German-Soviet battles, remembering all the anti-Polish crimes committed by both sides. We regard both partitioning powers as our eternal enemies. In this new phase of the war the Polish people should continue the policy it has been following up to now of not expanding its strength, but conserving it for the reconstruction of the new Republic. . . .'

The Government and its Delegation in Poland ordered the AK not to launch full-scale anti-German terrorist attacks and sabotage. The Germans had an answer to 'terrorist' attacks—savage reprisal. For every German killed, the Nazis would kill a number of Polish hostages. The underground AK was therefore only committing acts of *selective* terror against Germans with particularly bloody records. This was reckoned to be a deterrent to the extremes of Nazi brutality. Unrestrained AK terror, the Delegation thought, would have exactly the opposite effect. Apart from the reprisal problem, the soft-pedalling of AK sabotage was thought by many to be in Poland's strategic interest. Sabotage in Poland would help Russia and hinder the German advance eastwards. These Poles saw no reason why they should expose themselves to danger in order to help one enemy against another.

To the newly-formed PPR the issue was much clearer. The Soviet Union was in danger and must be helped, even at the cost of Polish lives. This fact was recognised by Nowotko and his Party, and expressed in a radio message from him to the Comintern leader Georgy Dimitrov on 19 June 1942: 'The leaders of the old parties—the Socialists, the Sikorski-ites, the Piłsudski-ites, the National Democrats—have come out strongly against our partisans. Their idea is to wait until the two enemies, Hitler and the Soviets, destroy each other. We are fighting against this idea. For the moment, however, we have not come out against these parties themselves.'[17]

Two months later, on 17 September, Nowotko sent another telegram. He was becoming impatient at the instructions he had received not to attack the London Government forces directly: 'Up to now we have not come out strongly against the leaders of the old parties and their political ideas. We have confined ourselves to explaining in our press and in our propaganda the harmfulness for Poland of these ideas, and to calling for a united front. Because of the violence of the attacks being made on the Soviet Union, we now regard it as essential that we express ourselves more strongly. . . .'

It is interesting to see that in his message, Nowotko did not differentiate between the political groupings of the London government. To him they were all hostile. Sikorski 'moderates' were tarred with the same brush as Piłsudski 'fascists'. This was contrary to the then Soviet policy and also contrary to the modern Polish communist line, which is to see Sikorski as a reasonable man, with whom socialists and communists might have been able to negotiate. In 1962 Władysław Gomułka in a well-known speech claimed that at this time the PPR 'did not exclude the possiblity that he (Sikorski) might stand at the head of the government after the liberation of Poland'.[18] In the opinion of Antoni Przygoński, a modern Polish historian:

'The group centred round the person of Sikorski was that group which in certain circumstances, if the situation were to change, might feel itself inclined to cooperate with the Left.

'At the same time all Sikorski's opponents were flatly opposed to such cooperation. Even though, as it turned out later, the rifts in the *émigré* camp were not as deep as

all that, and even though the Sikorski section of the bourgeois camp was not entirely consistent in its policy towards
the Soviet Union, there was still a chance at this time for
the PPR to split the bourgeois camp and cooperate with a
part of it, if not in 1942, at least some time in the future.'

In mid-1942 there was still no sign that Nowotko's trouble-
making telegrams would receive a favourable response from
the Kremlin. Sikorski's stock with the Russians, on paper at
least, stood high. In December 1941 he had visited Stalin in
Moscow and signed a second treaty, a 'Declaration of Friendship and Mutual Assistance'. Stalin's military position was still
weak. Moscow and Leningrad were still in danger. Stalin was
in no position to get tough with his allies, even an ally-in-exile.
He was still not ready to give a free rein to the Polish communists, of whom he was probably just as suspicious as he was of
Sikorski. The Polish and Soviet governments had, incredibly,
been on reasonably good terms for a whole year.

V: THE UNDER-
GROUND LIMELIGHT

The early months of 1942 were for the Allies some of the most unhappy of the war. On 15 February the Japanese took Singapore, on 10 March Rangoon. In North Africa in late January the Germans retook Benghazi and began their advance towards the Egyptian frontier. On the Russian front the Germans launched a spring offensive, a drive towards the oil-fields of the Caspian Sea and the Caucasus. Within a few months they had captured Sebastopol, Rostov, and Krasnodar, and were beginning their all-out attack on Stalingrad.

In occupied Poland relations between Premier Sikorski's representatives and the newly-created PPR should, by the laws of common sense, have been excellent. Premier Sikorski had signed two treaties with the Soviets—one with Ivan Maisky, Soviet Ambassador in London, the other with Stalin himself. Poland and the Soviet Union were, on paper, firm allies. This was the logical situation. For Poland and the Soviet Union not to be allies would have been absurd. The common enemy was so very strong. He was in military occupation of all Polish territory and much of the best and most productive Soviet territory. This is why the weak points in the Sikorski-Stalin agreement struck many outsiders as silly and hair-splitting. Why should they quibble about frontiers when the frontier did not even exist, when the very existence of both countries was in peril?

With hindsight it is clear that the Polish-Russian 'allied unity' of those months was largely illusory. It was as if both sides had to go through the motions of agreeing. Their 'friendship' was to impress the British and Americans, their suppliers, as well as the Germans, their enemy. Sikorski himself was one of the few to come out of the business with credit. He genuinely believed here at last was a chance to end the centuries of Polish-Russian enmity. He was prepared to swallow his pride and negotiate in the national interest with Stalin, the man who had

done so much harm to Poles in previous years. He was determined to get the best possible deal for Poles *in the present
situation*. To do this he had to lose personal face, and even be
called a traitor by the more hot-headed, vengeful and unrealistic of his countrymen.

As for Stalin's approach to 'friendship' with Poland, it is
hard to see it as any less hypocritical and insincere than his
usual schemes. As the balance of power changed, so his attitude
to Poland changed. In 1939 it was in his interest to invade
Poland. In 1940 it was in his interest to deport and imprison
vast sections of her population, to keep them in such inhuman
conditions that thousands died. In 1941 it was in his interest
to sign treaties with Poland and assure her of future independence 'irrespective of her internal social system'. In 1944 and
1945 it was in his interest to go back on this pledge at Yalta
and Teheran, and insist on a 'friendly' Poland, which in practice
meant a pro-communist Poland. Communist and capitalist
are now agreed that Stalin was no saint in his treatment of
Russia. In his treatment of Poland he was not far short of
devilish.

Divided Poland fell and divided Poland was enduring
German occupation. Inside the country there was little of
Sikorski's and Stalin's civilised diplomacy. There was no need
for the various Polish political groups to keep up a show of
unity. The communists had always been outside the mainstream of Polish politics. Between them and the 'London'
groups there was little common ground, even in wartime. In
1942 the PPR's numbers were still small. By the end of the year,
by their own figures, their Warsaw organisation numbered only
750 men. But from the beginning they were taken seriously
by the 'Delegation' and the AK. Since 1939 Sikorski's men had
operated an 'anti-communist agency', codenamed 'Antyk'.
There was no move in Poland itself towards underground
unity or a common anti-Nazi front. Instead both sides accused
the other of disloyalty. The 'Delegation' saw the PPR purely
as agents of Moscow. And they saw Moscow, whatever Sikorski might say or sign, as a hostile power. The PPR saw the
Delegation as full of fascists and collaborators, ready to cooperate with the occupying Nazis against the Soviet Union
and communism. Communist and anti-communist sometimes did
negotiate with each other, but they made little effort to keep up
the show of unity on which Stalin and Sikorski had set their seal.

This was, moreover, the honeymoon period of AK-communist relations. As the war continued the mutual abuse grew more intense and finally degenerated into open hostility, in deed as well as word. Both sides then accused the other of actively collaborating with the Gestapo. For instance, Władysław Gomułka in the first volume of his published *Articles and Speeches* makes the following charges and implications:

'In the internal affairs department of the Delegation and in the AK high command there existed special cells engaged in "processing" left-wing activists and organisations. From the year 1939 a so-called "Anti-Communist Agency" (code-name "Antyk" or "Blok") was financed by the Delegation and the AK high command. It distributed anti-communist propaganda, and also coordinated the anti-communist intelligence activity of various Delegation cells, reactionary military organisations and political parties. Among other things it prepared lists of left-wing leaders and activists, which more than once found their way *into the hands of the Gestapo*' [author's italics].[1]

On the other hand the AK leaders constantly accused the communists of exactly the same crime—of treachery, of being ready to give information to the Germans in order to strengthen their own position. These are allegations which it is impossible to confirm or disprove. The most extraordinary thing about them, perhaps, is that they were made at all, that it was even *thinkable* that two Polish groups of differing political views might denounce each other to the German Gestapo. For instance, Marceli Nowotko, the 1942 communist leader, is accused specifically of treachery by a number of anti-communists.* Józef Światło, a member of the post-war Polish security police who defected to the Americans in 1953, is one of the accusers:

'Parachuted into Poland as a man trusted by Moscow, he [Nowotko] had two tasks. He had to organise the PPR

* For example, Richard F. Staar on p. 79 of *Poland, 1944–62*, writes that Nowotko was killed by Mołojec 'who discovered the collaboration with the Gestapo and thought Nowotko to be a traitor'. The same implication is contained in the *History of Poland* by Władysław Pobóg-Malinowski, p. 403.

and fill it with Moscow men. At the same time he was to unravel the net of the Polish underground movement and liquidate it by all available methods. To this end he brought specific Soviet instructions ordering him to form close political collaboration with the Gestapo . . . immediately after his arrival Nowotko began to organise a secret disinformation cell which gathered data on AK activity: names, addresses and details of locations. This information was then sent to the Gestapo by letter.'[2]

On the face of it, it is an unlikely story. But 1942 was an unlikely year for Poland and its communist party. On 28 November 1942 its Secretary thus accused by Światło, Marceli Nowotko, was murdered. A few weeks later *Trybuna Wolności* (Freedom Tribune), the communist underground journal, announced he had been shot in the street 'conspiratorially'. No further details were given. The death was a mystery, one that has not been fully explained to this day. After the war part of the truth was told, that Nowotko was killed by a member of his own communist Party. In November 1949 the communist leader Bolesław Bierut said: 'It is a fact that comrade Nowotko, the first Secretary of the Central Committee of the PPR, was murdered by an *agent provocateur* who was sent into the Party by the *deuxième bureau*.' In 1952 a booklet about Nowotko's life and work claimed he was killed by 'a Polish fascist'. Even then there can have been few communists who realised their former leader was killed by his own 'number three', Bolesław Mołojec, a member of the original triumvirate. The truth is that Mołojec and his brother Zygmunt killed Nowotko. The outstanding question is, why? Here the mystery remains, one which old communists in Poland still discuss with bated breath. In unofficial Party circles two theories are mooted: firstly, that the deed was done by French intelligence; secondly, that the Mołojec brothers were pure Soviet agents who killed Nowokto because he was showing signs of excessive independence. As usual when no official explanation is forthcoming, rumour takes over, and rumour is always ready to believe the worst.

Polish communist historians no longer claim Mołojec was an agent of the London Government's *deuxième bureau*. They try to gloss over the unpleasant business with vague sentences— all of which increase the mystery, and lend weight to another of Światło's allegations: that Mołojec killed Nowotko because he discovered him giving information to the Germans, refused to believe he was doing this on Soviet orders and assumed Nowotko must be a traitor. It is a theory which fits the facts but, of course, cannot be proved or disproved until the day the PPR archives are thrown open to historical examination. After Mołojec killed Nowotko, he was condemned to death by a Party court and executed. The full truth probably died with him, but there are men alive, Gomułka among them, who were in the PPR leadership at the time, and who must know something of what happened. Until they tell what they know the rumours will continue. Światło's theory, however incredible, has the merit of being the only one on record.

Apart from such murder, treachery and internal Polish strife, November 1942 was a good month for the Allies. By 4 November the battle of el-Alamein was won and Rommel was in full retreat. By the end of the month the 300,000-strong army of General Paulus was surrounded by the Russians in Stalingrad. A year which had begun badly was ending well. Nowotko and Mołojec were both dead, so the surviving member of the PPR triumvirate, Pawel Finder, was elected Secretary of the Party. Władysław Gomułka, from being an ordinary Central Committee member, became Finder's deputy. The third member of the new trio was Franciszek Joźwiak-Witold. It was at this time that Gomułka's political career began to assume some importance.

Gomułka's appointment as the PPR 'Number Two' was part of an extremely rapid promotion. He was young, thirty-seven, and his political career, interrupted by five years of imprisonment and two years of political stagnation in Russia at the beginning of the war, was quite a short one. He had not been one of the leaders of the pre-war communist party. The KPP leaders had mainly been intellectuals who had little in common with Gomułka, a man with little formal education who relied on his common sense, gift for oratory and what he had managed to teach himself from books in his 'university'—a prison cell. In Soviet-occupied Lwów and Białystok in 1939–41 it was the communist intellectuals who got the good jobs in journalism and administration. Gomułka had to take a minor post in a factory.

Under occupation conditions Gomułka's situation was quite different. The intellectual qualities which he lacked became suddenly less important. His natural cunning, genuine socialist idealism, limitless energy and enthusiasm were just what was needed. He had valuable experience as an underground conspirator. The tricks he had learnt and used against the Piłsudski-ites could now be used against the Germans.

The 'Initiative Group', the founder members of the PPR, had left Russia late in 1941 with instructions not to 'rock the boat' with the London Government. But things had changed since then. The PPR leaders had a wireless link with Moscow. They were loyal communists, and so were expected to be obedient. But during 1942 links and communication with Moscow were no more than sporadic. Gomułka revealed in 1962 that

'up to 1944 the amount of arms we received from Soviet parachute drops was a mere trifle. Only after a partisan department was organised in the Polish Army in the Soviet Union did this situation change at all.

'In spite of the lies put about the London camp that the PPR was "a richly paid agency of Moscow", throughout its activity it received no financial help whatever from outside. . . .'[3]

In spite of its numerical weakness, the PPR longed to be able to go into the attack, to take a tougher line with the 'London' Poles. Many of its leaders had been in the illegal pre-war communist party, and had been imprisoned for their political activity. It stuck in their throats to be forced to tolerate the supremacy of the 'bourgeois' politicians they so disliked. By the end of 1942 some PPR leaders thought their party should break completely with 'London'.

Only a month after Gomułka joined the PPR three-man leadership, an attempt was made to patch up the differences between the PPR and 'London'. Significantly Gomułka was the man the communists put in charge of the peace offensive. His first move, and his first important piece of political writing was a long 'Open letter to the Home Delegation of the Government of General Sikorski', printed in *Trybuna Wolności*, the PPR's main underground journal on 15 January 1943.[4] The substance of it was an attack on the Home Army's policy of limiting anti-German terror and sabotage. The Home Army journalists were heading their articles with such slogans as 'Now is not yet the time', 'Armed action? Yes, but within limits.' 'National uprisings cannot be launched every three months,' said the Home Army's *Information Bulletin.* It urged its fighters to keep 'arms at the ready', and to conserve their strength for one great battle with the occupying army. Gomułka's 'open letter' was a strange mixture of deference, sympathy, threat and plain invective. Admitting that his party, the PPR, was 'the youngest member of the Polish underground', Gomułka claimed that 'we still extend the hand of friendship to other Polish political parties. We encourage joint cooperation and organisation of the struggle of the whole Polish people against the Nazi occupier.' He still drew a distinction between the unspecified 'democratic' elements in the 'London' camp, and the *sanacja* remnants of the pre-war government, whom he accused frankly of treachery:

'The PPR calls all political parties to national agreement. We think, though, that an agreement on the basis of inaction and political trickery would be a traitorous agreement. Such an agreement would be easy to make, even with the occupying army. . . .

'Unreliable elements, under the pretence of fighting communism, are feverishly trying to launch civil war among us, and have even taken the first steps towards this end. . . . It is no secret to us who prepares lists of names of members of our party, so as to give them into the hands of the Gestapo. . . .'[5]

In this situation, with both communists and anti-communists accusing each other of the ultimate crime, it seems strange there could have been any talk of peace between them. But there was, and Gomułka was to be the peacemaker. His aim was not to woo 'London' as a whole, but to split it. Even so, his words marked him out as a 'liberal' within the PPR, many of whose leaders were more inclined to reject 'London' altogether. The question of the correct attitude to 'London' was one of the main controversies within the communist PPR—one which assumed greater and greater importance as the day of liberation drew nearer. Should they rely on their own strength and on that of their Soviet ally, or should they try to broaden their support and attract sympathetic non-communists? Gomułka clearly held the latter view.

Early in 1943 Gomułka was known in underground circles, because of his 'open letter', as the leading exponent of the PPR 'broad front' faction. His work was partly military, partly political and partly editorial. Using his conspiratorial pseudonym 'Wiesław', he was active in planning anti-German sabotage and terrorism. He personally directed an attack on the Warsaw 'Café club', where German soldiers met to drink beer, on 24 October, 1942. Two grenades were thrown into the club. Several Germans were killed and wounded. Of course, the Germans took immediate reprisal action and arrested fifty hostages. It was just the sort of action that the 'London' AK regarded as pointless. But it was better, in Gomułka's view, than nothing. It was better than the inaction and vacillation that in his view characterised the 'London' military leaders and politicians. Still, his attitude to them was far from implacable, as is demonstrated by this excerpt from his 'open letter': 'If the London Government and its Delegation in Poland were to take a firm stand, reject and condemn the policies of the pre-war *sanacja*, especially with regard to the Soviet Union, then the questions of national front and national unity would become much more real and easy to negotiate.'[6]

In February 1943 there was a follow-up to the 'open letter'. Talks took place between the 'London' groups, the Delegation and the AK Home Army, and the 'communist' groups, the PPR and the People's Guard (the PPR's military arm), with a view to burying their differences and forming an anti-Nazi national front. Władysław Gomułka was the PPR's representative at the talks. His colleague from the People's Guard (the 'Gwardia Ludowa' or 'GL') was Jan Strzeszewski. The idea was that the units of the GL should join the more numerous and more powerful AK, stop inhibiting each other's activity, and become allies. But this plan, so clearly in Poland's interest, was soon bogged down in a mess of politics and 'matters of principle'. Gomułka and Strzeszewski, while admitting that the AK as the superior force had the right to lead, would not surrender the autonomy of their GL detachments. They also demanded the creation of a government *in Poland* 'that would express the opinions of the whole of society and supersede the *émigré* government'. The AK and the Delegation saw this as a direct threat to their existence as the legal rulers in Poland, subordinate to the authority of the legal government in London. They came back to the PPR with a series of demands:[7] the recognition of the London Government as the only legal government; the recognition of the 1939 frontiers of Poland; a declaration of their 'complete independence from non-Polish organisations'. This last demand was, of course, a reference to the PPR's supposed subservience to the Comintern and the Soviet Union.

The talks got off to a bad start. The 'London' delegate, Jan Piekałkiewicz, was arrested by the Germans the day after the talks opened. Then during April, while the talks were temporarily adjourned, there came crisis in relations between the Soviet Union and the London Government. The Germans announced the discovery in the woods of Katyń, near Smolensk, of a mass grave of several thousand Polish officers. Documents on the bodies seemed to show the men were killed while the area was still under Soviet occupation. It was clear the officers had been originally deported by the Soviet authorities. The question was, who had killed them?

Goebbels and his propaganda machine made the most of their chance. Soviet-Polish relations were already bad. Katyń was the last straw. Accused of mass murder, the Soviet authorities defended themselves by the best method they knew—by attack. To them, Goebbels was a murderer and a *provocateur*. Therefore, anyone who failed to treat his lies with the contempt they deserved was an enemy. At this point there was pressure on the 'London' Poles, from West as well as from East, to withdraw their demand for a Red Cross investigation into the massacre. When they refused, Stalin broke off diplomatic relations with the London Government. This was on 26 April 1943.

It was now clear there could be no link-up between the Home Army and the communists. Gomułka and Strzeszewski rejected all the demands of the 'London' delegates. The demand for recognition of the 1939 frontiers was seen as clearly unacceptable and 'reactionary'. It was pointed out that such a demand was not made even by Sikorski's government, whose policy it was for the Polish-Soviet frontier to be settled by mutual agreement after the war. The 'reactionaries' in Poland were therefore seen as more reactionary even than the 'reactionaries' in London.

The recognition of 'London' as the only real Polish government was rejected by the PPR for the same reason that it was later rejected by Stalin—because it was unfriendly and

anti-communist. But now the PPR began to make new accusations. They claimed the 'London camp' was unrepresen-
tative of the Polish people, that it was *not even a government at
all*. Its legal justification rested on the April 1935 constitution which had been written at Piłsudski's dictation, and
it was certainly dictatorial. The communists claimed the
constitution was 'fascist', and could therefore not provide a
basis for a Polish government that was in the process of fighting
fascism.

The call to declare themselves 'independent of non-Polish
organisations' was seen by the PPR as a provocation. The
Party's connection with the Comintern had always been a
difficult question. In fact most of the Party leaders had been
educated at Comintern schools, and the Party was the Comintern's creation. The fact that the PPR was not a *member* of the
Comintern was a purely tactical move to free the PPR of the
'unpatriotic' stigma that was attached to the pre-war KPP.
But the PPR was just as attached to the Comintern and Moscow as any other communist party. To quote a modern Polish
historian, 'it [the PPR] was linked with it [the Comintern]
ideologically, politically and organisationally'.[8] Therefore,
although for tactical reasons it could not admit itself a *member*
of the Comintern, it could equally not admit itself *free* of the
Comintern.

It was a problem from which the PPR was soon to be freed.
A month later, on 22 May, the Comintern was dissolved by
Stalin, ostensibly as a gesture of goodwill to his western allies.
This move was seen by many in the West as a blow to international communism. In fact, it was nothing of the kind. The
Soviet Union continued to provide moral help to foreign communist parties, even though it was not yet in a position to give
much physical help. And the plain fact still existed that Poland
and other east European countries were geographically closer
to the Soviet Union than to the West, and would probably
soon be occupied by the Red Army as it advanced towards
Germany. Regarding the PPR's chance of achieving power in
Poland, the Comintern was neither here nor there. But from
the point of view of a small communist party like the PPR, it
was an annoyance, a source of supervision and control. Polish
communists had special reason to dislike the Comintern, since
it was on the Comintern's initiative that the KPP had been
dissolved in 1938. So it was with some satisfaction that the

PPR viewed the dissolution of those who had five years earlier dissolved them:

> 'This resolution satisfies the needs of the international situation and the strategy of the workers' movement that arises out of it.
>
> 'It will help the consolidation of the anti-Hitler bloc, which is the main task at the present time. . . . Judging from our own one and a half years' of experience as a national [sic] workers' party, we consider the dissolution of the Comintern to be appropriate. . . .'[9]

So, in the space of a month, the PPR was free of two of the main millstones round its neck—the Comintern and the London Government—both of which it had previously been bound to support. The way was suddenly clear for it to act by its own rules and in its own interest. Many members, Gomułka among them, had hoped for an understanding with 'London' and had tried to achieve it. Others were only too pleased at last to be allowed a free hand.

The dissolution of the Comintern was useful to the PPR in another way. They could now claim with justification that they were no longer connected with 'non-Polish' organisations. Dependence on the Comintern had often been flung in the teeth of the PPR not only by the 'reactionaries' but also by their potential allies, who, though socialist, were anti-Soviet. These allies could now be pacified and wooed. As a contributor to a PPR journal wrote on 1 June:

> 'This [Comintern] question was continually raised during our conversations with Sikorski's delegation in January and February. Our supposed dependence on the Comintern stopped certain Peasant Party and village bourgeois groups from coming to an understanding and a way of cooperation with us. These objections, in so far as they were not only a pretext, now cease to hold water, and therefore great opportunities are opened up for our party.'[10]

This was quite true. The PPR membership had been slowly but steadily increasing. In June 1942 it was 4,000. In January 1943, the first anniversary, it was 8,000.[11] Fortune was being as kind to the communists as it was being cruel to 'London'.

On 30 June the Home Army commander Stefan Grót-Rowecki was arrested by the Gestapo and later executed. He was replaced by Tadeusz Bór-Komorowski. Then on 4 July Władysław Sikorski, Premier of the Polish Government-in-exile, was killed on his way back from the Middle East. Late that night his Liberator aircraft crashed into the sea shortly after leaving the Gibraltar runway. Everyone on board was killed except the pilot.

The mass of Poles, even the opponents of 'London', were shocked and dismayed by the death of Sikorski. Officially the PPR mourned his death, but from their own political point of view, if the tragedy had to happen, it was lucky that it happened so soon after the Soviet breach with 'London'. The communists were now able to credit the dead Premier with all the good that had ever come out of the London Government. Praise was heaped upon him by the Western Allies, and also by the Soviet Union. Just as when Franklin D. Roosevelt died three years later, the Russians were applying their rule that there is no good 'bourgeois' statesman so good as a dead one.

It was during the summer of 1943 that the PPR really began to challenge the London Government and to claim an influence, if not actual control, over the future government of Poland. The 'London' authorities realised this. The Russians were making definite progress in their fight against Germany, and every step the Red Army advanced westward strengthened the influence of their PPR comrades in Poland. 'London' and the Home Army had, on the other hand, been weakened by the breach with Moscow, the loss of Sikorski and Rowecki, and the mutual dependence, if not trust, that was growing between Stalin, Churchill and Roosevelt. The supporters of 'London' in Poland now felt bound to take more desperate measures. The work of the Home Army's anti-communist committee (Antyk) was intensified, as were attacks on the communists in the underground press. On 8 September the Labour Party (Stronnictwo Pracy) journal *Naród* wrote that 'the Germans have ceased to be enemy number one . . . the struggle against communism is today the most important, and perhaps the only task'. On 27 October *Wielka Polska*, organ of the National Party (Stronnictwo Narodowe), wrote: 'There are now operating on Polish territory two enemies, two occupying powers—the Germans and the Bolsheviks.'

It may now seem absurd, even monstrously unjust, for the

Polish journalists to have compared their Russian ally with their Nazi oppressor. Their feelings perhaps cannot be understood by anyone who did not live in occupied Poland during those years. For these opinions were not the anti-communist ravings of fascists. They were expressed by middle-of-the-road politicians, men who in other circumstances might be called 'liberals'. The point was that the German occupation, horrible as it was, was viewed optimistically by the Polish population. They knew it could not last. Germany was bound, sooner or later, to be defeated. They believed, naïvely perhaps, in the strength and support of their Anglo-Saxon allies. From 1943 onwards, to the optimistic and news-starved Poles, victory over Germany and occupation of Germany by the British and Americans seemed a mere few months away.

These politicians saw the German danger, although real enough at present, as insignificant in the long term. But Russian oppression, non-existent at present, they saw as a potentially more lasting and therefore a greater evil. If Poland were to fall under Russian domination, they thought, it would remain there not merely for a few years, but for decades. After all, 130 years of Russian domination had only just ended. The Poles were frightened of history repeating itself, and their fears were not without justification.

In March 1943 the PPR felt established enough to publish their party programme. This document, called 'What we are fighting for', was composed largely by Gomułka and Pawel Finder. It was hardly a revolutionary document. Indeed, it was not so much Marxist as liberal-reformist. It called for the elimination from the government of *sanacja* 'fascists and reactionaries', but not of the members of other 'London' parties. The camps and ghettoes should be emptied and destroyed. There should be complete freedom of speech, conscience, press and assembly. Banks and large industries should be nationalised, but not the smaller capitalist enterprises. Estates larger than fifty hectares should be confiscated and distributed among the peasants. There would be free education and a free health service. There was nothing in this programme that had not been proposed before the war by the anti-*sanacja* liberal parties. As a manifesto for a communist party it was so unexceptionable as to be quite unrealistic. Most Poles remembered that freedom of speech, assembly and suchlike were guaranteed by the Communist Manifesto and the Soviet Constitution, but they had still never existed. The whole thing seemed moderate and half-hearted, and therefore quite unconvincing to most Poles.

In the summer of 1943 the PPR leadership was strengthened by a new arrival. Bolesław Bierut was thirteen years older than Gomułka and, unlike him, had been high up in the pre-war KPP. During the 1930s he worked in a Comintern office in Prague. Then he was ordered back to Poland. He was arrested by the *sanacja* 'blue police' and imprisoned in Rawicz, from which he only emerged in 1938 after the dissolution of the Communist Party of Poland. In 1939 he crossed into Soviet-occupied territory. But two years later he was caught in the German advance and therefore separated from the main communist groups. Only in the middle of 1943, after escaping from a prisoner-of-war camp, did he manage to travel from German-occupied Minsk to Warsaw and join the PPR.

He was immediately elected to the Central Committee and to a high position on the 'central editorial board', the group that watched over the expanding communist underground press. Although a more experienced communist and more trusted by Moscow, he had arrived on the scene late, and was therefore subordinate to Gomułka. A rivalry began between the two men that was to become very important in Poland. Bierut and Gomułka vied with each other from the beginning, for the leadership of the Polish party as well as for the ascendancy of their particular political views. For although both men were communists, there were important differences between them, differences which were to grow with time and end in disaster.

In 1943 in Poland disaster was all too frequent, but when it came it often meant promotion for the survivors. On 14 November Gomułka's boss, the PPR Secretary Pawel Finder, was arrested. He and another Central Committee member, Małgorzata Fornalska, who was the common-law wife of Bolesław Bierut, were at a communist hide-out at 10 Grottger Street, Warsaw, ready for a meeting to be held at 8 a.m. Just before eight the Gestapo raided the flat, arrested Finder and Fornalska, and drove them away to the Pawiak prison. Gomułka and three other communist leaders—Franciszek Jóźwiak-Witold, Aleksander Kowalski and Hilary Chełchowski—saw the unfortunate pair being driven away. Following instructions specially designed for such occasions, they walked away from the place of their rendezvous. If they had gone in they would doubtless have been arrested themselves.

For the second time in less than a year the communist party leader was violently removed from office. Finder and Fornalska were horribly tortured in Warsaw's Pawiak prison. On 26 July of the following year they were shot.

The arrest of Finder and Fornalska is now seen as the greatest blow the PPR suffered during the occupation years. The reason why it happened is still not entirely clear. In 1949 Poland's Stalinist leaders were to imply that the Gestapo were tipped off, told about the rendezvous either with the connivance of Gomułka and his friend Spychalski, or at least through their negligence. Pobóg-Malinowski, a pro-*sanacja émigré* historian, implied Finder was given away by the Russians. The most probable explanation—that it was a coincidence, that the Gestapo did not know there would be a meeting—was laughed out of court by the Stalinists after the war, and only put forward in the early 1960s. Coincidence now seems the most likely explanation, and this view is now supported by Hilary Chełchowski who, in a contribution to the book *Ludzie, Fakty, Refleksje* (People, Facts, Reflections), published by the Warsaw Ministry of Defence in 1961, gives a vivid and terrifying eyewitness account of the arrest. If the Gestapo had been tipped off, by whoever it was, they would hardly have been so clumsy as to leave their car outside the door of the flat they were raiding. If they really knew the communist leadership was to meet in this place, they would surely have gone to some trouble to spring an effective trap.

Nine days after Finder's arrest his comrades met to choose a new leader. On such an important matter it would have been normal to communicate with Moscow. But this was impossible. Finder and Małgorzata Fornalska were the only two who knew the code.[12] The PPR went ahead and elected a leader nevertheless—a Polish communist who had spent very little time in Russia, and of whom the Moscovites had probably never heard. Władysław Gomułka was elected Secretary of the Polish Workers' Party on 23 November 1943. He became leader of a small group of a few thousand political idealists. Their popular support was meagre and their backing—the military strength of the Soviet Union—still tentative. The Nazi authorities were calling them bandits and hunting them to death. Many Poles were calling them traitors and slaves of Moscow. It was clearly unlikely at this stage that Gomułka's job would one day be the most important in Poland. Yet this is exactly what happened.

His job became the key to government, and a quarter of a century later Gomułka still held it.

At this time in the eyes of the world the London Government was still the legitimate government of Poland. It was recognised by Great Britain, the United States and almost all the non-Nazi countries of the world. It was not recognised by the Soviet Union, but Stalin had still not yet come up with an alternative. He had to admit as much when, five days after Gomułka's election, he met Churchill and Roosevelt in Teheran. During their four days of talks, 28 November to 1 December, the Polish question came up more than once. It was not, as in subsequent 'Big Three' conferences, a matter of the composition of the future Polish government. They were discussing the frontiers of the future Polish State.

The Polish-Soviet frontier had changed many times between the two world wars. Several attempts were made, both by negotiation and by force of arms, to resolve the allegiance of western Byelorussia and western Ukraine, areas which were declared part of Poland by the Treaty of Riga. The trouble was that their population was not Polish except in certain defined districts and in the city of Lwów. In September 1939 the Soviet Union occupied these areas according to the terms of the Nazi-Soviet pact. Stalin was now unwilling to lose them. He was fortunate in that the September 1939 demarcation line had been agreed not only by Molotov and Ribbentrop a month earlier, but also by Lord Curzon, the British Foreign Secretary who had made an unsuccessful attempt in 1920 to solve Polish-Soviet differences.

The shrewd Stalin saw that a frontier ironically named the 'Curzon Line' would be more acceptable to the Anglo-Saxons than a 'Molotov-Ribbentrop Line'. And it was not his plan that Poland should suffer. His demand for the 'Curzon Line' was coupled with the offer of compensation to Poland at the expense of Germany. It was suggested the other frontier of Poland be moved westwards into Germany and established along the Oder and Neisse rivers. (*Which* Neisse river they meant, the eastern or the western stream, was a detail it was too early to discuss.) The Germans, of course, would be in no position to object to this encroachment on their territory. But the Polish Government was an ally. They might well dislike their country being shunted like a railway wagon 200 miles to the west. They would certainly dislike the idea of losing the Polish city of Lwów. Their views could not be entirely ignored.

It became clear to Stalin at the Teheran conference that Churchill was losing his patience with the Polish Government. He was finding them as overbearing and unaccommodating as he was finding de Gaulle's Free French. Here was the government-in-exile of an occupied country, maintained and financed by the British exchequer, adopting an attitude to the Russian ally so hostile that it was actually endangering relations between the Soviet Union and the British and Americans. It was not a matter of right and justice. It was not that the Poles' hostility was without foundation. It was a matter of practical warfare. Churchill felt a sense of obligation towards the Poles. He admired their bravery, even if he felt little sympathy or kinship with them. Several times he told Stalin that Britain had declared war on Germany because of Poland, that Poland must not be wronged in the final peace treaty. But his disillusionment with Mikołajczyk's 'intransigent' Polish Government, coupled with his fear of a serious breach with Stalin on the Polish issue, was leading him to place Polish interests in the second category of importance.

The Polish Government was not represented at the Teheran Conference. The future frontiers of their country were discussed by Americans, Britons and Russians. Important decisions were made about Poland without the Poles' participation. It was decided Churchill should present a 'formula' to the London Poles, that 'it is thought in principle that the home of the Polish state and nation should be between the so-called Curzon Line and the line of the Oder. . . '. Churchill knew he could never get the Poles to agree to this. He told Stalin as much, remarking petulantly that 'we should never get the Poles to say that they were satisfied. Nothing would satisfy the Poles.'[13] But he went ahead with his 'formula'. The Poles' dissatisfaction he could tolerate. Stalin's he could not.

Churchill's thinking on the Polish issue was becoming more clear. In spite of his liberalism and his lack of orthodoxy, he was an imperialist. To him, when two great powers were struggling in a given area, as the Soviet Union and the western allies were in Europe, it was natural and advisable that they should agree on 'spheres of influence'. It was by such agreements that great powers avoided conflicts of interest. Churchill had also had an English classical education—at least the rudiments of one. When it came to Europe, there were certain countries he knew about and loved—France, Italy and Greece. The Slavic culture was entirely alien to him. It seemed natural that the Slavic nations should be allowed to move closer together and work things out for themselves without interference from the Anglo-Saxons. Poland, and later Yugoslavia, he saw as matters for the Russians rather than for himself. He saw the Slavs as a family of nations to which he was in no way related. His family was the English-speaking peoples, whose culture was based on those of Rome and Athens.

In 1941 Stalin had assured his allies that his only desire after the war was for a free and independent Poland. Now, at the end of 1943, his hopes were not quite so modest. He told Churchill he wanted a Poland 'friendly to the Soviet Union'.* This seemed to Churchill an entirely legitimate request for Stalin to make. He had heard plenty about injustices done by Russia to Poland. But he knew enough recent European history to know there was injustice on the other side as well. When the Soviet Union was weak, a hostile Poland had been a considerable danger. Poland had attacked Russia in 1920 and won large areas from her in battle. These areas Poland had tried to colonise and 'polonise'. The Ukrainian and Byelorussian populations had been oppressed—not violently oppressed, true, but culturally. Facts were facts. The Soviet Union was bearing the brunt of the war against Nazi Germany. Surely, after the war was won, the Soviet Union had the right to security on her western frontier? Was not Stalin justified in expecting the future Polish Government to be 'friendly'?

It may have been coincidence, if so it was a happy one for the Polish communists, that a few days after the Teheran Conference was over steps were taken to create a communist-dominated representative body in occupied Poland. Although some dozen organisations were involved in it, the dominant role was played by the Communist PPR. By mid-December its Manifesto, written by Gomułka, was ready and signed. Some of the signatories were well-defined groups, such as the Central Committee of the PPR and the leadership of its military arm, the GL. Others were more vague, so vague as to make one wonder if they ever really existed. There was 'A Group of

---

* This was a departure from the assurance he gave Polish Ambassador Kot in Moscow in 1941 that he hoped for a free and independent Poland 'irrespective of her internal political system'.

Independent Democrats', 'A Group of Polish Writers', 'A Group of Socialist Activists', even 'Field Groups of Home Army (AK) Soldiers'. One wonders what was the Manifesto's definition of a 'group', whether it was anything more than 'two or three gathered together'.

If Home Army soldiers did sign the PPR-led Manifesto, they certainly committed a grave breach of military discipline. Their civil rulers, the London Government, were taken to task by the full spate of Gomułka's oratory. 'Citizens!' he wrote:

'The policy of blind hatred of the Soviet Union, the policy of mobilising the people to war with the Soviet Union at a time when the powerful Soviet Army is standing at the gates of Poland, is pushing Poland into a chasm, and bringing the Polish people face to face with a catastrophe the extent of which cannot be estimated. Even today, after the conferences in Moscow and Teheran, the London Government has not recognised the great alliance of the three Allied powers. Instead of cementing Poland's co-operation with the Allies, instead of preparing a proper place for Poland in a Europe which today is fighting, but tomorrow will be rebuilding itself, the London Government's policies are making Poland more and more isolated. . . .'[14]

The importance of Polish-Soviet accord, the absolute necessity of restoring good-neighbourly relations with Russia, and the London Government's clear refusal and unwillingness to do this—these were the lynchpins of Gomułka's argument. And there were many non-communist Poles in Poland, feeling themselves closer and more dependent on Russia than the politicians in London, who saw some sense in what Gomułka said. It was thus easier for them to believe Gomułka's later exaggerations and distortions: that the 'reactionaries' in London were mobilising the Polish people to fight the Soviet Union, that they had rendered moral support to the Germans on the eastern front. Gomułka was developing a tactic that was to become very useful during the four years that followed. He was tarring the whole London Government, the whole spectrum of *émigré* politicians, many of whom were liberal and, in the western sense, socialist, with the brush of the few fanatical right-wingers in their midst who saw Bolshevism as a greater threat to Poland than Hitlerism. In his language anti-Soviet meant pro-Nazi. The Pole who was anti-Soviet and *anti*-Nazi, as most of the *émigrés* were, was bound by his attitudes to resist and deplore the liberation of Poland by the Red Army. He would prefer the *status quo*, Nazi occupation, and was therefore pro-Nazi. There was a certain strange logic in these arguments, at least from the point of view of a communist as convinced as Władysław Gomułka.

Gomułka's Manifesto called for the foundation of a 'National Council for the Homeland'. It was to be 'the factual political representation of the Polish people, entitled to act in the name of the people, and to guide their destiny until the time of Poland's liberation from foreign occupation'. It was, of course, a piece of monumental bluff. What right this group of left-wingers had to call themselves representatives of the Polish people, Gomułka alone knew. For a start the 300,000-strong Home Army was opposed to it, even though a small number of them may have signed the Manifesto. The broadly-based support was clearly a façade. The Manifesto was no more nor less than a clear bid for power by Gomułka and his communist party, the PPR. The time had come for them to spell out their plans: 'The National Council for the Homeland will at an appropriate moment summon a PROVISIONAL GOVERNMENT in which will be included representatives of all democratically-based groups.'

This was fair enough in theory. The trouble was, though, that the word 'democratic' means different things to different people. Gomułka's idea of democracy was hardly the same as Churchill's or Roosevelt's. To his mind Anglo-Saxon democracy was a lie. It was political democracy only. It was not *economic* democracy, it did not include equality of wealth or opportunity. To Gomułka as a Marxist, true democracy meant socialism, and it was his long-term intention to exclude from government all those who did not accept the principle of Marxist socialism.

This is not to say that the communists aimed at monopolising the Polish government immediately. They were realistic enough to see that as yet only a tiny percentage of Poles supported them. They wanted to attract sympathisers, men who were not with them, but not against them. They wanted to broaden their appeal, and put themselves forward as the voice of reason, a viable alternative to the London Government, and the solution to the Soviet-Polish impasse.

This was not as difficult as might be expected. Their membership was only a few thousand. In July 1942 it was 4,000, in January 1943 it was 8,000, but by July 1944 it had risen to 20,000, and a year later to 160,000. The PPR was able to appeal to those Poles who, though not communists, were able to see that Poland was, geographically at least, an east European country and therefore bound to be influenced by Russia after the war. Though some still hoped the British and Americans would bring Poland freedom from the west, others realised by sheer military logic that the meeting point of the eastern and western armies was bound to be in Germany. The Red Army would soon pass through Poland and occupy it. The consequences of this were obvious to all but the most optimistic Poles. Many took the view that the communists were the strongest power in their particular area. They could not beat them, so they joined them.

Gomułka was not at this stage making any assumptions about his party's mass support. He believed the American axiom that 'a politician's first duty is to get elected'. How it was done was not so important as that it should be done effectively. Support and popularity would come later, as soon as the virtues of communism, in which Gomułka firmly believed, became apparent to his fellow-Poles. Meanwhile there was one way of 'getting elected', by the physical support of the Red Army. Gomułka made no bones about this. On 12 January 1944, he wrote a long letter to the Central Bureau of Polish communists in the Soviet Union explaining the 'state of the nation' and the balance of power. It was a letter designed probably for Soviet eyes as much as Polish. There was a revealing paragraph on the problem of power: 'In its political calculations the PPR is starting from the assumption that the Red Army will cross on to Polish territory in its pursuit of the German enemy. This will greatly facilitate the struggle of the freedom-loving, democratic and progressive elements against the fascist and reactionary elements that still linger within the Polish people both at home and abroad.'[15]

The 'National Council for the Homeland' came into being only a month after Gomułka's election to the leadership of the communist party. It was very much *his* council. He wrote its Manifesto and was the leader of its dominating party. 'In this Manifesto my ideas are most faithfully recorded,' he said in 1948 when he was under attack and his role in the Council was being minimised. He was sensitive on this very point. The Council was founded on *his* ideas which *he* wrote. Clearly he regarded it as one of his greatest achievements.

The Council (called in Polish the 'Krajowa Rada Narodowa' or the 'KRN') was intended to become a government, and therefore had a President. This was Bolesław Bierut, the recent arrival from Minsk whose views and communist background were so different from Gomułka's. 'For conspiratorial reasons' Gomułka was not present at the meeting where the KRN was founded. This was in a worker's flat in Warsaw's Twarda Street. There were two rooms, one full of armed young men, members of the communist 'People's Army', ready to fight off a surprise German raid. The other room contained the politicians. They assembled there early on the evening of 31 December 1943, before curfew, at different times and by different routes. It was dangerous for any group of people to assemble anywhere, and so only those essential to the inaugural meeting were there, a couple of dozen of them: Marian Spychalski, head of the 'People's Army' intelligence; Władysław Bieńkowski, a member of the Central Editorial Board; Kazimierz Mijal, a prominent military underground leader;* Stefan Zółkiewski, a writer; Władysław Dworakowski, a trade-union leader, and Bolesław Bierut. Once there they could not leave till the night was over. They talked until dawn and made their plans.

A speech written by Gomułka was read out, a passionate appeal for immediate and widespread anti-German resistance and sabotage. By now the full extent of Hitler's plans for Poland were becoming clear. He had already almost exterminated the Polish Jews. The Poles themselves would be next. The German armies were retreating, and in a bitter mood. A Nazi leader, Sauckel, had declared his armies would leave Poland only when 'no stone was left on top of another stone'. The war was nearing its end, but for Poland the outcome was entirely in the balance. Anything might happen. Millions of Poles might be deported and exterminated. Or there might be an orderly resumption of power by the 'London' leaders. Gomułka was determined that neither of these two extremes should happen.

* The same man who in February 1966 escaped illegally from Poland by disguising himself as an Albanian trade delegate and using an Albanian passport. He has now adopted the 'Chinese' line and lives in Tirana, the Albanian capital.

When the KRN's declaration was reported on the Home
Army radio to London, it made little impact on the Polish
Government there. To the *émigrés* it seemed ludicrous that this
group of left-wingers, of whom nobody had ever heard, should
set themselves up against such known Polish statesmen as
Premier Stanisław Mikołajczyk and Kazimierz Sosnkowski, the
new Commander-in-Chief. The 'London' leaders did not feel
their existence threatened. They underestimated the KRN's
potential. They were concentrating their attention and influence on the matter of the eastern frontier. This was their
mistake—one which they continued to make until the middle
of 1945. They got their priorities wrong. They held out for
their 'rights' in the face of the practicalities of power politics.
By trying to extend their power, they annihilated it.

Stalin's attitude to the KRN was not yet clear. Clearly his
sympathies were with them, but he did not yet want to make
trouble with his western allies by publicly acknowledging
them. The KRN needed Stalin more than he needed them.
They would be helpless without his support. So he could afford
to wait. The KRN was not Stalin's idea. He learnt about it
only after its creation, a month after Pawel Finder's arrest,
when there was no Moscow-Warsaw radio link. Stalin's main
Polish contact was still the Union of Polish Patriots and its
leaders Wanda Wasilewska (a colonel in the Red Army),
Andrzej Witos (a Peasant Party leader), Jakub Berman,
Stanisław Radkiewicz and Roman Zambrowski (these last
three were to become prominent in the post-war administration). The beginning of the KRN marked the beginning of the
diplomatic battle of Poland. It was a three-year struggle that
ended early in 1947 in victory for the forces of Soviet-style
socialism.

At first Gomułka himself played only a small part in the
game. As leader of the communist party his position was too
patent. He was too committed to be thrown into the mêlée.
Churchill and Roosevelt had admitted Stalin's right to a
Polish government 'friendly to the Soviet Union'. So Stalin had
his toe in the door. But both western leaders were against a
communist take-over. So Stalin had to move carefully. Socialist
power had to be cloaked in the guise of 'parliamentary democracy'. The western leaders would admit his right to have
some communists in the government, but they would not allow
it to be dominated by communists.

VI: ASPIRING TO
THE SUPREME POWER

When in mid-March 1944 a KRN delegation set out from
Warsaw to Moscow, two of the Council's chief communist
creators—Bierut, the President, and Gomułka, who had written
the Manifesto—stayed behind. The delegation's leader was
Edward Osóbka-Morawski, a member of the Socialist Party
prepared to work fully with the communists. The other members were Marian Spychalski (later Vice-Minister, then Minister of Defence, then President of Poland) and Jan Stefan
Haneman. Their chief aim was to obtain deliveries of arms and
supplies. The communists had received very little from the
Soviet Union—a fact which Gomułka was raising in telegrams
to his 'Union of Polish Patriots' comrades in Moscow. The
journey to Moscow took two months. It involved travel across
marshy, enemy-occupied country and a meeting with a special
aeroplane. They arrived in mid-May.

The talks about supplies went excellently. On 19 May the
delegation met Stalin and asked for 20,000 machine-guns.
Stalin promised 50,000.[1] The Red Army's spring offensive was
going well. They were advancing across the Ukraine and had
entered Romania. A week earlier they had driven the Germans
out of the Crimea. Stalin was at last in a position to think about
incidental problems like Poland, and to be generous with his
hitherto scarce supplies.

The talks about recognition were more complicated. They
told Stalin they had come to Moscow, writes one of the delegates, 'to inform him that the London "government" was not
the representative of our people, that it did not represent our
political ideas or national aspirations, that the true representative was the National Council for the Homeland [the KRN]. . . .'

At first Stalin was cautious. The future of Poland was becoming a diplomatic game. Everyone was wooing Stalin—Roosevelt,
Churchill, Gomułka, even Mikołajczyk. They knew and he knew

73

that he and his Red Army were the key to the Polish question. He told the KRN delegates that 'the London Government in the form it exists today will never be recognised by the Soviet Union'. It was a statement that promised very little. None of the 'Big Three' leaders were satisfied with the London Government 'in the form it exists today'. They agreed its composition must be changed. The intransigent anti-Russians and anti-communists must be removed. But would that be enough? Churchill, Roosevelt and Mikołajczyk hoped it would. Stalin wanted more, but even at this stage he was not sure how much he would be able to get.

The London Government's position was becoming weaker and weaker because of its conflict not only with Stalin, but also with the western Allies. Early in 1944 Churchill tried hard to get the Poles to accept the frontiers he had agreed to in principle at Teheran, the Curzon Line and the Oder. He failed absolutely. 'I have no authority to yield forty-eight per cent of our country,' said Premier Mikołajczyk. To the 'London' Poles the issue was as simple as that. How these eastern territories had been originally won by Poland they did not care to remember. The frontier question became a matter of honour on which they would not yield. They became bogged down in it so much that the more important question—whether post-war Poland should be an independent country at all—was allowed to go by default.

Churchill had made a mistake at Teheran. He had agreed in principle to Stalin's demand for the Curzon Line without realising, from the Polish point of view, the enormity of what he was doing. He now became like a shuttlecock, to be beaten to and fro by the Soviet and Polish governments. The Poles could call him an ungrateful ally, ready to connive at yet another partition of Poland. To this Stalin had a simple answer. He could remind Churchill of what they and Roosevelt had agreed at Teheran. Neither side would yield. And Churchill, the unwilling 'honest broker' between them, was cast as villain by both. The matter was degenerating into one of politics and power. Stalin's demands were backed by strength. Mikołajczyk's were not. This was the deciding factor. It became a matter of brute force. Justice did not come into it. For once Churchill was out of his depth. How he must have longed to be rid of the whole affair.

What would have happened if the London Government had

been more amenable to Allied demands, more realistic about the extent of their influence and power? If Churchill and Roosevelt had not become so irritated by their Polish allies, would they have been able to plead their case more effectively? The 'London' Poles demanded justice—a luxury few Polish governments have ever been able to aspire to. If they had moderated their frontier demands, would they have been able to salvage their existence and their country's independence?

In early 1944 the Polish communists began to reveal signs of internal discord. The 'Polish-Polish' communists were not quite at peace with their 'Russian-Polish' comrades. This disagreement, scotched by Stalin's influence in 1945, was to flare up again three years later. It was the old matter of communist upbringing. Gomułka had spent only a short time in the Soviet Union. Though a communist, he had remained thoroughly Polish in character and temperament. Some of his comrades, though, had spent longer in the Soviet Union and had become partially Russianised. Perhaps it was a matter of national characteristic rather than of political interpretation.

The importance of this 'split' in the Polish communist movement has sometimes been exaggerated by western historians. In 1944 the issue was important enough: which was to become the next Polish government, the KRN or the Moscow-based 'Union of Polish Patriots'? But it was discussed amicably between the two organisations and resolved, for a time at least, quite simply when the proper time came. On 18 July 1944 the Peasant Party leader Andrzej Witos revealed that: 'In the second half of 1943 and the beginning of 1944 the Union of Polish Patriots asked the Soviet Government to agree to the preparation of a Polish administration by the Poles *who were living in the Soviet Union*. It would then be able to take over the administration of the liberated territories.'[2]

In other words, the Union of Polish Patriots in Moscow was duplicating the actions of the KRN in Warsaw. According to Witos, Stalin soon put a stop to the Union's plans. But word of the scheme did reach the communists in Warsaw, and on 12 January Gomułka wrote tetchily to Moscow:

'It has recently come to our knowledge that the Union of Polish Patriots is organising a representation of the Polish people outside the country. . . . This news has been received by us with great joy. It will make our work here considerably easier. We are not quite sure, however, exactly what form of political representation the Union of Polish Patriots has in mind. We assume it will consist of authorities confined to the present phase of events, i.e. that it will not be an actual government. We feel that at present such a government would be premature.'[3]

It is hard to know to what extent it was a misunderstanding that the KRN and the Union duplicated their claims. It was the time of the break in the Moscow-Warsaw radio link. And the problem was resolved quite soon. The Union of Polish Patriots recognised the KRN during their delegation's May visit to Moscow, and were the first to reveal its existence to the world, in a statement on 24 May. Still it is significant that it was two 'Polish Patriot' men—Jakub Berman and Stanisław Radkiewicz—who with Bolesław Bierut, the recent arrival from Russia, were later most responsible for the Stalinist terror in Poland. There were important differences between these Polish communists, even if for the moment they were being kept in abeyance by the need for unity and by the practical dependence of both factions on Stalin and the Red Army.

Stalin saw that time was on his side. There was no need for him to strain allied unity by a premature public recognition of the KRN. The Red Army would soon be in Poland (it had already crossed the pre-war frontier). The KRN would then have something more important than Soviet recognition. It would begin to govern. It would possess power, which would be nine-tenths of the law, especially in wartime.

The KRN delegation stayed several weeks in Russia. They travelled around the country. They visited the Polish Army of General Zygmunt Berling, created out of those Poles who were not evacuated to Iran with General Anders. It was Stalin's idea to bring the KRN together with Berling. 'The KRN has no army,' he told them at a secret meeting, 'and the Polish Army has no government.' The delegates awarded General Berling a medal and behaved generally as if they were a government, to all of which Stalin was able to turn a blind eye and smile sadly, for it was none of his doing.

In mid-June Churchill and Roosevelt were able to arrange for Mikołajczyk to visit Moscow. He was received by Viktor Lebedev, later Soviet Ambassador to Poland, and by Stalin.

The Russians were in such a strong position over the Curzon Line *vis-à-vis* Churchill and Roosevelt that they were able to twist Mikołajczyk's arm. They sent him away with three conditions, all of which he had to agree to before talks could begin on the question of him and his colleagues entering the new government. The conditions were recognition of the Curzon Line, withdrawal of all anti-Soviet accusations on the Katyń forest murders, resignation from the London Government of the three most anti-Soviet members—Sosnkowski, Marian Kukiel and Stanisław Kot. It was a clever move by Stalin. On these three points he could count on support from Roosevelt and Churchill. They might well insist that Mikołajczyk accept them, or else wash their hands of his case. The western leaders were committed to the Curzon Line and to accepting the Soviet version of Katyń. Equally Mikołajczyk was committed, as Premier of the London Government, against the Curzon Line and against Katyń. He was in another cleft stick, forced to choose between his own government and the 'Big Three', who were on this particular issue united.

Churchill and Roosevelt could not put their finger on any point where Stalin was being clearly unreasonable. The three of them had agreed to a principle—the need to build a new government of Poland, friendly to the Soviet Union and consisting of men of every political shade. Stalin was sticking to this principle. While Miłołajczyk was in Moscow, Stalin received the KRN delegates again and told them they would probably have to accept a few 'London' politicians into their midst. 'Not all the London *émigrés* should be regarded as lost,' he told them, 'there are many good officers in Anders's army.' There was really nothing specific for the Anglo-Saxons to complain about.

There was no point in the KRN delegates returning to Warsaw. The Red Army was advancing quickly across Byelorussia and the Ukraine. On 18 July they crossed the River Bug, now part of the Polish-Soviet frontier. On 21 July they captured the first place they recognised as Polish territory, the small town of Chełm, near Lublin. With them was General Berling's 'First Polish Army'. Ten days later they were approaching the banks of the Vistula, more than a hundred miles further west, and the outskirts of Warsaw. Suddenly a large area of Poland, about 75,000 square kilometres, was free of German occupation and in need of government. Immediately the Polish communist leaders converged on Chełm and Lublin. Gomułka, Bierut, and several other leaders left Warsaw and crossed the German lines. Berman, Spychalski, Zambrowski and Radkiewicz came from the east with the Red Army and General Berling. The comrades from Russia were coopted into the PPR leadership.

The very day Chełm was taken, the KRN formed a 'Polish Committee of National Liberation' to govern the freed areas. It was a mark of the caution with which they were acting that they did not at once form a Provisional Government, as foreseen in the KRN manifesto. This was to come only at the end of 1944. The total Party membership in these areas was only a few thousand. The number of political workers was only twenty-four. When Lublin fell, two days after Chełm, the communists and the 'Committee' moved there, naming Lublin the temporary capital of Poland. They occupied a house in Bernadyńska Street, where for the first time they were able to operate legally and publish openly their newspaper *Trybuna Wolności*. Gomułka held no official position in the Committee of National Liberation, but his job as Secretary of the Party was still a key one.

He and his colleagues were lucky to get out of Warsaw when they did. A few days after they reached Lublin, on 1 August, the Home Army launched the Warsaw Uprising. This event—one of the most controversial of the Second World War—came about because the Home Army and the London Government thought mistakenly that the Red Army would take Warsaw very soon, within a day or two. They wanted to capture Warsaw first, and then to be able to receive the Red Army as their 'guests'. It did not work out that way. The Red Army either would not (the 'London' version) or could not (their version) force the Vistula and help the insurgents. The Home Army had counted on being able to hold the city for a few days, long enough for help to arrive. Instead they found themselves besieged and abandoned, except for the occasional frantic parachute drop, for week after week. The population, military and civilian, was slaughtered. 150,000 died. Finally on 2 October the Home Army leader Tadeusz Bór-Komorowski surrendered to the Germans. He and his men became prisoners-of-war, and the Home Army was rendered largely ineffective as a fighting force.

Four days after the start of the Uprising, Gomułka addressed a meeting of 150 local communist leaders in Lublin. 'Our main task,' he told them, 'is to organise the whole nation to fight against the occupying army for a free, independent and democratic Poland. Our eventual task in the historical perspective is to introduce socialism.'[4] During the following weeks, while the Uprising was in progress, Gomułka devoted his attention more to consolidating socialist power than to fighting the Germans. He did not concern himself with the Warsaw Uprising, which he was later to call 'the criminal fruit of the policies of the London camp'.[5] The PPR Central Committee spent August and September organising a propaganda network: a press centre, a Party school, an information centre. They set up agricultural and trade-union offshoots of the Central Committee. In October Zenon Kliszko, a close friend of Gomułka, was put in charge of the personnel department, which controlled Party appointments. In November Gomułka himself took over the Party's military department. He arranged for the officers' corps to be 'democratised'. On 29 September, three days before Bór-Komorowski surrendered, Gomułka delivered a speech in Lublin in which the Uprising was not even mentioned. In an uncharacteristic attack on the German people (the usual communist target was the German Nazi ideology, not the German people), he called them 'a nation of aggressive plunderers, ever bent on conquest'. His attacks on the 'Polish reactionaries' were only slightly less severe. Clearly to him they were public enemy number two. He was establishing his role as leader of the 'anti-reactionary' movement in Poland—one which, as leader of the communist party, could hardly be denied him.

When the Uprising broke out Mikołajczyk was in Moscow. He reportedly asked Stalin to have him parachuted into Warsaw.[6] 'My presence there will make possible the creation of a new government,' he told him. Presumably Stalin did not take him seriously. Stalin and the Polish communists were for the moment ignoring the Uprising, pretending almost that it did not exist. 'The Home Army consists of a few detachments misnamed divisions,' Stalin wrote to Churchill on 5 August (the Home Army in fact had a potential membership of 300,000).[7] 'I cannot imagine such detachments taking Warsaw.'[8] 'There is no fighting in Warsaw,' Wanda Wasilewska told Mikołajczyk.

On 6 and 7 August Mikołajczyk conferred with Bierut (just

back from Lublin), Osóbka-Morawski and Wanda Wasilewska.
They offered him the premiership of a coalition Polish government. But fourteen of its members were to be 'Lublin' men,
only four 'London'. Mikołajczyk refused. He also failed to
persuade Stalin to provide any help at all for the Warsaw
Uprising. The Germans had counter-attacked east of Warsaw.
The Red Army, he claimed, was not even in possession of the
east bank of the Vistula, let alone in a position to force it. The
most dubious of Stalin's acts was his refusal to allow allied
aircraft supplying Warsaw to land and refuel in Soviet-
occupied territory. There is no doubt that Stalin could have
done more than he did to help the Uprising. On the other hand
the accusation still made by many Poles that the Red Army
could easily have taken Warsaw, but held back for political
reasons to allow the Home Army to be destroyed, cannot be
proved and may rest on shaky foundation.[9]

Stalin would equally make no concession on the Polish
frontier and the Curzon Line. His position here was well
entrenched. All he had to do was leave Mikołajczyk to fight it
out with the Americans and British. Mikołajczyk arrived back
in London on 13 August. There was nothing he could announce
to his government except his total diplomatic failure.

While the Uprising was still in progress, there was some
resistance to the Lublin Committee's take-over. According to
a modern Polish historian representatives of the London
Government 'Delegation' made a bid for power, but 'their
efforts to take power into their own hands ended in failure. The
Delegation representatives were unable to gain wide support
from the population who in the broad mass subordinated
themselves to the Committee for National Liberation.'[10]

Could it be, one wonders, that the presence of large Red
Army forces in the area influenced the population's choice?
The writer continues: 'In this situation it became necessary to
disarm and re-form Home Army units in the liberated territories and to liquidate the Delegation civil administration
supported by them.'

The Lublin Committee did not let the grass grow under its
feet. On 6 September a land reform decree was signed, the
basis of a law that confiscated the landowners' estates and
limited each private holding to fifty hectares (123 acres). Basic
nationalisation measures were put into effect—all this while

fighting was still going on in Warsaw, and when the diplomatic battle for control of Poland was only just beginning. On 31 August the Committee set up courts to put war criminals on trial. At the end of November the guards and officials of the notorious extermination camp at Majdanek were tried in Lublin and executed. This popular move clearly lent authority to the Committee and its courts, which were then able to pass on to more controversial business. Already Stanisław Radkiewicz, one of the more brutal communist leaders, was in charge of 'public security', a post he was to hold for nine years. There were frequent arrests of 'London' supporters. When this fact was reported to London and representations were made, through western Allies, to Moscow, the reply was always the same. The Soviet Government would counter-claim that 'fascist bandits and reactionaries' were harassing the Red Army and threatening its lines of communication. The British and Americans had no observers in the liberated areas, and only shaky, second-hand intelligence. They could not therefore prove or disprove the charges of either side. Having no men on the spot they could have no control over the situation other than what they could negotiate diplomatically at the highest level.

Early in October Churchill was in Moscow. This time he found the going with Stalin easier, and was encouraged to send for Mikołajczyk and make another attempt to solve the Polish problem, now the greatest bone of contention between him and Stalin. Mikołajczyk and his Foreign Minister Tadeusz Romer arrived on 10 October. Mikołajczyk immediately told Churchill, first, that he would not talk to the Lublin Committee, only to the Soviet Government, secondly, that there was no chance of his changing his mind and recognising the Curzon Line. This made Churchill angry. He knew that without these two concessions there was no hope of agreement whatever. He was becoming thoroughly exasperated by this Polish problem which was beginning to sour the moment of victory. Several times he lost his temper with Mikołajczyk. An account of their talks was kept by Romer, the Foreign Minister.[11]

'In that case I wash my hands of you [said Churchill]. We do not intend to destroy the peace of Europe for these inter-Polish quarrels. You are blinded to what is happening. I shall tell the world you are being unreasonable. You want another war, which will cost the lives of 25 million people. . . . I will leave you to your troubles. You have no sense of responsibility, if you want to sacrifice your people in Poland. You are quite insensitive to their sufferings. You don't care about the future of Europe, you care only about your narrow, selfish interest.'[12]

At the same time the Lublin Committee were at pains to present a reasonable image and to assure everyone of their good intentions. 'We very much want to reach an understanding,' Bierut told Mikołajczyk, who had finally been prevailed upon to meet the Committee: 'we want a democratic Poland, and it is our responsibility to see that it becomes so. We trust you, and believe you are a democrat. We ask you to come to Poland. We guarantee you complete freedom of political action there. We are not Soviet agents. We do not want to sovietise Poland. All we want is a democratic Poland and the destruction of the reactionaries.'[13]

There was nothing Mikołajczyk could do, even if he believed Bierut's assurances, which he did not. He knew Bierut had been a Soviet NKVD agent before the war. He did not trust him one inch. Nor was his own personal power as strong as it had been. He had been sent to Moscow as representative of a split government, with very little power to negotiate. As he told the British Foreign Minister Anthony Eden on 19 October, even if he gave in to the immense pressure there was upon him and accepted the Curzon Line, it would still do no good. His action would at once be repudiated by his government colleagues in London who saw their premier as dangerously liberal and 'soft' in his approach to the communists. Again the talks achieved nothing.

Mikołajczyk, Eden, Churchill, Romer and the rest returned to London. Their plan now was for Mikołajczyk to try to set his house in order. It was now clear that some of the 'London' Poles were ready to talk. There was a 'Mikołajczyk group' of 'liberals' and a 'Sosnkowski group', led by the conservative and anti-Soviet commander-in-chief, who were against any truck with the Lubliners.

As every day went by the Lublin Committee became more established in Poland, and the 'London' case grew weaker. Stalin was quick to point this out to Churchill, who passed on the bad news to Mikołajczyk. The Polish Premier tried hard to bring his government round. But the situation was slipping away from him. His opponents justified their intransigence by predicting that the military situation in Europe was about to change, that the German army would soon collapse on its western front, allowing the British and American armies to sweep across Germany and meet the Red Army near the borders of Poland. The western Allies would then be in a far stronger position to negotiate with Stalin on the Polish issue. It was a dangerous theory that left no contingency plan in case the German army should hold out. In fact, the Germans did hold out. They even launched an offensive in the Ardennes which put paid to the pipe-dreams of men like Kazimierz Sosnkowski.

On 29 November Mikołajczyk and Tadeusz Romer, his Foreign Minister, resigned from the London Government. A week later a new government was formed under Tomasz Arciszewski. This body of men, committed to a stern, anti-Soviet line, was still *recognised* by the United States, Great Britain, France and many other countries as the government of Poland. But it was *supported* by hardly anybody. It still disposed of military strength: an army corps commanded by General Władysław Anders which had been fighting valiantly in Italy and played an essential part in the capture of Monte Cassino during May; also the remnants of the Home Army (the AK) commanded, after Bór-Komorowski's Warsaw Uprising surrender, by Leopold Okulicki. These were considerable forces, and they gave the 'London' leaders false confidence in their own strength and influence. For in comparison with the presently united armies of the 'Grand Alliance', they were insignificant.

The Polish non-communists were now irrevocably split. The word 'traitor' was being bandied about among them, and was frequently applied to Mikołajczyk and others who were now willing to talk with the Lublin Committee. The 'London' case was going by default. Mikołajczyk and his men were by now prepared to throw in their lot with Churchill and Roosevelt. They now knew this was the only way anything could be salvaged from the mess. But they were now mere individuals, no longer ministers even of a government-in-exile, let alone of a government with power. The whole situation was thoroughly encouraging to the Polish communists.

On 7 December an interview with Gomułka was published in the newspaper *Rzeczpospolita* (Republic).[14] It was a clever piece of writing, designed partly for foreign consumption, to pave the way for the next stage in the communist assumption of power. The 'National Liberation Committee' was to be transformed into a provisional government. Gomułka explained that only natural self-restraint and modesty had prevented the KRN from declaring themselves a government as soon as Polish territory was liberated. 'There was not then enough indication,' he said, 'as to the Polish people's attitude to the KRN's political line.' This situation, he said, had now changed: 'Our five months of work have proved that the democratic camp, being the basis of the Liberation Committee and of the KRN, has proved itself in times of great difficulty, has broadened its base among the masses and become ideologically stronger. Around this camp, around our four democratic political parties, the whole Polish nation is now rallying.'

This was, of course, a distortion of the truth. The KRN was supported only by a minority of the Poles in its area of influence, and Gomułka knew this. There was more justification, though, in some of his other claims: that the Committee had already begun to set up the machinery of government and was in control of the liberated areas; that they had rebuilt a Polish army that was fighting its way together with the Red Army towards Berlin. Life under the Committee's guidance was being slowly brought back to normal, said Gomułka. They had set up schools. These, apart from a few elementary and trade schools, had not existed under the German occupation. They had introduced their land reform, with which even Mikołajczyk had little quarrel, and put industry back on its feet. They had already begun to negotiate a treaty with the Soviet Union which in their view would provide the only viable foreign policy for the future of Poland.

Continuing to build up his reputation as a moderate and reasonable man, Gomułka revealed why a provisional government had not been created as soon as eastern Poland was liberated:

The KRN was at that time of the opinion that in the face of the new situation . . . the so-called London Government's policies would change, that they would move towards close and friendly relations with the Soviet Union, and that the attempts to restore *sanacja* government to the new

Poland would be rejected and condemned. The KRN was able to expect that these eventual changes in the London *émigré* 'line' would make it possible to set up a Provisional Government in Poland consisting of representatives of the Lublin Committee and of the democratic elements in the London emigration.

It was easy to say this, of course, when the offer of cooperation no longer held good. 'The situation now,' said Gomułka, 'is that the Polish people has ceased to be interested in the London *émigrés*.' This was a strange remark. How could Gomułka possibly know what the Polish people thought? Half the country was still occupied by the enemy. It would be wrong, though, to dismiss his words as mere politician's rhetoric. Since mid-1944 the controversy within the PPR had sharpened. Should they try to broaden their front and cooperate with the non-communist but non-fascist London leaders? An article on this subject by Władysław Bieńkowski, a leading communist journalist, was printed with Gomułka's approval in *Trybuna Wolności* on 1 July 1944. It was a conciliatory piece, dangerously so in the eyes of the more dogmatic communists. It treated with sympathy the problems of Mikołajczyk, who had recently had kind words to say about the Poles fighting under Soviet orders. He was described as weak, and influenced by his right-wing government colleagues, but not in himself reprehensible. It called for 'a consolidation of the democratic camp' which would include Mikołajczyk and several other of the moderate London leaders, 'We believe,' wrote Bieńkowski, 'that this consolidation, in spite of the forces that oppose it, will become a fact.'

Gomułka and his supporters in the PPR would in mid-1944 have been ready to work with some of the London leaders, and probably with Mikołajczyk. Four years later Bierut, who by then had the upper hand, was to claim that Gomułka's policy smacked of defeatism, but by then freedom within the Party had disappeared, and Gomułka's entirely reasonable view was seen as heretical, or even criminal. One cannot know whether Gomułka's mid-1944 desire for compromise was dictated by a respect for moderation in government or whether his un-doubted wooings of 'London' were simply a ruse, a political tactic aimed at splitting the London camp and thereby strengthening communist influence. In the event, although the

'London' camp *did* split, it was probably not because of this communist tactic. The London leaders were not sensitive to the differences in the two communist factions. They took no notice of the olive branch offered by Gomułka, Bieńkowski and the other 'moderates'.

The events of the second half of 1944 did nothing but harm to the 'London' cause. They quarrelled among themselves and with their Anglo-Saxon supporters so bitterly that they created an image for themselves, with Churchill and Roosevelt as much as with Stalin, Bierut and Gomułka, of a reactionary, intransigent group of men. It became clear to Gomułka that it was no longer politically wise or tactically necessary to woo 'London'. The turn of 1944–45 marks the turn of Gomułka's attitude. From being the communist leader most ready to compromise, he became the most violent in opposing the non-communists who aspired to enter the government of Poland. For two years he played the part of a 'hard-liner', the ring-leader of attacks upon 'bourgeois' forces. Mikołajczyk became his special victim.

Mikołajczyk, dismissed from office by his right-wing colleagues for being 'soft' on communism, was simultaneously being labelled a reactionary by the leftists in Poland. Stalin went further than this. On 27 December, 1944 he accused Mikołajczyk of terrorism. In a letter to President Roosevelt he wrote: 'A number of facts which took place after the last visit of Mikołajczyk to Moscow . . . with all palpability prove that the negotiations of M. Mikołajczyk with the Polish National Committee served as a screen for those elements that conducted from behind Mikołajczyk's back criminal terrorist work against Soviet officers and soldiers on the territory of Poland.'[15]

Again these were accusations which Churchill and Roosevelt, having no direct information about Poland at their disposal, could not confirm or deny. In the same note Stalin went on: 'I have to say frankly that if the Polish Committee of National Liberation will transform itself into a Provisional Polish Government then, in view of the above-said, the Soviet Government will not have any serious ground for postponement of the question of its recognition.'

The ground had been well prepared. On 31 December the Lublin Committee formed itself into a provisional government which was recognised by the Soviet Union on 4 January. The western leaders could do little. They had no control over the events for which they were supposed to be responsible. From being President of the Committee Edward Osóbka-Morawski became Prime Minister. Władysław Gomułka was made one of the two vice-premiers. Bolesław Bierut retained the key position of President of the KRN. Stanisław Radkiewicz became Minister of Public Security.

The western leaders protested. The three-power Yalta conference was already planned for early February, and the Polish issue was to be high on its agenda. The only hope was to thrash the matter out there. Both Churchill and Roosevelt were prepared to take a tougher line at Yalta. They both felt Stalin had gone too far. He had acted unilaterally and high-handedly in recognising the Lublin leaders. He had prejudged the issue of a difficult problem which, it had been agreed at Teheran, should have been solved by the three powers jointly. This they could justly complain about.

For once the western leaders' view coincided with that of the London Government. But it was too late to think of an improvement in relations between them. Arciszewski's newspaper could declare with accuracy that 'the [London] Polish Government is still the only legal representation of the Polish state recognised by all the United Nations and the neutral countries'.[16] This was still the legal position. But that same week Roosevelt was informing Stalin that his refusal to recognise the new government 'in no way entailed any special links with the Government in London'.[17] That was the practical position. The London Government was out, even if there were a few months of half-life still left in it. The westerners were backing Mikołajczyk. Roosevelt called him 'the only significant Polish politician who it seems can ensure a proper solution to the hard and dangerous Polish question'. He became the only card the westerners were left with, a man of moderate, liberal views, not a communist but ready to work with communists, and with a considerable following inside Poland. As their only card, they were forced to place their whole stake upon him. The question was, would the card prove of high enough value to justify such an investment?

In mid-January the Red Army resumed its offensive, much to the gratitude of the British and Americans whose armies were hard pressed by the German counter-attack in the

Ardennes. On 17 January Warsaw was finally liberated. For five months the Red Army had inhabited its outskirts across the Vistula. Now they were moving westward at high speed. By the end of the month they were in German territory.

The communist-aligned Provisional Government moved its seat at once from Lublin to Warsaw and began to plan the reconstruction of the city which was largely a pile of rubble. Seventy per cent of its buildings were totally destroyed, deliberately dynamited on Hitler's order as an act of revenge for the Warsaw Uprising. The new government's decision to move to Warsaw, in spite of the difficulties entailed in living and working there, was a popular one. The work of rebuilding began immediately. Again the communists could claim the role of hero. It was *they* who were doing the work and facing the physical hardship of life in a devastated land, while the *émigrés* were living comfortably abroad. Everywhere the non-communists found themselves cast in the role of destroyer, while the communists were doing the building. In January too the London-controlled AK was disbanded by its leader Leopold Okulicki. Many of its members joined an avowedly anti-communist organisation called NIE, which had been started as soon as the Red Army reached Poland in the summer of 1944. NIE was short for *niepodległość* (independence), but *nie* is also the Polish word for 'no'. This was how the situation was being presented. The 'London' groups were acquiring an entirely negative image. They were non-communists, the men who said 'no'. It was not an attractive political platform.

On 4 February the Yalta Conference opened. The Polish question was discussed at seven out of the eight plenary meetings. Churchill was making his final attempt to negotiate a just settlement for Poland. It had been the invasion of Poland in 1939 which had brought Britain to war and himself back into the government. For him Poland was a matter of British honour, not of her national interest. He was prepared to give Stalin much of what he wanted, but would do his best to prevent communist rule being imposed on Poland against the wishes of its people. As will be seen, Churchill's best was on this occasion not good enough.

The eastern-frontier issue was by now almost a dead letter. Churchill still hoped for some concession. He told Stalin that for Russia to give up Lwów would be 'an act of generosity'. But Stalin felt no obligation to be generous. He contrasted the western leaders' attitude to the Polish provisional government with that to the French government of de Gaulle. This was also provisional, and no more elected than the Polish one. So why treat them differently? Why recognise de Gaulle and not the Lublin Poles? Stalin was the only one of the 'Big Three' with continuous reliable information about Poland. He could tell the other two any story he liked. For instance, he told Churchill: 'It was well known the Poles had not liked the Russians, because they had three times tried to partition Poland. But the advance of the Soviet troops and the liberation of Poland had completely changed their mood. The old resentment had disappeared and had given way to goodwill and even enthusiasm for the Russians.'[18] He assured Churchill also that 'the Lublin Government was really very popular, particularly Bierut, Osóbka-Morawski and General Żymierski. They had not left the country during the occupation, but had lived all the time in Warsaw and came from the Underground movement.'

If Churchill was properly informed he knew Stalin's statement contained many distortions and at least one lie. Bierut had not lived all the time in Warsaw. He had been there only eighteen months, having arrived there from Russia in mid-1943. General Żymierski was a man with a shady political past who was by no means popular among Poles. Stalin also told Roosevelt he would see elections were held in Poland 'within a month' In fact they were not held for two years. He was not in one of his more honest moods.

Now that the eastern frontier was agreed along the lines of Stalin's wishes, the western frontier was beginning to cause trouble. All three leaders had roughly agreed at Teheran on an 'Oder-Neisse line'. What they had not decided was *which* Neisse they meant, the eastern stream, which would leave Wrocław (Breslau) in Germany, or the western stream, in Polish the Nysa Łużycka. On this point the leaders agreed to differ. It was omitted from the final *communiqué*. The western leaders felt at the time that a frontier on the western Neisse would give Poland more territory than she could control. Events have proved them wrong, although Poland still suffers from these western doubts.

On the main issue, the future government of Poland, agreement of a sort was reached. The final *communiqué* contained the paragraph:

'A new situation has been created in Poland as a result of her complete liberation by the Red Army. This calls for the establishment of a Polish Provisional Government which can be more broadly based than was possible before the recent liberation of western Poland. The Provisional Government which is now functioning in Poland should therefore be reorganised on a broader democratic basis, with the inclusion of democratic leaders from Poland itself and from Poles abroad. This government should then be called the Polish Provisional Government of National Unity.'[19]

It was the best the western powers could get. Throughout the Yalta Conference they had had to negotiate from weakness. On the western front the British and American armies had been making very slow progress. On the eastern front the Red Army had just made a breakthrough and over-run most of Poland. It looked then as if the meeting point of the two Allied forces might be well to the west of the point originally conceived. The agreement on Poland meant really very little. Stalin was not committed to accept Mikołajczyk or any individual *émigré* leader into the Polish government. The agreement was vague, leaving plenty of scope for each point to be argued at the detailed stage. All this time, Stalin hoped, the position of the Soviet Union and of the the communist-dominated government of Poland would be growing stronger.

The Yalta decisions were then debated in the British House of Commons. 'Our honour is pledged,' said Sir William Beveridge, 'to see that Poland gets an independent government, chosen to please the Poles and no one else.' They were brave words, but hardly enough to combat the influence of the Red Army and the insincerity of Stalin. And it is now strange to think that Churchill chose this debate as the occasion to speak in extravagant terms of Soviet virtue and honesty. Hard pressed in the House of Commons, and shortly before a vote in which eleven members of his government abstained, Churchill said: 'The impression I brought back from the Crimea, and from all my other contacts, is that Marshal Stalin and the Soviet leaders wish to live in honourable friendship and equality with the western democracies. I feel also that their word is their bond. I know of no government which stands to its obligations, even in its own despite, more solidly than the Russian Soviet government.'[20] In volume six of *The Second World War*, first published in 1954, Churchill explained the reason behind this statement: 'I felt bound to proclaim my confidence in Soviet good faith in the hope of procuring it. In this I was encouraged by Stalin's behaviour about Greece.'[21] But it is still a mystery why Churchill had to be quite so effusive, why one of history's greatest defenders of democracy had to praise so warmly one of history's worst dictators and mass-murderers.

The implementation of the Yalta agreement was left to a commission of three: V. Molotov, the Soviet Commissar of Foreign Affairs, and the British and American ambassadors in Moscow, Sir Archibald Clark-Kerr and W. A. Harriman. But the weeks went by, and no useful result came from their talks in Moscow. It was clear Stalin was once again stone-walling, playing for time in the comfortable knowledge that time was on his side. By the end of March he had strengthened the Soviet position in Poland quite dramatically. A number of prominent non-communist Poles, including Leopold Okulicki, leader of NIE, the Home Army's successor, and two or three of the men actually being proposed by the British-Americans for inclusion in the Polish government, were tricked into revealing themselves to the local Red Army command in Poland, arrested and sent to Moscow. In reply to anxious telegrams from Churchill, Stalin announced they would stand trial for diversionary activity in the rear of the Red Army and for operating illegal wireless transmitters. For all anyone in the West knew the charges might be justified.

Gomułka was not yet involved in the diplomatic game. Up to mid-1945 Polish politics were the concern not of Poles but of Russians, Americans and Englishmen. As a communist Gomułka was identified with the Russian side, but he was not close to the Russian authorities. Bolesław Bierut, on the other hand, had been an NKVD officer and was thoroughly Soviet-orientated. Gomułka's usefulness, from the Soviet point of view, was to come later. As one of the few genuine Polish 'national' communists he was a trump card to be played at the conference table at the proper time. As leader of the communist PPR, he was to lead the party political battle against the legal opposition, Mikołajczyk. Meanwhile Bierut, Hilary Minc, Stanisław Radkiewicz, Jakub Berman and Roman Zambrowski were the 'men from Moscow' whom Stalin trusted.

Gomułka's tasks lay inside Poland. As vice-Premier he helped restore order in the devastated country and implement the early socialist reforms. The Provisional Government, as yet unrecognised except by the Soviet Union and one or two other countries, had two sorts of opposition, the political and the violent. Non-communists were in two minds. What was the best way of preventing Soviet domination of their country? Should they trust the assurances of their American and British allies, play the game according to the rules, and rely on 'free elections' and 'parliamentary democracy' to give them independence? This was the view of Mikołajczyk. Or would they have to use force to gain their independence, as they had been doing for the past five years against the Germans? This was the view of the London Government, its NIE armies in Poland, and the even more right-wing NSZ. Old habits die hard, and to many Poles, even honourable men, violence seemed the only possible way of avoiding their country's rapid fall from one occupation into another.

The violent opposition was opposed by Radkiewicz's security service, aided when necessary by the Red Army. Organisations like NIE superseded in April by Jan Rzepecki's WiN (after '*Wolność i Niepodległość*' or 'Freedom and Independence'), became involved in an armed struggle with communist forces that soon turned into civil war. Lavish figures are quoted by both sides of the murders done by the other, but both sides have a vested interest in exaggeration and the figures are too unreliable to be quoted. Certainly there were tens of thousands of Poles killed by fellow-Poles. The communist forces had the advantage that they possessed prisons and places of interrogation. They could arrest. The anti-communists had to kill, in the manner of *Ashes and Diamonds*, Jerzy Andrzejewski's vivid novel about this period later made into a film by Andrzej Wajda.

Civil war is incomprehensible after the event. Perhaps it was too much to expect the violence of wartime Poland suddenly to disappear. After five years in which it was as easy to be killed as to catch a cold, Poles developed a strange attitude to death. They learnt to live with it. Rule by foreigners they never learnt to live with. So it was that many of them, instead of breathing a sigh of relief that the war was over, carried on fighting for what they believed was justice. Only this time Pole had to fight Pole, and justice had become a debatable point. Before 1945 the anti-German struggle was manifestly just. After 1945 it all depended on one's political attitude. It divided the Polish people and was morally more painful, if less bloody, than the fight against the Nazis.

The press of the time, from being resolute and reasonable, became fanatical. Communist and 'reactionary' wrote of each other in terms scarcely less virulent than those used against the Nazis. A typical piece, written in a sort of semi-poetry, appeared in the communist *Trybuna Wolności*:

THE ENEMIES OF THE PEOPLE MUST STAND TRIAL

Today Poland is ruled by the Polish people.
Theirs is the army, our democratic army.
Theirs is the people's militia, the guard of democracy.
Their child is the security apparatus, built by the popular masses.
Let accurate blows fall from our hands. Let every saboteur and traitor be arrested. May our courts issue stern and just sentences. The Polish people have grown up out of your care. They have had enough of you. Times have changed.
You will stand before justice, you traitors of the people, accomplices of Hitler.
You will be sent into prison![22]

On a more mundane level, a foretaste of the new government's ideas was printed in the same newspaper on 31 January: 'In democratic Poland the rights and achievements of democracy will be enjoyed only by those citizens with democratic views and tendencies. Democratic Poland cannot and will not give democratic rights to its opponents.'*

The British and American governments seemed quite unaware of all this. Their trust was still in Polish 'national unity' and Stalin's 'good faith'. In 1945 it would have been hard to find two more doubtful quantities.

The Government had another vast administrative problem. The Red Army's early-1945 offensive re-established the Polish state within new boundaries. Gomułka began to take a special interest in the 'Recovered Territories', the former German lands east of the Oder-Neisse line and along the Baltic. A special ministry to run these areas was created in November 1945, and Gomułka was appointed the Minister. They presented

* Neither of these extreme views is reflected in Gomułka's speeches of the time.

many special problems. Much of the German population had retreated with the German army, so that the area was half-empty. The plan was now to empty them completely of Germans and to move in Poles from beyond the Curzon Line, from the areas taken over by the Soviet Union. 'It is not a question of thousands of people to be transferred,' said Gomułka in February, 'but of millions. This operation will involve literally the whole people.'[23] At the May Plenum he was more specific: 'During the current year the entire German population must be removed from the Recovered Territories. We must settle there three and a half million Poles, of whom two and a half million must be settled before harvest time, otherwise the crops will spoil. . . .'[24]

The Yalta agreements gave the Poles the go-ahead for this vast operation. A mass deportation was arranged. Millions of Germans (a German census of September 1950 claims it was about seven and a half millions) were being removed under conditions of some hardship. Understandably, the Poles who organised the exodus did not treat the Germans particularly gently. Suddenly the roles of the conqueror and victim were reversed. Many Germans died.

Gomułka's third task was to build up PPR party membership. By January 1945, after six months of legal activity, the PPR had increased its numbers by fifty per cent. But the membership was still only 30,000, a small figure indeed for a party that aspired to dominate the Polish political scene. Gomułka, as Secretary General, had to promote the PPR as a 'mass party'. He did this with some success. By April there were 300,000 members. Those who applied were given membership quite easily, without the months of checking and probationary training which applicants now have to go through. While many joined out of belief in the new, socialist Poland, there were inevitably many who joined out of opportunism and careerism, who saw which way the wind was blowing and acted accordingly. There were many also who believed in the new régime and wanted to work for it, but would not go so far as to join the communist party. They joined the other parties in the government—the Socialist Party (PPS), which while sympathetic to the communists was not yet dependent on them, and the Peasant Party (the SL, not to be confused with Mikołajczyk's Peasant Party which was still based in London). The Party was at this point handicapped by the decision to avoid the name 'communist' and to call itself the Polish Workers' Party (PPR). Most of the people who joined were workers. Those who were not were largely administrators, officials and intellectuals. There were very few peasants. This was especially dangerous because Poland was an agricultural country, and because it was now clear that the only political opposition to the régime would be provided by Mikołajczyk, who was a peasant leader.

In Moscow the Commission of Three were making no progress at all. The Soviet interpretation of Yalta was that the already functioning Provisional Government should be the *nucleus* of the future government of national unity. The British and Americans claimed that the new government should consist largely of new people, men of goodwill from inside and outside Poland. The Provisional Government should provide some of these men, but not a majority. Nor could the three powers agree on any specific names. Stalin had insisted that no Polish leader 'hostile to the Soviet Union' could be consulted. This at once excluded the majority of Polish leaders. But it was a condition neither Roosevelt nor Churchill could quarrel with. It was taken as read that the future Poland must be friendly to Russia. On this basis Stalin could still with justification object even to Mikołajczyk, the least anti-Soviet of the 'London' leaders. He had proclaimed his desire to live at peace with Russia, but he still had not accepted the position agreed by the 'Big Three'. Stalin could therefore criticise the western powers thus:

'They absolutely insist on inviting to Moscow for consultation, for instance, Mikołajczyk, and this they do in the form of an ultimatum. In this they take no account of the fact that Mikołajczyk has come out openly against the decisions of the Crimea Conference on Poland. However, if you think it necessary, I would be willing to use my influence with the Provisional Polish Government to make them withdraw their objections to inviting Mikołajczyk, if the latter would make a public statement accepting the conditions of the Crimea Conference on the Polish question and declaring that he stands for the establishment of friendly relations between Poland and the Soviet Union.'[25]

Mikołajczyk duly made this declaration on 16 April. Stalin described it as 'a great step forward'. But he was still not satisfied. Determined to get as much purchase out of the statement as possible, he next asked Mikołajczyk to amplify his views on the Curzon Line, to declare himself in favour of it. Mikołajczyk knew that if he did this he would cut himself off from most of the *émigré* Poles. But it was either that or resign from the political running. 'With some misgivings', as he later wrote, he swallowed this bitter pill and announced his readiness to accept the new Polish frontiers. In the words of Churchill, 'the Dictator was for the moment content'. Stalin withdrew his objection to Mikołajczyk, and the Provisional Government of Poland predictably followed his lead.

On 12 April President Roosevelt died. The new President Harry Truman was from the beginning prepared to take a tougher line with the Soviet Union. One of his first acts was to join with Churchill in firmer and more concrete demands. He wrote to Stalin demanding the formation of 'a new Provisional Government'. This was exactly the point at issue. Stalin did not want a new government at all. He insisted on the same government, with certain changes. Still, the two sides were by now closer together. The final agreement was that twelve Poles should meet in Moscow on 17 June to work out the composition of the government. Four of these were already members of the Provisional Government (Bolesław Bierut, Władysław Gomułka, Edward Osóbka-Morawski and Władysław Kowalski), five were from Poland but not in the government, and three were from abroad (Stanisław Mikołajczyk, Jan Stańczyk and Julian Żakowski). Invitations were sent to these last three who were in England. Mikołajczyk and Stańczyk accepted. Żakowski refused. His place was taken by Antoni Kołodziej, a leftist trade-union leader who had already recognised the Provisional Government.

The communists' position was further strengthened by a Polish-Soviet non-agression pact, signed by Osóbka-Morawski and Stalin on 21 April. On 8 May Germany surrendered, leaving the Red Army in control of Berlin. The PPR was able to hold its May Plenum in a Poland at peace for the first time for nearly six years. But although the war was over, many Poles felt their country was still not independent. The Red Army was there. They had to be, for Poland was the main road between Russia and Germany. The question was, how long would they stay? Poland had for centuries longed for freedom. She had had a taste of it in the 1920s. Was the old cycle of partition and Russian and German occupation now to return? Gomułka took some pains to allay these deeply felt fears. He spoke of

'lying propaganda about our so-called intention of "sovietising" Poland and turning her into a Soviet republic. The Provisional Government, and especially our party, is accused of having this intention. This sort of agitation is part of the general political line of the reactionaries. . . . [They] will be destroyed not by Poland as a Soviet republic but by a democratic Poland. In spite of their lying propaganda Poland is not going along the road of "sovietisation" but along the road of democratisation. The Soviet Union has stated quite clearly and unequivocally its attitude to Poland through the lips of Marshal Stalin, who has several times stated that Poland must be strong, independent and democratic. For this is in the Soviet Union's interest.'[26]

Gomułka was to repeat this message many times. Englishmen and Americans found it thoroughly reassuring. Poles found it less so. They knew that Gomułka's idea of democracy was political and *economic* democracy, i.e. socialism. Words had other meanings for him than for Churchill or Truman. Gomułka was being sincere. He wanted socialism, in the marxist sense, for his country. He also wanted a close alliance and treaty with the Soviet Union. He did not want the Soviet Union to control Poland's internal affairs. It was here that he differed from Bierut and some of the Russian-orientated members of his party.

About this time non-communists began to conceive an idealised, optimistic image of Gomułka. Here was a man until recently quite unknown in political life. Suddenly he was vice-Premier of Poland. Poles judged him by his words and actions. Some noticed his quick temper and fiery oratory, and judged him a typical communist fanatic. Others thought they saw in him a patriot. It was these who were right. But they were wrong to make the assumption that came naturally to any Pole who had lived through the previous thirty years—that if he was a patriot he could hardly be a genuine communist. A myth grew up which lasted for decades of Gomułka 'a Pole first and a communist second', as if the two were self-contradictory. This was a grave mistake, but one understandable to most Poles. It was Gomułka's task in life to try to prove these people wrong. He saw no reason why he should choose between country and ideology. He wanted both.

VII: NATIONAL UNITY?

The conference which finally decided the government of Poland took place in Moscow from 17 to 21 June 1945. Gomułka was one of the Provisional Government delegates. It was the first time he had been out of Poland since 1941. Since that time his life had undergone a staggering succession of changes. From being a factory official in Lwów he had been first an underground conspirator, later a reformist administrator. The Moscow consultations gave him his first chance as an international diplomat.

Gomułka's two main colleagues at the consultations were Bierut and Osóbka-Morawski. The choice of the new government was still nominally in the hands of the Commission of Three: Molotov and the two western ambassadors. But they agreed to step aside for the present, and to reassemble only when the three Polish groups had reached an agreement among themselves. The Anglo-Soviet-American commission of three was replaced by a Polish commission of three: Stanisław Szwalbe (a socialist), Władysław Kiernik (Peasant Party) and Gomułka.

Both Szwalbe and Kiernik were in sympathy with the communist-dominated régime. They and Gomułka presented a strong pro-communist force. Mikołajczyk was almost on his own. He was the only important delegate committed to a definite non-communist platform. The Peasant Party elder statesman Wincenty Witos was unable to attend because of illness. This was a further blow. Witos enjoyed great respect in Poland. He had been premier of Poland several times before the 1926 Piłsudski *coup d'état* and in 1931 had been imprisoned by the *sanacja* authorities. Mikołajczyk had been relying on him. When he heard Witos was not to be in Moscow, he nearly withdrew from the consultations. Only another Churchill ultimatum made him change his mind.

With little or no support from his fellow Poles in Moscow, Mikołajczyk was forced to fall back on the understanding and confidence he enjoyed with the British and Americans. He was fond of invoking the name of Churchill, whom many westerners hero-worshipped as the conqueror of Germany. But in Moscow people did not see things that way. Churchill's name did not cut so much ice there as it did in London. And many Poles, not only communists, distrusted Great Britain as an unreliable ally. After all, she had not given any worth-while help to Poland in 1939. Why should she in 1945?

Mikołajczyk was on his own in Moscow, but he thought that once he got to Poland he would not be on his own. His plan was to return to Poland in some high position. There he would be known as the American and British 'man'. He would then rally the Polish people (who were predominantly non-communist) and win the 'free and unfettered' elections guaranteed to Poland by international agreement. Therefore he reminded his Polish communist opponents of the offer they had made to him the previous August, the premiership of a coalition government. The communists were prepared to offer him only one of two vice-premierships. According to the communist journalist Jerzy Borejsza (whose account makes Mikołajczyk sound very silly and is probably distorted), Mikołajczyk said: 'I cannot accept the Provisional Government's proposals. They are against the declaration made by Anthony Eden in the House of Commons. Before I left for Moscow I had a long talk with Premier Churchill. Premier Churchill gave me an assurance. In his view, either I should be appointed President, or else I should be made Premier.'[1]

This speech gave Gomułka the opening for an important outburst of oratory. Gomułka, as the official leader of the communist party, was to be given a task roughly in line with the western idea of party politics. He was to be Mikołajczyk's special adversary. This was Gomułka's first salvo in a battle that was to last more than two years at the end of which one of them was to be forced literally to flee from the field of combat. According to Jerzy Borejsza, Gomułka spoke slowly, 'splitting up every sentence, painfully but clearly formulating every idea, with that characteristic grimace on his face bearing witness to the fact that every word was uttered by an effort of the nerves and the heart':[2]

'. . . it is not Mr Eden or Mr Churchill who will decide what sort of government Poland will have, but the Poles themselves. The proposals put up by the Provisional Government cannot be treated as a matter for bargaining. . . . In Warsaw during the occupation, the PPR suggested an understanding to the *émigré* government's Delegation concerning the fight against the occupying army and the creation of an inter-party body in Poland, which would decide the form of Poland's government at a suitable moment after the liberation.

'Our hand of friendship was rejected. The *émigré* government politicians in London and Poland could not properly evaluate the situation. They lived on the thought of involving the Soviet Union in a war with Germany. . . .

'Twice there were meetings held in Moscow between Mr Mikołajczyk as Premier of the then *émigré* government and representatives of the Committee for National Liberation. *Then,* for the good of the Polish people, to show our good will and our wish to reach an understanding, to mobilise the whole people against the occupying power, we offered Mr Mikołajczyk the premiership of a government in Poland. And he rejected our proposals. We are now not going to make such generous proposals. There can be no reward for the false standpoint taken at that time by Mr Mikołajczyk, for the damage endured by the Polish people as a result of the false *émigré* government policies for which Mr Mikołajczyk, whether he likes it or not, must bear a responsibility. We shall never forget that one of the most tragic results of these policies is the fact that our capital is now in ruins.

'We are now rebuilding Poland and working eighteen hours a day, and it is impossible to treat the Provisional Government and Mr Mikołajczyk as two equally important sides. It is only to *democrats* from abroad that we offer a place in our house, and by this we emphasise that even today we have not changed our policy. We still want an understanding. For this would be in the interest of Poland, and is connected with the need to liquidate that governmental fiction that still exists and operates abroad in the person of Mr Arciszewski. Do not take offence, gentlemen, that we only offer you as many places in the government as we think possible. Because we are the

hosts here. You too can become co-owners of Poland if
you will understand your mistakes and continue along the
road begun by the Provisional Government. We desire
an understanding with all our hearts. But do not think
it is a condition of our existence. Once we have attained
power we shall never give it up. . . . You have the choice,
either we come to an understanding and work together to
rebuild Poland or else we part once and for ever.'³

Poor Mikołajczyk! He could either take it or leave it.
Bullied and friendless among a crowd of hostile Poles, he could
do little but look to America and Great Britain for support.
But what measure of support could he count on?
Truman was new to high office and Churchill was in the
middle of an election campaign. Peace was only a month old.
The British and Americans were weary of war and crisis.
Churchill was thoroughly weary of the Polish question which
was 'threatening to darken the hour of victory'. He writes of
the month of June:

'This month was therefore hard to live through. Strenuous
motor tours to the greatest cities of England and Scotland,
with three or four speeches a day to enormous and, it
seemed, enthusiastic crowds, and above all four laboriously
prepared broadcasts consumed my time and strength.
All the while I felt that much we had fought for in our
long struggle in Europe was slipping away and that the
hopes of an early and lasting peace were receding.'⁴

If Churchill had his doubts about the Moscow talks, the
western press had few. Victory was won and the future of
Poland, for which the war had originally begun, now seemed
of minor importance. A leader in *The Times* on 14 June was
headed 'Progress over Poland', and reflected the opinion now
widely felt in the West that central Europe was not their
concern, it was the concern of the Russians. Now that Britain
was at peace her mood had changed. It was now very similar
to that of September 1938 of Munich. Three days before the
Moscow talks began *The Times* wrote:

'The presence in London of the reactionary and intransigent Arciszewski government, whose anti-Russian pro-
clivities have been no secret, has been not the least of the

many obstacles in the way of a settlement. The success of the negotiations ... would lead automatically to the joint recognition by the Three Powers of a provisional Government of National Unity established in Warsaw. This step would by itself go a long way to remove the wholly unnecessary friction which the Polish imbroglio has generated.'

The tone of this article was reflected elsewhere in the British and American press and can hardly have been much encouragement to Stanisław Mikołajczyk, alone in a hostile city trying to negotiate independence for his country. Not only Poland's freedom was in danger. Mikołajczyk thought there was a chance that *he* might be arrested on charges, already mentioned in Stalin's correspondence with Churchill, of supporting anti-Soviet 'bandits'. The day after he arrived in Moscow in an RAF aircraft, the sixteen ex-Home Army leaders arrested by the Russians in March appeared on trial in the Hall of Columns. Their trial and the political talks were carried on simultaneously—a piece of timing which must have been a deliberate attempt to intimidate Mikołajczyk. Seldom can a man have been forced to negotiate such an important issue under such threats and pressures.

On the very day of Gomułka's outburst, a short distance away across Moscow, Leopold Okulicki, a former leading member of the Home Army of the London Government which Mikołajczyk had once led, was pleading guilty to forming an underground army after the Home Army's dissolution, to ignoring Red Army orders to surrender arms and equipment, to having secret wireless communications with London. 18 June presented a tense, gloomy situation in Moscow. But it did not deter the optimism of *The Times*'s diplomatic correspondent. 'Wide field of agreement' and 'High hopes of success' were the headings to his article which began: 'The Moscow talks on broadening the Polish Provisional Government seem to have made a good beginning.' One wonders from what reliable source he got his information. A similar article on 21 June claimed the talks were continuing in a 'friendly atmosphere'. The British public, at any rate, were to be satisfied that the affairs of Poland were in good hands.

For three days the trial and the talks continued in Moscow. Mikołajczyk kept up his lone stand for a day, after which he realised his opponents would not make concessions. He was given a 'take it or leave it' choice. Gomułka told him, probably correctly, that if he said no and returned to London, the western powers would recognise the Provisional Government in two or three months anyway. By 19 June he knew he had no alter- native but to take what he was offered. 'The train will not always stand waiting with open doors for the passenger to get in,' one of the delegates told him.[5] Mikołajczyk capitulated.

On 21 June the Commission of Three were told that the Polish delegates had reached an agreement. Bierut was to be President of Poland, Osóbka-Morawski to be Premier, Gomułka and Mikołajczyk to be joint vice-Premiers. Mikołajczyk's Peasant Party was to receive one-third of the governmental posts. The details of this share-out was to be finalised in Warsaw. The same day came the verdicts in the trial of the sixteen. Okulicki was sentenced to ten years imprisonment, Stanisław Jankowski to eight years, the others to shorter terms. Two of the accused were acquitted. Amazingly, the result was seen abroad as an example of Soviet leniency. The end of the trial, said a leader in *The Times*, 'will clear up many misunderstandings': 'Nothing in [the prisoners'] confessions will cause surprise to those who have followed with anxiety the increasingly outspoken anti-Russian activities of Polish agents here and elsewhere during the past twelve months. . . . The trial ended in the general expression of a desire to let bygones be bygones and to do nothing that might prejudice the chances of a genuine Russian-Polish settlement for the future.'

In the West there was widespread relief and delight. The 'London' military leaders were not to be executed. They would only have to serve a few years in one of Stalin's prisons—an inconvenience hardly worth making a great protest about. The agreement between the Polish leaders, though, was hailed by *The Times* as a triumph. 'A wide welcome' and 'Proof of allied concord' were the headings to the report (25 June): 'There is the deepest satisfaction in that the problem, seemingly so intractable, should have been settled in a manner consistent with Polish dignity.'

This was ten days before polling day in the British general election. The war against Japan was going well, but the end of it still seemed a long way off. The Americans and British had other things on their minds than the future of Poland, which was for Britain 'a matter of honour' only, not a matter of security or practicality. There was a sudden revival of the issue that had started the war in the first place—whether or not Britain should interest herself at all in eastern Europe. In September 1939 the reluctant conclusion had been that Britain should. In June 1945, after fighting for nearly six years on the basis of this decision, Britain was taking a step backwards towards her old insularity and policy of appeasement. On 14 June the *Times* leader contained the sentence: 'It would be folly to pretend that Britain has an equal claim and desire with Russia to speak in the affairs of eastern Europe. . . .' There was a feeling that Britain had already spent too much money and energy on Poland. There were complaints on the amount of money—about £120 million —the British had given Polish government and administration in London. The vast contribution that Polish armed forces had made to the British war effort was conveniently forgotten. Polish detachments were not even invited to take part in the British victory parade.

Great Britain, war-weary and immersed in a general election, wanted to wash her hands of the 'Polish imbroglio'. The idea of a crisis with the Soviet Union, much less a war, was intolerable. Anything was better than that. So Britain gave up her 'matter of honour' and broke her word towards the Poles, just as she had done in 1939.

Anthony Eden had said in the Yalta debate (28 February): 'We would not recognise a government which we did not think representative. The addition of one or two ministers would not meet our views.' This was exactly what happened in June in Moscow. The government of 'national unity' that emerged from the talks was dominated by communists. They were not the junta of villainous revolutionaries depicted in 'London' propaganda. But equally they were not representative of the will of the Polish people. And Great Britain recognised their government.

Almost at once the western powers broke off relations with the London Government and recognised the new Government of National Unity. De Gaulle did this on 4 July, President Truman on 5 July and Churchill on 6 July, the day after polling day. It was one of his last acts as wartime premier, and not one of his most glorious. 'It is difficult to see what more we could have done,' he said, sounding uncharacteristically pathetic.

Mikołajczyk and Gomułka, though politically at loggerheads, were now governmentally linked. They were joint vice-Premiers. As such they gave a joint press conference in Moscow on 26 June, the day before they all left to take up office in Warsaw. The two opponents dutifully assured the press that their government was supported by most Poles at home and abroad. The date of the 'free and unfettered' elections, they said, would depend on how quickly the Poles abroad, most still centred on England, could be repatriated. Gomułka then gave the press a further proof of his 'Polishness' by presenting an emphatically patriotic view of the Cieszyn question. The Polish delegation, the Czech Premier Fierlinger and vice-Premier Gottwald had for two days been negotiating about Cieszyn (Teschen), a part of Czechoslovakia mainly inhabited by Poles which was seized by Poland after the 1938 Munich agreement. Gomułka, in answer to a journalist's question, declared that the Cieszyn area was ethnically Polish and should remain so. The Polish Minister of Defence Rola-Żymierski had occupied Cieszyn on 19 June, the place was under Polish administration and there was no point whatever in putting the matter before a peace conference of the Three Powers. This was patriotism almost to the point of chauvinism, and it was a line Gomułka was shortly to have to modify.

Gomułka also rejected the idea that western recognition of the new government should be withheld until the election date was fixed. Poland was now fully competent to conduct her own affairs, he told the newsmen. Many westerners, meeting Gomułka for the first time at diplomatic paries and suchlike, found his bluntness encouraging. Clearly he was no left-wing dogmatist. If Polish communists were like this, they thought, there was no point in being unduly alarmed.

That evening Stalin entertained all involved in the new government—Polish, Russian, American and British—to a banquet in the Kremlin. He was in a good humour and spoke with feeling of the bitter Polish-Russian conflicts of the past, of his hope that these were now ancient history and that the Soviet and Polish peoples would now live in friendship. The next day (27 June) the Poles piled into Soviet transport aircraft and flew to Warsaw. They landed at Okęcie airport, there were speeches, and they drove in a procession of cars to their temporary buildings in Praga, the least-destroyed part of Warsaw on the east bank of the Vistula. The streets were festooned with banners and national emblems, and the schoolchildren were given a holiday.

VIII: CO-VICE-PREMIER

The Moscow agreement awarded Mikołajczyk's party one-third of the places in government and administration—enough for a voice but not enough for power. Their allotment was spelt out in detail: one vice-President (Wincenty Witos), one vice-Premier (Mikołajczyk), and five of the fifteen ministries. One of these, the Ministry of Public Administration, usually an important department in countries where political feeling runs high, went in fact to Władysław Kiernik, a Peasant Party member. But the vital internal security department was made into a special ministry led by Stanisław Radkiewicz. He had spent most of the war years in the Soviet Union and was well qualified for his job.

Everyone knew the government had been constructed in a rough and ready way. But June 1945 was a difficult time, when democracy and free elections were hard to arrange. In theory the situation was clear-cut. The new government was bound by international agreement to hold free and unfettered elections 'as soon as possible'. All democratic and anti-Nazi parties would be allowed to compete. The western press and diplomatic missions would be allowed to observe the administration of the country and the conduct of the elections. Most westerners, if in this first flush of victory they cared for Poland at all, had the impression that justice of a sort had been done. In the opinion of *The Times* (25 June): 'The provisional administration thus constituted will be as fully representative and as deserving of confidence as any government established anywhere in the liberated countries of Europe. . . . The suspicion entertained in some quarters that Russia will be concerned with the political complexion of the new government is not borne out by what has happened in the other countries of eastern Europe.'

The government contained a sprinkling of anti-communists,

but the key posts were held by communists or else by men ready to support communists. The government enjoyed the physical strength of Radkiewicz's ministry, known informally as the 'UB' (for *Urząd bezpieczeństwa* or 'security office') which was being expanded in preparation for the expected civil strife. If this was not enough the UB could if necessary count on the support of the Red Army. The communists were still a small force, but tightly-knit and efficient and with ready access to arms and equipment.

The opposition, just as it had been in London, was split. There were the political anti-communists and the violent anti-communists. Mikołajczyk was one of the first group. Though thoroughly opposed to communist domination of Poland, he could not now oppose the principles on which it was based, the three-power agreements of Teheran, Yalta and Moscow. To have any chance at all in the forthcoming political battle he had to maintain what support he had from the British and Americans, who alone had the force necessary to press his claim. He had to stand by the agreements they and the Russians had signed.

This meant he could not support his natural allies, the militant anti-communists. These consisted of two main organisations. One was 'WiN' (Wolność i Niepodległość or 'Freedom and Independence'), the successor of 'NIE' (whose leaders, Okulicki and others, had just been imprisoned) and of the AK. The other was the 'NSZ' (Narodowe Siły Zbrojne or 'National Armed Forces'), a more right-wing, fascist-style group, some of whose members collaborated with the Nazis.

There were thus three main groups opposing the communists: Mikołajczyk and the legal opposition, the 'respectable' anti-communist 'bandits' of WiN, and the disreputable, reactionary bandits of the NSZ. But of course the distinction was not clear cut. The three groups overlapped. WiN openly supported Mikołajczyk, but since WiN were 'bandits' Mikołajczyk could not support them. The NSZ sometimes supported Mikołajczyk, though he openly rejected them. Both 'bandit' groups by supporting Mikołajczyk gave him a bad name with the western Allies and with many peace-loving Poles. It was here that the communists found a slender basis [but a basis] for charges that he was a reactionary, and even pro-Nazi. The 'bandits', by supporting Mikołajczyk, made it easier for the communists to destroy him.

Mikołajczyk tried to keep himself 'clean' of the 'bandits', but many members of his party did not. Not all anti-communist Poles had his touching faith in Anglo-American promises and international agreements. He had resolved to get rid of the communists by legal means, without bloodshed. Many of his supporters saw this as moonshine. They knew the communists would never allow themselves to be voted out of office. They would not resign and depart gracefully from the scene as the Conservative Government had just done in Great Britain. In their view Poland's only hope lay in violent civil strife. They were probably prepared if necessary to provoke a war between the western Allies and the Soviet Union. They began to kill communist leaders and activists. By doing this they provoked the UB to kill them, and not only them but anyone suspected of being sympathetic to them.

The strife that was to come was exemplified by the rivalry between the two vice-Premiers, Gomułka and Mikołajczyk. This very quickly turned to hatred. They were the leaders of the two main political parties, the communists and the Peasant Party. Mikołajczyk was Minister of Agriculture, a job soon to be diluted by Gomułka's appointment as Minister of the Recovered Territories. Their struggle was soon to become Poland's struggle. Mikołajczyk's attitude to his co-vice-Premier was simple. To him Gomułka was a communist fanatic. During July he had a confrontation with Gomułka over ministerial appointments. He describes it in lurid terms:

'. . . I called on Gomułka in his office and told him I planned to take this to the people unless it stopped immediately.

' "Don't you go too far with the people," he roared in a gale of fury. "The people are already against us. They are crazy! You watch your step or you'll be as sorry one of these days as they are."

'It is interesting to study maniacs of this kind.

' "You can't kill all of us, Gomułka," I said to him. "You can't exterminate a whole people or crush its determination to be independent. You know you can't win. Poles are essentially anti-communist. It is barely possible that over a long period of time you might win them to your way of thinking, if that way of thinking included even an elementary kindness. But, by God, you'll never *beat* communism into us!"

'He leaped from his chair and charged me, his hand on the revolver in his pocket and the outline of the gun pointed at my chest. I sat there, for there was nothing else to do, while he stood over me, twitching and speechless with rage.

' "Give me a cigarette, please," I asked.'[1]

Such melodramas were hardly what the British and Americans had hoped for when they had agreed to and recognised the new government. But in 1945 it was party politics, Polish style. 'Parliamentary democracy' and 'free elections' became mere words written into documents to salve people's consciences. Mikołajczyk was one of a tiny number of Poles who believed in the power and effectiveness of Anglo-American influence. He believed touchingly that right would triumph. He did not realise he was dealing with the Anglo-Saxon temperament, with men who thought all they had to do was create the basis and trappings of democracy—parliament, opposition parties, free elections and the rest—and democracy would follow. He underestimated the Anglo-Saxon cynicism of men who believed themselves obliged merely to give their creatures a start, a push into the unknown. What they did then, whether they did well or went to the devil, was not the king-makers' business. They were content to mix Gomułka and Mikołajczyk like oil and water, stand back, observe and deplore the insoluble result.

Stefan Korboński, a Peasant Party leader, gives another unflattering description of Gomułka, an entry he made in his diary after watching him speak in the Sejm in the summer of 1945:

'His broad square chin and prominent cheekbones suggest strength of character, stubbornness and an iron will, of which qualities his enemies have daily evidence; his burning eyes and energetic manner suggest a strong, independent personality; his high, protruding forehead enlarged by a bald pate suggests a certain kind of intelligence—the narrow kind, as each of his pronouncements today testified. He is notoriously lacking in humour, so I was not surprised that his vigorous speech, although consistently to the point, lacked the light touch. When he spoke of the "enemies of the people" his eyes flashed and his sonorous voice expressed hatred. I knew that I had before me a communist fanatic, a mediocrity raised above his level by events.'[2]

These two descriptions show the reason for the lack of communication between the western democracies and their allies in Poland. The Polish democrats (in the western sense) fell between two stools, unable to play either the cool, polite political game of Great Britain, France and America or the brutal political game which has until recently been the rule in eastern Europe. To the western mind there is a hysterical, dangerous sound to the above quotations from Mikołajczyk and Korboński, two Peasant Party leaders. They saw Gomułka as a maniac and a fanatic. But westerners who had met Gomułka knew that this was not true, that he was a fervent communist liable sometimes to lose his temper, but still on the whole a moderate from among his colleagues. They were embarrassed by the frantic labels of hatred the 'liberal' Poles stuck onto everything 'red', and may well in moments of stress have wished for a plague on both Polish houses. Churchill and Truman saw no reason why Mikołajczyk should not deal normally with the communists. After all, *they* had to.

There were no such differences between the Polish communists and their allies in Russia. Although the former had many resentments against Stalin and the Soviet leaders, they were (or at least most of them were) ready to put them aside in favour of the great link which bound them together, their common ideology and their common interest in foreign policy. As such they made a far more serviceable, compact team at the negotiating table than their 'western' opponents. Proof of this came at the final 'Big Three' meeting which began in Potsdam on 17 July. Polling had already taken place (5 July) in Great Britain. Churchill knew his political fate lay with the ballot papers in sealed boxes, ready to be opened on 26 July, and that there was a chance (a small chance, he believed) that he would not see the conference through as leader of the British delegation.

On the opening day Truman and Churchill received momentous news. An atomic bomb had been exploded in the New Mexican desert. Suddenly the western bargaining position was strengthened, more so perhaps than people realised at the time. There would be no need now to woo the Soviet Union into the war against Japan. The United States could finish the job herself, and this she did a few days later. On 6 August she dropped an atomic bomb on Hiroshima, on 9 August another on Nagasaki.

None of the 'Big Three' planned to raise the question of the Polish government's composition. This had been settled a month earlier in Moscow, apparently to everyone's satisfaction, and the three powers were glad to have the matter off their agenda. Now the most difficult issue was that of her western frontier with Germany. In principle the three powers had agreed to an 'Oder-Neisse line' but Churchill, whether through ignorance or sheer pressure of work, had not envisaged Poland's occupation of territory as far west as the *western* Neisse. Polish forces, supported by the Red Army, were now in control of this area which included the city of Wrocław (Breslau). The coal was being dug by Polish miners. Polish farmers, most of them from east of the Curzon Line, were preparing to harvest the corn. It was yet another *fait accompli*, in the opinion of Churchill an unjust one.

It was decided that on this occasion, unlike what happened at Teheran and Yalta, the Poles should be consulted on matters that vitally concerned their country. On 23 July President Truman, the conference chairman, invited the Polish Government to send a delegation to Potsdam. With great haste a group of men was assembled—Bierut, Osóbka-Morawski, Gomułka, Mikołajczyk, Wincenty Rzymowski (Foreign Minister) and six others. Their arrival lent weight to the Soviet case. Their first act was to meet the Soviet delegation and agree on a common cause against the British and Americans. Again Mikołajczyk was torn between two courses of action. As a patriotic Pole he thought it right that Poland should be fully compensated at German expense for her territorial losses in the east. To deny this would be to cast himself in an anti-Polish role, and into a minority of one in his delegation. On the other hand he knew that Churchill, on whom he relied for so much, held a different view. He could not join the rest of the Polish and Soviet delegates in flatly opposing the man whose influence, he hoped, was soon to bring him to power in a non-communist Poland.

Mikołajczyk tried to kill two birds with one stone. He told his colleagues the British and Americans might be ready to withdraw their objections to the western Neisse frontier, but only if he and his party were given a more equitable share of government posts, and more influence in Poland. Predictably, the communists objected to this line of argument. Gomułka was the one to protest: 'Władysław Gomułka reacted sharply to what Mikołajczyk said. He told him he had the impression the so-called condition he referred to had been invented by Mikołajczyk himself, and perhaps suggested by him to the English. Gomułka condemned Mikołajczyk's unpatriotic behaviour, aimed at benefiting his own political career or his own party.'[3]

On the morning of 25 July Churchill had a 'stern talk' with Bolesław Bierut. Bierut told him war provided an opportunity for 'new social developments'. Churchill wrote:

'I asked whether this meant that Poland was to plunge into communism, to which I was opposed, though of course it was purely a matter for the Poles. Bierut assured me that according to his ideas Poland would be far from communist. She wanted to be friendly with the Soviet Union and learn from her, but she had her own traditions and did not wish to copy the Soviet system, and if anyone tried to impose it by force the Poles would probably resist.'[4]

Bierut then said: 'Poland will develop on the principles of western democracy'—an extraordinary statement to come from the lips of a man who had spent so many years as a militant communist and in the service of the Soviet Union. Amazingly, Churchill seems to have accepted Bierut's words at their face value. It is doubtful how much he knew of Bierut's background. Perhaps nothing. At any rate he thought it worth while appealing to Bierut for press and judicial freedom in Poland. Again Bierut reassured him, and apparently was believed. Churchill said nothing about the violence and repression that Polish communists and anti-communists were already visiting upon each other. Did he know about it? Perhaps not. Or perhaps his mind was on other things. Whatever the explanation, Churchill thus wasted his last chance to influence events in Poland. It was a unique opportunity. For eighteen months he had negotiated about Poland from a position of weakness and ignorance. But now the war was won. Britain no longer needed to rely on her Soviet ally. Potsdam was his first chance to speak from strength, knowing that in the last resort the atomic bomb could deal with the ultimate crisis. He did not take that chance. That same afternoon he flew to London to attend the counting of the British people's votes, hoping to be able to resume the negotiations in a few days after re-election. He had allowed several issues to stand over until his return. He did not return. The Conservative Party was defeated and Clement Attlee became Prime Minister.

After a four-day break Attlee and Ernest Bevin flew to Potsdam to resume the talks. Although there was no immediate change in British foreign policy, the change of government hardly helped the Polish 'liberal' case. Mikołajczyk had had a warm, if erratic, personal relationship with Churchill. He and the new British delegation were still trying to obtain a package deal from the Russians and communist Poles on the major outstanding issue—the Polish western frontier. In a note dated 31 July they indicated they would approve the western-Neisse frontier only in exchange for assurances about the internal future of Poland—freedom of press, religion, travel for foreign correspondents—as well as guarantees of fairness in the forthcoming elections. But it was now no longer easy to press these points. Bierut was able to claim that Poland was now an independent country with a government recognised by the major world powers, who no longer had any right to meddle in Poland's internal affairs. It was hard to counter this argument. The package deal collapsed and all that was achieved was an assurance that Soviet troops would be withdrawn from certain areas—a promise of doubtful usefulness. Short of using the nuclear threat, the western powers neither had nor would have the power to enforce the promise, or even to know for certain whether or not it was being broken.

The extent to which the British and Americans finally agreed to accept the Polish western frontier has been a matter for controversy ever since. One of the Potsdam resolutions, dated 2 August, delineates the frontier according to the Polish-Soviet claims, an almost-straight line running from just west of Stettin, north to south. The former German territories, says the resolution, 'should be placed under the control of the Polish state'. The question is, was this a permanent decision? Western Germany claims it was a temporary decision, valid only until the signing of a peace treaty which will determine the final frontier. Poland and the Soviet Union (and now East Germany) claim the present 'Oder-Neisse Line' is the final frontier, that no revision of it was contemplated in the Potsdam resolution, and that a peace treaty can only confirm it. While the issue has recently been losing momentum in Germany itself, in eastern Europe it is much more important—a bitter source of anti-

German feeling, of accusations of German 'revanchism' and potential aggression.

The Polish delegates returned home, all except Mikołajczyk well satisfied with the Conference's outcome. 'The Polish victory at Potsdam' was the title of an article by Gomułka on 8 August in the communist daily *Głos Ludu* ('Voice of the People').[5] The Potsdam decisions, he said, made it clear Poland was becoming 'the greatest potential of strength in central Europe'. At last the lands of the 'Piast', the first dynasty of Polish kings which flourished in the fourteenth century, were returned to Poland, together with their rich natural resources and formerly German-owned property. And this had only been possible because of the support given to the Polish cause by the Soviet Union. 'Without their help,' said Gomułka, 'it would have been hard for the Polish delegation to convince our other allies, especially England, of the justice of our cause.' He quoted the 'wonderful words' of Stalin spoken a month earlier in Moscow, double-edged words which ten years later were to sound all too meaningful: 'We do not ask you [the Poles] to take our word for it. Nobody should take our word for it. Let facts and deeds decide the relationship between Russia and Poland. In politics faith should be based only on facts.'

Gomułka's arguments then took a more original turn. The new frontier, he said, was correct not only because it strengthened Poland, but also because it weakened Germany. 'The weakness of Germany,' he said, 'will be a condition of peace in Europe and the whole world for many decades yet.' This view, fair enough perhaps in the Poland of 1945, was to persist. A quarter of a century later it was still the basis of Gomułka's foreign policy, almost his obsession. He was to propound anti-Germanism as a constructive idea, a contribution to the good of the world. Peace in Europe was only three months old, but already Gomułka was taking the lead in the anti-German (not anti-Nazi but anti-German) crusade. Several times he reminded Polish audiences how the Nazis were supported by 'almost the entire German people'.* However much he might deny it, he was to become the spokesman for a national prejudice. Gomułka's anti-Germanism was originally as justified as any such feeling possibly can be, but it was later to become

* For instance his speech delivered on 8 September 1946, in reply to US Secretary of State Byrnes.

a negative ideal, a barrier in the way of a *rapprochement*, and as such probably detrimental in the long term to Polish interest.

The immediate aftermath of Potsdam was in some ways an agreeable time for Poland and its new government. Though many Poles felt a sense of hopelessness, that they had been betrayed once again by their western allies, abandoned to the Russians just as in 1939 they had been abandoned to the Germans, many others were excited at the thought of starting with a clean slate in a devastated but compact and potentially rich country. The Polish cities were in ruins. Factories, works of art and the most talented of Poland's people had been carried off to Germany and destroyed. Twenty per cent of the population had been killed—one of the most appalling population losses in the history of any country. Now those who were left had to begin from zero. There was hunger and violence. Poland had plumbed the depths, suffered from the war more than any other country. But at least now there was peace. The cities were being rebuilt. The rubble was being cleared, by hand if necessary, and brick piled upon brick.

Although the new government was certainly not constituted according to the will of the majority of Poles, it did enjoy support from many moderate, realistic men. The number of convinced communists was still tiny, but communism—the ideal towards which the PPR leaders, Gomułka included, were aiming—was not mentioned in their speeches or interviews. They were putting up a liberal façade, partly for the benefit of the British and Americans who might rebel at the prospect of Poland being communised overnight, partly for domestic consumption, to reassure the population whose support they needed for the tasks ahead. They did not offer their fellow Poles the absurdities they proclaimed at international conferences. Bierut did not speak in Poland of his belief in 'western democracy' as he had to Churchill in Potsdam. Such words from a communist of twenty-five years' standing would have been an insult to his audience's intelligence. But he did, in his function as President, attend services in Catholic churches and speak of the importance of private initiative in the post-war economy. It was an ideological concession to necessity and tactics. Rome was not built in a day and neither was stalinist rule in Poland.

This is not to say the communists had no case. Whether by coincidence or not, the need to present a façade gave the PPR the chance to present their plan as the only realistic course for

Poland after the war. This case is eloquently set out by Gomułka in his speeches during 1945–46, the consolidation period of communist power. He repeated again and again the points that lay in his party's favour. In a long speech delivered on 7 December at the PPR First Congress[6] he effectively outlined recent Polish history to show his party's policy in a favourable light. He spoke of prewar Poland, a backward, second-rate power, exploited by foreign capitalists, frantically wooing Hitler and Goering, forming useless and dangerous alliances with Germany, France and Great Britain in attempts to oppose her natural ally, Soviet Russia. It was these policies, he said, that were responsible for the disaster of September 1939. The French, the British and the 'reactionary' Poles had all betrayed Poland. The 'reactionaries' had counted on Hitler's assault being directed first against Russia—a move they would secretly have supported. They were afraid to ally themselves with Russia, since this might threaten their personal position as rulers of Poland and possessors of its wealth.

The Anglo-French declaration of war on 3 September, 1939, Gomułka claimed, had 'a formal rather than a factual character'. Her 'allies' did not lift a finger: 'From every Polish heart came a cry for help joined with a determination to fight. But Poland received no help. In the West the Munich-ites played a comedy of war and treated us to radio broadcasts which nobody listened to.'[7]

Gomułka mentioned the (for him) embarrassing question of the Soviet invasion of eastern Poland on 17 September 1939. He claimed the Soviet attack on his country was quite justified. The Soviet government had no other alternative. First, there was the *sanacja* Polish government's rejection of all Soviet offers of an anti-Nazi pact. Secondly, when the Red Army crossed the frontier, the Polish state apparatus had already collapsed and the government fled into Romania.* Thirdly, there was a clear

---

* This may be a distortion of fact. Most reports claim the Red Army attacked in the *early morning* of 16 September. The Moscow daily *Izvestiya* quotes a *communiqué* of the Red Army General Staff dated 17 September, confirming that they crossed the Polish frontier that *morning*. According to most sources the Polish government did not cross into Romania until the *evening* of 17 September (see Włodzimierz Kowalski, *Walka Dyplomatyczna o Miejsce Polski w Europie, 1939–45*, p. 10).

intention on the part of the French and British to direct Hitler's aggression against the Soviet Union, which had to be countered. Fourthly, the territories the Red Army occupied were inhabited mainly by Ukrainians and Byelorussians, whom the Soviet government had a moral right and duty to protect. These four points led Gomułka to the conclusion that the Red Army attack 'was a measure of necessary self-defence and security on the part of our eastern neighbour. Anyone not poisoned by anti-Soviet propaganda must accept this. However painful for us and for all Poles were those September days, the step the Soviet government took was the first basic step towards the future victory over the Germans, won by the Polish people together with the peoples of the Soviet Union.'

But there were two important points which Gomułka ignored. He did not explain why the Soviet authorities found it necessary to arrest and deport so many hundreds of thousands of the people living east of the River Bug, whom they had supposedly come to liberate. And he ignores the fact that in the twenty-one-month period that followed September 1939 the Soviet Union was no neutral bystander, no non-participator in Hitler's westward-directed aggression. She was Hitler's ally. She supported him in the Soviet press and supplied him with military equipment.

Gomułka has no time or understanding for those Poles (the vast majority) who saw the 1939 Russian attack upon them, the subsequent brutality and NKVD terror, the stage-managed elections and the absorption of forty-five per cent of prewar Poland into the Soviet Union as clearly hostile acts. Although there is some truth in his arguments, he knew well that in the eyes of most Poles they did not vindicate the Soviet actions. After 1939 most Poles blamed the Russians and Germans equally for their miseries, creating the so-called 'theory of two enemies'. It was this that became Gomułka's next target.

Most Poles took delight in Germany's attack on Russia in June 1941 and in the initial disasters that befell the Red Army. There were extremists who deplored the agreement with Russia signed by Sikorski. The Home Army, at the height of the German-Soviet battles, did 'go slow' on their resistance to the occupying army, seeing little reason why they should run risks in helping the Russians who had so recently attacked them. As so often in their history, the Poles had put their pride before their interest. Even moderate Poles like Mikołajczyk had supported the 'go slow'. Gomułka eagerly seized on a speech made by Mikołajczyk on 30 December 1942, during the height of the battle of Stalingrad: 'These cases show that the Germans would like to provoke our defenceless population to premature resistance. This must not be allowed. Endure steadfastly and with caution. The end of your sufferings is near.'[8]

Gomułka was on weaker ground with his next point, the Katyń affair. His case here depended on a straight acceptance of the Soviet version of the murder of 8,000 Polish officers near Smolensk. Gomułka is one of very few Poles indeed who still defends the theory that these men were killed by the Nazis. He called and still calls the affair 'Goebbels's provocation' and compared it to the burning of the Berlin Reichstag. 'They believed the [German] accusation because they wanted to believe it,' says Gomułka of his 'London' opponents. One might say the opposite of Gomułka himself. Gomułka would like to believe the Soviet version of this still controversial affair, but it is unlikely that he does.

Another partly valid point Gomułka made was that he and the communists had several times offered to make peace with the other political groups during 1943, that each time their hand of friendship had been rejected. This was true, but it was not quite as simple as that. During 1943 the communists were weak. They numbered only a few thousand inside Poland, and they had as yet scant support from Soviet Russia. When the communists became strong they became less conciliatory. For a short time they had been a force directed towards national unity. But it is doubtful whether this was for patriotic motives as much as out of political self-interest.

Gomułka was able to show, however, by carefully selected quotations from the Polish émigré press, how fanatically anti-Soviet most of the 'London' politicians had been. The words he quoted revealed an attitude which, even to Poles with no love for Russia, seemed quite ludicrous and unrealistic in the face of the wartime situation. Gomułka was right when he claimed that men like Sikorski, ready to bury the hatchet and collaborate with the former Russian enemy, were few indeed. He could also show that Mikołajczyk was not entirely guiltless of anti-Sovietism. After all, it was known he had only accepted the Soviet terms for the formation of the new government under pressure from his American and British friends.

There were numerous accusations against the 'London' Home Army: that they had collaborated with the Germans, that they had fought and killed communists and members of the rival People's Army (AL). The greatest Home Army crime, Gomułka claimed, was the destruction of Warsaw after the 1944 Uprising. This he blamed as much on the opportunism of the 'reactionaries' as on the villainy of Hitler. The Warsaw Uprising, he said, 'gave the Hitlerite criminals a pretext for the complete destruction of our capital'. By this he meant presumably that the Home Army should have soft-pedalled their actions and waited for Soviet liberation. In fact he was now making use of the 'London' argument for restraint during 1942–43. But he was probably right in claiming that the timing of the 'adventure' had a basically political character. The Home Army wanted to liberate Warsaw before the Red Army arrived. They would then be able to welcome the Russians there as their 'guests', under their jurisdiction. They miscalculated, over-estimating their own strength, ignoring the inability of the western powers and the reluctance of the Soviet Union to come to their aid.

On the frontier question too Gomułka had just cause for complaint against the 'reactionaries'. They were guilty at best of lack of realism, at worst of treachery. Their anti-Sovietism had led them to press their demands for the largely non-Polish lands east of the River Bug, and to reject the more attainable, less spacious but richer lands east of the Rivers Oder and Neisse. Jan Kwapiński, Economics Minister in Arciszewski's London Government, had said, 'We do not want Szczecin [Stettin], we do not want Wrocław [Breslau].' It was a rash statement which Gomułka was to quote again and again, especially to the Poles who had been resettled in the West and whose livelihoods were threatened by the 'London' attitude. The 'London' demands for the eastern territories, now a part of Russia, he dismissed as pie in the sky: 'Among all our allies we could not find one country that would support our demands for the territories east of the Bug.'

Gomułka took some pride in what his government had already achieved. He and his colleagues had been presented with a raw material, a country in ruins. The population, twenty per cent of which had perished, was debilitated by illness and starvation. In the face of these immense difficulties the government had done well. The agricultural reform was historically overdue and generally accepted, even by Mikołajczyk. A start had been made in rebuilding the cities, providing schools, hospitals and social services. The countryside, stripped of equipment and livestock, was being replenished, admittedly with the help of UNRRA and other foreign-aid groups. By the end of 1945 industrial production had reached fifty per cent of its pre-war level, a fact rightly hailed by Gomułka as a success.

These were the facts on which Gomułka hoped to build his movement. Regarding his own party, his own colleagues, he was on the defensive, ready to play down the communist nature of his movement in the hope of ridding it of the stigma it had acquired before the war of being a 'Moscow agency'. With his own plans he was a moderate, partly a tactical moderate, partly a genuine one, certainly more of a moderate than Bierut, Minc, Berman and the other Moscow-orientated men in the PPR. His passion and fervour he reserved for attacks on his opponents: the 'bandits' who were physically fighting communist power, the London-based 'reactionaries' who were scheming and plotting his overthrow, and the Warsaw-based legal opposition, Mikołajczyk and the Peasant Party.

Gomułka was pressing his party's case with a strange mixture of moderation and ruthlessness. He was trying to broaden his party's base, give it a more general image, turn it into a 'mass party'. He was quite prepared to accept non-communists. provided they had a 'positive attitude' to the new Poland: 'We must accept into our Party, into our Party school, all those good workers and good democrats who fought for democracy even without knowing what that is. Ideological conceptions cannot be crystallised immediately.'[9]

Again Gomułka used the word 'democracy' in his own specialised sense. It was a word he was fond of, and many Poles unused to Marxist terminology were confused by it. Maybe they did not understand 'democracy', Gomułka said, but 'these people came into our Party because they recognised as correct what our party leaders said. They recognised as correct the call to fight for peace against the reactionaries, to nationalise our industry. This is why they came to us. We would like to take a million of such men and women into our Party.'

In these words there are, of course, the self-assurance and condescension of the convinced communist. But they also show the flexibility which Gomułka as a young man possessed and used with advantage in the chaos of Poland immediately after the war. His foreign policy also was then, on the face of it, unexceptionable: 'We have always emphasised and we emphasise today Poland's need for friendly relations with the western countries, especially with France, England and the United States. But the unbreakable canon of our political line in foreign policy is the basing of the security of Poland frontiers on the Polish-Soviet Alliance.'[10]

There were, of course, Poles who accepted none of this, who insisted that the PPR, in spite of its proclaimed, temporary moderation, was a straightforward communist party, and as such dependent on the Soviet model. In their view it was only a matter of time before Poland's régime became a replica of the Soviet system. To such Poles Gomułka addressed a carefully worded message of moderation. Here are some quotations from his speeches:

'We completely reject the accusation made against us by the reactionaries that we will impose a one-party system. We do not want a one-party system and we are not moving towards it.'[11]

'The path of evolutionary social change, of an evolutionary transformation to the socialist system, is entirely possible. People's democracy can be transformed in a peaceful manner into socialist democracy.'[12]

'. . . enemies of democracy and People's Poland have been spreading lies, saying the government confiscated the large estates because it intends to introduce the *kolkhoz* [collective farm] system into our villages. . . .'

'Their second lie was to try to convince the people that the government of our newborn Poland, lead by the PPR, intends to annex Poland as the seventeenth republic of the Soviet Union.'[13]

'In the Soviet Union power is exercised by the soviets which combine legislative and administrative functions. In Poland there is a division of functions, and state power is based on parliamentary democracy. . . . The dictatorship of the working class or of a single party is not essential nor would it serve any useful purpose. . . . Poland can proceed and is proceeding along her own road.'

It is difficult to know how sincerely felt were these moderate views. Certainly the last quotation shows Gomułka in an unjustly liberal light. There may be differences in eastern and western terminology, but it is hard to see how Gomułka, a marxist, could speak up for parliamentary democracy and mean what he said sincerely. Still, some of the moderate views were his own, as later events were to prove. His views on the collectivisation issue did differ from those of Bierut and the other 'Moscow' leaders. He did believe that the 'Polish road to socialism'—a phrase that was to become, in political defeat as much as in victory, his special trade mark—existed and had as much validity in Poland as the edicts of Lenin and Stalin had in Russia. All these months, while putting forward these 'liberal' views partly as a tactic to reassure the Polish people, partly to emphasise his sincere beliefs which were already being questioned by his more dogmatic comrades in the PPR, he was establishing himself, perhaps without even realising it, as a 'national' communist. The Gomułka myth was founded in this campaign of erratic, moderate caution.

Gomułka was not being consistent. His mildness and lack of communist dogma were in strange contrast to the hard and ruthless way he dealt with the opponents of 'people's power', especially Mikołajczyk and the Peasant Party. In June 1945, when the two vice-Premiers met for the first time on the political stage, Gomułka played the role of Mikołajczyk's particular gadfly. No sooner had the two men taken up office in Warsaw than they were at daggers drawn. Mikołajczyk saw Gomułka as a maniac. Gomułka saw Mikołajczyk as the focal point of the whole 'reactionary' movement. He saw this mild, plump, unimposing man, whose politics were by western standards left-of-centre and by no standard extreme, as the enemy incarnate. A few days after they had been appointed joint vice-Premiers Gomułka said: ' . . . Mikołajczyk's politics may not suit certain of the reactionary groups, but this is not what counts. For them what counts is to make of Mikołajczyk a symbol of all anti-democratic elements, a standard of everything that is hostile to democracy and the Soviet Union.'[14]

Mikołajczyk had arrived in Poland in June 1945, to find a Peasant Party, quite separate of his 'London' Peasant Party, in existence and already represented in the January 1945 provisional government. He tried to absorb this party (Stronnictwo Ludowe or SL) but failed. So on 22 August 1945 he founded his own party, the Polish Peasant Party (Polskie Stronnictwo Ludowe or PSL). The new party immediately acquired a mass membership. Whole local groups of the SL joined Mikołajczyk and the PSL. The veteran Peasant Party leader Wincenty Witos gave him his blessing, but could not give his support. He died on 31 October. While his policies were harmless and liberal enough, Mikołajczyk's main quality in the eyes of Polish anti-communists was that he was supported by the British and Americans who, many of them hoped, would soon liberate Poland and the rest of eastern Europe from Soviet control with their new atomic weapon. Gomułka was in some ways right. Mikołajczyk *was* supported by many anti-communists of extreme views, warmongers who thought their future freedom depended on Soviet defeat and nuclear destruction. But he was wrong to lump these extremists together with the supporters of Mikołajczyk, whose sinister scheme was merely to win the promised free elections, to see the same orderly change of power and government that had just taken place in Britain. In this Mikołajczyk was perhaps being naïve and unrealistic. But he was not being vicious or reactionary, except in the technical sense. He had no more intention of working permanently with the right-wing extremists than he had of working with the communists. He had contacts with both extremes, official ones with the left, unofficial with the right, but these were on a day-to-day basis, administratively essential since Poland was still keeping up the façade of a coalition government, a coalition of men who hated each other.

The United States, Great Britain and the Soviet Union had airily 'guaranteed' Poland free elections. For their benefit, or rather for the benefit of the two western nations, the 'coalition' was necessary. It was they whom Gomułka was thinking of when he made such un-communist, liberal statements as: 'No government and no social system sympathises with those who oppose them. Nor do we have sympathy for the PSL, who oppose us. But we do not wish to take away anybody's democratic right of opposition. We do not take away this right from the Polish Peasant Party (PSL).'[15]

This is perhaps the most insincere statement Gomułka ever made. He said this at a time when police terror and intimidation, organised by the PPR which Gomułka led, were being ruthlessly applied to Peasant Party members and organisations all over Poland, with the express purpose of taking away their right to oppose. Mikołajczyk's book describes what was happening, probably with some exaggeration since it is an emotional, rather wildly written book. But the basic content of the book is confirmed by other authorities on the subject and is certainly true. It is also indisputable that the PSL was being terrorised and that Gomułka was one of the main instigators of the terror. After the death of Władysław Kojder, allegedly murdered by the UB, Mikołajczyk demanded an inquiry into Radkiewicz's ministry. Gomułka opposed him. 'To form such a commission,' he said, 'would constitute a vote of no confidence in the Ministry of Security.'[16] In a speech on 27 February 1946 he said:

'The security organs as a whole are healthy and extremely devoted to their work. And we shall defend them against all unjust and slanderous accusations. For the security apparatus is a sharp tool in the hand of democratic Poland in her fight against the reactionaries. The Peasant Party would like to disarm the democrats, to deprive them of power in the face of the reactionaries. This we shall not allow. There are no unjustified arrests of Peasant Party members.'[17]

This was an emphatic enough assurance. But Gomułka went on to tell of incidents where underground 'bandits' were captured or killed and found to be carrying Peasant Party cards. Known Peasant Party men, he said, had been found with firearms or with 'illegal literature': 'If such men as this are arrested, then they are correctly arrested.' He then contradicted his earlier statement. Apparently unjustified arrests *did* occasionally occur: 'I do not say there may not be incidents in which some Peasant Party member or other is arrested, although innocent, during the liquidation of some bandit gang. But this is something which happens with all security organisations all over the world.'[18]

The speeches of Gomułka and Mikołajczyk make sad reading. Both men use the same sort of language to describe the same sort of horrors, the wholesale murder and kidnapping of their supporters by a ruthless enemy (either 'communist' or 'reactionary'), backed by alien powers (either Soviet or Anglo-Saxon). Only the proper names need to be changed. The story is the same. Here are some quotations from the Mikołajczyk version:

'In the Wrocław region all members of the Polish Peasant Party's executive committee for the area were arrested; some were tortured. In Bochnia the security police station became a house of horrors. Bartkowicz, commander of the station, who had worked closely with the Gestapo during the occupation. . . . On 8 September 1945 he murdered mayor Józef Kołodziej of Bogucice. . . . He then ordered his torturers to seize Józef Szydłowski, the Peasant Party's local executive committee member, whose tongue was cut out, fingernails ripped off and eyes seared with a hot poker before he was finally shot. . . . On 30 November and 1 December of that year, Security Police and Red Army units fell on the villages of Lempiec and Kobusy in the Bielsk district. They shot nine Polish Peasant Party men. . . .'

'Security Police arrested Franciszek Nygowski and Jan Brzozowski in Mława. Their naked bodies were found the following day in a near-by forest. . . .'[19]

Gomułka had a simple answer to these charges. In the first place they were lies. In the second place, even if they were not lies, the men who suffered were reactionary bandits who thoroughly deserved their fate. There was no government in the world, he announced, that would tolerate armed rebellion, murder and larceny committed by its political opponents. And with these murders and illegal acts he linked the entire Peasant Party, or at least its leadership:

'The Peasant Party leadership is pushing the party further and further to the right, closer and closer to the reactionaries. . . . In many parts of the country the Peasant Party has become a protection and a place of refuge for bandits and diversionary activity. . . .

'In the new Poland our system, our rule of law is democratic. But there is no democracy on earth which would passively and without resistance allow acts of bloody violence, terror and anarchy. This is why our democratic government is taking repressive action against this, and it regards such action as entirely justified.'[20]

Apart from the purely administrative work of running his Ministry and his Party, Gomułka's main task was to oppose the *legal* opposition, Mikołajczyk. The illegal could be dealt with by the police in its various forms, assisted if necessary by the Soviet Army. No western political leader could complain if Gomułka, the head of a political party, abused the head of the rival party. This was party politics. Nor could westerners complain if a properly constituted government asserted its authority and imprisoned 'bandits'. But there was a limit to what Gomułka and his party could get away with. The legal opposition could not be crushed by force, although force might sometimes be used against it. Mikołajczyk had to be crushed by defeat in 'free and unfettered elections'. Any other means would have run the risk of incurring British and American intervention in eastern Europe.

The Provisonal Government was bound by the Potsdam agreement to hold elections 'as soon as possible'. This was a vague phrase, so vague that the government was able to postpone elections until January 1947, a year and a half after they assumed power. They explained the delay by claiming that elections would be impossible to organise in a Poland torn apart by civil strife and 'bandit' activity, that before elections could be held the bandits had to be stamped out. Meanwhile on 30 June 1946 they held an interim referendum in which the electorate was asked three questions: (1) Are you in favour of the abolition of the Senate? (2) Are you for making permanent the land and nationalisation reforms?* (3) Are you for fixing the Polish western frontier on the Oder-Neisse Line? To these questions the communists invited Poles to vote 'three times yes'. The questions were cleverly formulated. To none of them was the answer an obvious 'no', and there was nothing communist, or even very socialist about them. The third question was a clear 'yes' to all but a handful of anti-Soviet extremists who still hankered after the lost lands in the east and saw the Soviet Union rather than Germany as 'enemy number one'. The second question, which concerned reforms already in effect, also probably had majority support. And the first question was seen largely as an irrelevance. The matter of whether the Polish parliament should or should not have an upper house was not the burning issue of the day. The only real issue—the struggle for power between pro- and anti-communist—was not part of the referendum.

Many of Mikołajczyk's supporters would have been ready to vote 'three times yes', as the communists were asking, on the strength of the issues themselves. But to do so would, on the face of it, be to give them a vote of confidence. Therefore Miko-łajczyk asked his supporters[21] to vote 'no' to the first question, 'yes' to the two others. He said: 'We decided to vote "no" on the first question as a protest against political terror, against dissolving local units of the Polish Peasant Party, against false arrests and censorship, and against the referendum itself. . . .'[22]

None of this had anything to do with the value or non-value of the senate. As it disappeared from Polish politics, the Senate's abolition became a symbol, either of political terror (the Mikołajczyk view) or of Polish democracy (the Gomułka view). Gomułka put the matter in his usual simplistic terms: 'To answer "no" will bring harm to the state and the people. All answers of "no" will damage our people's democracy and the very basis of the Polish state. To vote "no" to the first, second or third question is to deny the new Poland.'

Gomułka announced that 'a threefold "yes" will document

* These were the Land Reform enacted on 6 September 1944, confiscating all estates larger than 50 hectares (123 acres), or 100 hectares in the Western Territories, and the Nationalisation Act of 3 January 1946, which appropriated all industrial concerns which employed more than fifty workers per shift.

our unshakeable will to maintain our western frontiers for ever'. What the abolition of the Senate had to do with the western frontiers he did not explain. To him, the three questions were as one. To vote against abolishing the Senate, he implied, was to vote against the western frontiers. And anyone who voted against the western frontiers was a German-lover, a fascist and a traitor. His were the simple politics of the convinced communist: he who is not for 'people's power' is against it, and he who is against it is a traitor. To vote 'no' was to be 'against'. As usual his speeches made clever use of both stick and carrot. The ruthlessness with which he attacked those 'against' was balanced by the moderation with which he approached all those who, even though not communist or even socialist, broadly accepted the new régime. Part of the communist 'three times yes' programme, he announced on polling day, was 'a constitutional guarantee for the basic rights of private initiative, a guarantee of work and development for the non-nationalised branches of production'.[24]

In the face of such moderation the Peasant Party was hamstrung. Gomułka made his appeal: 'Everyone to the urns . . . everyone vote three times "yes".' On the issues themselves he might well have won an honest majority.

In the event Gomułka got his majority, but it was hardly an honest one. The communists needed a mandate, and they felt justified in using unorthodox, violent methods to influence the voting. Details of these methods are described by Mikołajczyk and others, and were observed by western diplomats and correspondents in Poland. There can be little doubt that physical pressure was exerted by the communists both on the voting and on the counting and issuing of results.

According to the official result, thirty-two per cent of Poles obeyed Mikołajczyk and voted 'no' to the first question. The real figure can only be guessed at. Mikołajczyk claims it was more than eighty per cent. Of course he protested at the published result and took the drastic step of explaining his view to a press conference of western correspondents. The Americans and British also protested at the violation of the Potsdam and Yalta agreements. All protests were rejected by the Soviet and Polish governments. Mikołajczyk was called a traitor for inviting foreign western powers to 'meddle in Poland's internal affairs'. In a speech delivered a week after the referendum Gomułka, while claiming the result as a victory for the régime, castigated those who voted the Mikołajczyk way, lumping them together with the extremist five per cent who voted 'three times no', i.e. against the western frontier with Germany. He spoke of 'our reactionary NSZ and WiN Mikołajczyk', thus directly accusing the Peasant Party leader of collaboration with bandits, both 'London' and plain fascist. He implied that Mikołajczyk was a Nazi, an accusation which if established would have enabled the Peasant Party to be legally banned, since by both international agreement and Polish law Nazi parties were not permitted.

The British and Americans did very little. The two ambassadors, charged by their governments to ensure that the Polish elections were 'free and unfettered', were soon obliged to report their task was impossible. Cavendish-Bentinck, the British Ambassador, kept himself well enough informed. He had a private aeroplane, which he called his 'peering machine', and used to fly round the country in it making reconnaisance. He had the ear of Mikołajczyk, of the cardinals Hłond and Sapieha, and many other anti-communist leaders. But all he and his American colleague Bliss Lane could do was report and protest. Cavendish-Bentinck had been in Poland before, just after the First World War, and he had friends among the former rulers. Several of these were arrested and one, Count Grocholski, was shot after a trial in which the British Ambassador was frankly accused of anti-Polish espionage, declared *persona non grata* and expelled. The communists had by now ceased to care about British and American susceptibilities.

The cold war was now well under way. East-west relations hardly existed. Protests did nothing but trigger off counter-protests and freeze the atmosphere still more. On 8 March 1946 Churchill made his famous 'iron curtain' speech at Fulton, Missouri. A lesser known aspect of the speech was his rejection of the Polish western frontier. He spoke of 'Slav penetration deep into German territory'. It was, from the internal Polish point of view, an unfortunate piece of timing. Once again Churchill was demonstrating his unwillingness to support the wishes of the Polish nation. Although no longer in power, Churchill was to many Poles the epitome of British thought and British policy. In their view he had been largely responsible for handing them over to Russian and socialist domination. Now he was trying to take away their one compensation, the western territories. To make matters worse, on 30 August the American Secretary of State James F. Byrnes confirmed Churchill's view in a speech at Stuttgart. He told his German audience the Polish western frontier was not necessarily permanent.

These two speeches were grist to Gomułka's mill and did great harm to the anti-communist case. Once again, he could claim, the western powers were proving themselves unreliable allies of Poland. They had done nothing to help Poland in 1939, nothing much in 1945, and now here they were again preparing to take the German side. It all lent authority to the argument Gomułka began to propound in 1943 and continued for decades, that for Poland an alliance with the Soviet Union was essential, that so long as Poland continued to rely on the untrustworthy British, French and Americans, she would always be open to attack from the west, constantly vulnerable to the German *Drang nach Osten*. Again and again he told his audience: 'If ever in the future the Germans should again fall upon Poland, without the Soviet Union's help, without a Soviet-Polish alliance, we should be threatened with the same fate we suffered in September 1939.' He certainly had a point.

Slowly the anti-communists lost heart. Their active supporters began to drift away into political inactivity. Others who had hitherto stood on the fence began to move towards a *modus vivendi* with the régime. The Poles were, as always, ready enough to fight for their freedom, but the price had become too high and the chance of victory too small. 15,000 pro-communists died in the civil strife and an unknown, probably larger number of anti-communist 'bandits' or 'patriots' (depending on one's point of view). A little island of resistance in Red-Army-occupied eastern Europe, abandoned by their wartime allies, they could not keep up the struggle indefinitely. Gomułka's views, set out eloquently in his speeches, wooed many hesitant 'bandits' and Mikołajczyk supporters away from opposition. To judge by what Gomułka said, if they persisted in opposition they could expect nothing but the most ruthless repression. But if they chose the path, not of communism, but of broad cooperation with the régime, they could expect moderation and understanding. The non-communists who preferred to work positively for 'people's Poland' rather than continue the civil war set much store by Gomułka and what they thought he stood for.

The promised elections to the Polish parliament (Sejm) finally took place on 19 January 1947. For several months attempts had been made to make Mikołajczyk join in an electoral bloc with the other parties. This would have meant Mikołajczyk's continued participation in a government under communist domination. He was offered twenty per cent of the seats in the Sejm. He said he would consider it if he was offered seventy-five per cent. Negotiations collapsed. The communists then set about making it impossible for Mikołajczyk to win. The electoral campaign became blurred into a civil war. The methods of war were used to win the electoral as well as the physical battle. Again, details of what happened are set out in exaggerated, but basically true detail in Mikołajczyk's book.[25] They ranged from the cutting off of the telephone from his party HQ to the alleged arrest of 100,000 Peasant Party members and murder of 130.[26] Two days before the elections Mikołajczyk gave a press conference and placed these accusations before the world press. The communists admitted there had been arrests, but the numbers were much smaller and all those arrested were guilty. A senior officer in the security service, Colonel Roman Romkowski, announced the number of arrested Peasant Party men was only 2,100.[27] This figure was a far cry from 100,000 and one may safely assume that both Mikołajczyk and Romkowski were exaggerating. Mikołajczyk was apt to be carried away, by emotion as well as by events. And the Colonel's honesty was hardly above reproach, as was revealed ten years later when he was convicted by a Polish court of faking evidence and torturing prisoners.

Even *The Times* of London was by now disillusioned with Polish democracy. Their leader of 18 January declared it was 'more than doubtful' whether the next day's elections could be regarded as the redemption of pledges made at Potsdam. Mikołajczyk announced that 138 of his parliamentary candidates were under arrest, and that the election results were already decided; he was to receive eight per cent of the votes— a surprisingly accurate forecast, as it turned out. On 1 January Gomułka made his last great attack on the Peasant Party. He painted an amusingly lurid picture of what would happen if the 'reactionaries' won—an unlikely eventuality as he must have known. Anders, Raczkiewicz, Kwapiński and the other 'reactionaries' would fly in from London to vie with Mikołajczyk for the best ministerial jobs. Plans would be made to invade Russia to regain Lwów, Wilno and the eastern territories. The land and industry of the country would be given back to the capitalists, and the western territories returned to Germany. The Red Army would be refused the right to cross Poland to their zone of Germany, and 'one can imagine how the Soviet government would react to such a situation'. It was rather unsubtle stuff, but then so is most political propaganda, and one can well believe that many who listened accepted Gomułka's thesis that, communist or not communist, Poland had no alternative to the present régime. Again he summed up his arguments by reducing everything to simple terms that every Pole ought to understand: 'He who votes for the reactionaries will vote in effect against Poland's frontier on the Oder and Neisse. . . . He who votes for the reactionaries, let him not forget that he votes for the warmongers.'[28]

Gomułka gave his audience promises as well as threats. Within three years, he told them, the worker's standard of living would exceed the prewar level, within five years all the postwar shortages would be liquidated. If anyone could have persuaded Poles to vote for a communist-dominated government in 1947 it was Władysław Gomułka. At least he showed some respect for his audience's fears and hopes, if not for their prejudices. He of course knew about the planned rigging of the elections and connived at it. In his case one must assume he genuinely believed that to rig the elections was a lesser evil than for the communists to lose power, for anarchy and 'the reactionaries' to prevail and for Poland to lose the support of the Soviet Union. Even so, he did not openly declare his belief in limiting the freedom of the elections as did some of his more dogmatic colleagues. Roman Zambrowski, for instance, a Politburo member who spent the war in the Soviet Union and took a more marxist-leninist view of the function of elections, declared that 'Democracy cannot mean freedom for the enemies of freedom. While powerful forces of political bandits are still active . . . there can be no privilege of democratic freedom for some people.'[29]

Ignoring the emotional anti-communist writings of Mikołajczyk and others and merely taking such communists as Zambrowski at their word, one can justly assume that the 1947 elections were not 'free and unfettered', at least in the western sense. The official results gave Mikołajczyk's Peasant Party 10·3 per cent of the votes cast and the government bloc over eighty per cent. Everyone protested—Mikołajczyk, the British and American governments—but by now protests were quite without value. By now there was nothing the British and Americans could do short of declaring war and occupying Poland. There was no question of their considering such a course, and so once again a largely unpopular government was imposed upon the Polish people.

Gomułka made full capital of his party's doubtful victory. At an open-air meeting three days after polling day he made no effort to be magnanimous in victory, or to spare his defeated rival. He said: 'Through the electoral urn the people have pronounced sentence of condemnation on Mr Mikołajczyk and his party for their harmful and destructive policies towards Poland. ... The people have condemned and rejected the Peasant Party leaders for their attempts to undermine People's Poland and to sow anarchy among us.'[30]

Mikołajczyk had lost the game. However much he might complain he had been betrayed, robbed and generally ill-used, the fact remained that he had lost and Gomułka had won. He and twenty-seven other Peasant Party men remained members of the Sejm, but they were an insignificant drop in the ocean of pro-communists. Some began to seek an understanding with the régime, others to think of escape to the West. The WiN (London) and NSZ (pro-fascist) 'bandits' also faced defeat. During 1947 the opposition to the régime, both the legal and the illegal, was effectively crushed. In November 1947 Mikołajczyk fearing for his life and his freedom made his final appeal to the British, and asked them to help him escape from Poland. This time the British were able to help him. They got him on to a ship to England, and thence to exile in America until his death in 1966. Even then he was forced to concoct a story about an escape overland, so as to avoid official British embarrassment over such an undignified, undiplomatic incident. The field was thus left clear for the communists and their allies. At last the country was at peace. There was no one to oppose the will of Bierut, Gomułka, and ultimately Stalin. Henceforward if the communists wanted a fight, they would have to fight among themselves.

If this account of Gomułka's career up to the year 1947 has concentrated on his political activities and his struggle for power, it is because this was the issue that consumed his time and to which he devoted most of his oratory, which is documented. The other important side to his work was his administration of the western territories, to whose ministry he was appointed on 9 November 1945. For more than three years he headed this important department and was responsible for the 'repolonisation' of 101,000 square kilometres of former German territory. He had to administer 'state property', which meant almost everything there since everything German was automatically nationalised. Much of the movable wealth was being packed up by the Russians and exported east, and there are stories that this was the first bone of contention between Gomułka and the Soviet Union. He resisted the Russian depredations, regarded by them as legitimate war reparations, and ten years later was to denounce them openly.

By March 1946 the expulsion of Germans from these lands was in full swing and 5,000 a day were being transported westwards, mainly to the British and American zones. One important problem was to decide who was or was not a German. In the former German lands of East Prussia and east of the Oder-Neisse line there had lived before and during the war many persons of doubtful nationality. Most of these had German as their native language, but Polish names, and were assumed to be originally of Polish origin. Some were bilingual in German and Polish, others kept only the most shaky ties with their former country. After all, its citizenship had not in recent history been a particularly valuable possession. These people were known after the war as autochthons. After an initial period in which they were lumped together with pure Germans and treated with the same rough justice by the new Polish administration, an attempt was made to separate the sheep from the goats, to get rid of the Germans and to accept and assimilate the Poles. This process was largely Gomułka's responsibility. He told a congress of autochthons in Warsaw in November 1946: 'We shall not give up one single Pole to the Germans, and we do not want among us Poles one single German.'[31] This entailed the need for 'a clear distinction between the Polish autochthons and the Germans, which can be accomplished only by a process of verification, and by giving Polish citizenship to those thus verified'. Already nearly a million had been 'verified', Gomułka said, and these men were 'a million witnesses declaring by their presence before the world and history that their forefathers were the sole owners of these lands, and that the Germans were there only as newcomers . . .'. Fortunately for them the autochthons, many of whom had no idea whether they were Polish or German, had become politically valuable. Now instead of being persecuted they were to be wooed, given back their property, some of which had already been settled by Poles from the east, and made Polish citizens with full rights.

The 'recovered territories' made up nearly a third of the new Poland. They contain most of Poland's coastline and much of her industrial wealth. Throughout his years in government they have been Gomułka's pride and joy, all the more so since they were won at the expense of Germany and gave Poland a recompense for the return of a much larger area in the east to Soviet Russia. They enabled Gomułka to present the new Poland, shunted 200 kilometres to the west like 'a country on wheels', as a more compact, more administratively viable and richer unit. Militarily too the country was less exposed. The length of its frontiers was reduced by more than a third, the coastline quadrupled. Gomułka regarded the new geographical location and shape of Poland, which he and his party had advocated since 1942, as a great victory won largely through the foresight and realism of Poland's communists. When this victory was threatened—whether by Churchill, Byrnes, German revanchism or 'London' anti-Soviet extremism—Gomułka's reaction was that of a mother whose favourite child is about to be stolen. He could see no reason why foreigners should withhold consent to the frontiers of Poland, the country whose wartime material and human losses were greater than those of any other country. Those who did, in his view, could be guided only by malice, by anti-communist or anti-Polish extremism. Such people, if within his jurisdiction, he proceeded to suppress, and if outside his jurisdiction, to abuse.

Gomułka can take pride in many of his achievements in the 'recovered lands'. The expulsion of Germans, the resettlement of Poles, the assigning to them of land, seed, livestock and (occasionally) machinery—all this was done during the years 1945–47 with some efficiency, considering the devastation which then covered Poland and the civil war which bled her, as if she were not bled enough already. He can take pride in the fact that these areas provided and still provide the nucleus of the Polish régime's support and of his own personal popularity. He defended the interests of the peasant settlers, his own kind, against the hazards of those early postwar years: Red Army looting, German revanchism, the Anglo-Saxon doubts as to their right to their new plots of land, and the Stalinist anti-peasant prejudices of his more dogmatic comrades in the Polish Workers' Party.

Yet the years 1945–47 mark one of the darker periods of Gomułka's career. The vitriolic way in which he persecuted Mikołajczyk—an uninspiring, imposed-upon man, not great enough for the role in which he was cast by political coincidence, but without evil and as patriotic a Pole as he was physically capable of being—and drove him out of his country will be judged in retrospect as a piece of stark political ruthlessness and cruelty. Excuse for what Gomułka did can only be found in Marx's belief that 'The end justifies the means', in Lenin's axiom 'You can't make an omelette without breaking eggs' or in the Russian proverb 'If you chop wood, then chips must fly'. Mitigation for what he did can be found in his achievements, in what he built in western and northern Poland.

After a few weeks of 1947 the political struggle for power was over and Gomułka could give his main attention to administration and Party affairs. The Polish Peasant Party (PSL) was in disarray and its leaders—Mikołajczyk, Stefan Korboński and others were shortly to flee from Poland. Gomułka's next political task was a mere mopping-up operation; he was to arrange a merger between the communist party (PPR) and the socialist party (PPS). This would present little difficulty since the socialist party, which had an impressive record over many decades of radicalism and anti-communism, was now controlled by a group of pro-communist left-wingers lead by Józef Cyrankiewicz, who was to serve so many years as Premier of Poland. Earlier the socialists had presented a problem. They had been in contact with Mikołajczyk's party and Gomułka expressed his fear that 'this policy could lead to the formation of a PSL–PPS bloc'.[32] But it came to nothing. The socialists soon realised their future lay in cooperation with the left. Their right-wingers, such as Zygmunt Żulawski, were pushed to one side and the party gladly entered into an electoral bloc with the communists. The merger of the two parties was a piece of administrative rationalisation that would simultaneously broaden the Party's membership, by absorbing allies from among the socialists, and provide a chance for a further purge of right-wingers, who could clearly not be allowed to join a united marxist party. It may be that for some of Gomułka's comrades the change was planned as a move in the direction of the Soviet model, the one-party system. But this was not Gomułka's idea. All along he had rejected the one-party system, and he took a severely practical view of the planned merger as a step along the Polish road to socialism. In May 1947 he was still showing his lack of dogmatism. The science of marxism, he said, 'does not give us any ready, universal indication or recipe which can be made use of with an identical result, without regard to time, place and the existing conditions'.[33]

The PPR–PPS unification, he said, could not be based on 'the abstract recognition by both parties of the correctness of marxist theory'. One can well believe that by now Gomułka's frank, practical attitude to communism was becoming, in the eyes of many of his Soviet-orientated comràdes, an embarrassment to the communist party which Gomułka officially led. They knew that in the Soviet Union no one, let alone the leader of a communist party would ever be allowed to speak so slightingly of marxism, the science which was then accepted in that country to have combined with leninism and stalinism to produce the ideal social system. They must have wondered how long their party could keep as its head a man so lacking in reverence for the thirty years of Soviet socialism. Was his frequently-expressed belief in private enterprise, his rejection of agricultural collectives merely a tactic to win the elections and broaden support, or did he really hold these outrageous views? Poland's more dogmatic communists were beginning to ask such questions.

The answer was not long in coming. Until 1947 Stalin had been happy to give the communist leaders of the east European countries a certain freedom of movement. He had interfered little in Polish affairs or in the un-marxist nature of many of the PPR policies. But now he decided was the time to gather his children about him and present a united front against the 'imperialist warmongers' of the West whom he genuinely believed were planning to attack the Soviet Union. He hoped to consolidate the whole force of the world communist movement against the Anglo-Saxon powers who possessed the atomic bomb, while the Soviet Union did not, to build up a moral pressure throughout the world which would create, at worst, an atmosphere in which a nuclear attack on Russia would be out of the question, at best, world revolution. He would form a new international movement, to be called the 'Cominform'.* The inaugurating conference was to be held on 22 September 1947 in a small town of Polish Silesia called Szklarska Poręba.

Gomułka, who with Hilary Minc was Polish delegate to the conference, viewed the whole affair with trepidation. The Cominform's predecessor the 'Comintern', dissolved for the sake of 'Allied unity' in 1943, had been no friend of the prewar KPP and had been responsible for its dissolution in 1938. Gomułka, who was in prison at the time, laid at the Comintern's door, rather than at Stalin's, the blame for the mass arrests and murders of Polish communists by the NKVD in the late 1930s. He compared the achievements since 1942 of the new Party, which had a certain independence of Moscow, with the notorious unpopularity of the KPP thoughout the twenty years of its existence. The support the PPR now enjoyed in Poland—that of a minority, but of a considerable minority—he realised would never have been achieved by the KPP with its 'dogmatism', its 'sectarianism' and its humble acceptance of Russian pressure. The Cominform, he thought, rightly as it turned out, might be the first step towards establishing that old authority, and he was against it.

It is perhaps Gomułka's greatest act that, being in Stalin's physical power, he was the first leading eastern-bloc communist openly to defy Stalin's will. The records of the Szklarska Poręba meetings are not open to public scrutiny, but accounts of them have been given. The atmosphere is best described by an Italian delegate, Eugenio Reale,[34] a communist who was under-secretary at the Italian Foreign Ministry, then Ambassador to Warsaw, and who broke with the Communist Party after the 1956 events in Hungary. The conference took place in a large villa, formerly the property of a German aristocrat. The welcome was lavish—eight or ten dishes for every meal, not counting caviar and other *hors d'oeuvres*. Every day each delegate would find a gift had been put in his room for him: a camera, or a suitcase, or a pair of pyjamas. Each of the leading communist parties of the world had sent two delegates. Gomułka and Minc represented Poland, but the tune was called by the leading Soviet delegate, Andrei Zhdanov.

---

* Communists were by now in effective control of Poland, Yugoslavia, Bulgaria, Romania, Hungary and East Germany. In Czechoslovakia they were to take power in the coup of February 1948.

Eugenio Reale found Gomułka at first acquaintance 'a difficult and stormy character, but honest and loyal'. He continues:

'I was also struck by the coolness with which he greeted the proposal to create a permanent consulting body between communist parties. This seemed to me strange, coming as it did from the representative of the party which had officially at least taken the initiative in arranging the meeting. On the subject of collaboration between communist parties he confined himself to generalities, speaking at greater length about the negotiations in progress to unite the PPR and the PPS into one great workers' party.'[35]

Milovan Djilas, then Marshal Tito's deputy in Yugoslavia and later imprisoned for his heretical writings, had the same impression: 'The only two delegations that were decidedly for the Cominform were the Yugoslav and the Soviet. Gomułka was opposed, cautiously but unequivocably holding out for the Polish road to socialism.'[36]

If, as it seems, Gomułka was cautious in expressing his opposition to the Cominform in general, he was not at all cautious when the time came to discuss a resolution calling all countries to collectivise their agriculture as soon as possible. This was directly contrary to everything that the PPR, and in particular Gomułka, had ever promised. Only a few months earlier he had reassured his country's peasants that 'we have completely rejected the collectivisation of farms'.[37] Stories of the PPR's eventual plans to collectivise he had dismissed as 'fantastic' and 'provocative' and 'insinuations of the enemy'. Now he was expected to vote for these enemy insinuations.

'Immediately I was told of the text of the resolution,' Gomułka said a year later, 'I expressed the view that the PPR would be wrong to vote for collectivisation, that the Politburo should refer such an issue to the Party's Central Committee.'[38] But in September 1947 he stood alone against the leaders of his own Party and of every other leading communist party of the world. According to Reale 'he underlined the difficulties of such a step in a country so basically agricultural as Poland'. His suggestion that the matter be referred to the PPR Central Committee was of course quite impractical in the context of a six-day conference. His co-delegate Hilary Minc later chided him for what was clearly a delaying tactic. Did he really expect, Minc asked, that the Polish delegates should leave the conference, drive to Warsaw, summon the Central Committee of hundreds of men, discuss the issue, put it to the vote and then return—all this while the delegates of the other eight parties waited upon the pleasure of the Poles?[39] Obviously it was absurd and Gomułka was summarily overruled. The delegates went home. Andrei Zhdanov—that stern, often cruel dogmatist —went home to Moscow presumably with dire reports of the man who had been elected leader of Poland's communists in 1943 without Russia's knowledge or consent, and who had learnt so little in those four years about the way Stalin's Russia liked to run her own and other countries' affairs. Here was a Polish communist who had refused to learn the lesson so painfully dinned into his comrades in the late 1930s. He had opposed Stalin. Towards such as him the Soviet leader was not known for his tolerance.

Gomułka was thus the first 'satellite' leader to defy Stalin. He opposed him over two issues, the Cominform and collectivisation, at a time when Stalin was consciously trying to tighten his control over eastern Europe and to standardise the various countries' administration. According to Milovan Djilas Stalin's ambitious aim was a complete re-drawing of the east European boundaries. Albania was to be 'swallowed' by Yugoslavia; Djilas gives a graphic, disgusting description of how Stalin tilted his head back and stuffed two fingers down his throat to demonstrate the 'swallowing'. Djilas quotes Stalin as saying 'we think a federation ought to be formed between Romania and Hungary, and also Poland and Czechoslovakia'. This would have effectively diluted the remnants of nationalism and democracy that could not be suppressed by force. If this were not enough, Djilas continues, 'it seemed the Soviet leaders were also toying with the thought of recognising the Soviet Union by joining to it the "people's democracies"—the Ukraine with Hungary and Romania, and Byelorussia with Poland and Czechoslovakia'.

Perhaps the Cominform was the first step towards the fulfilment of these grandiose plans. If so, it was a failure. After a second meeting in Belgrade something began to go badly wrong between the Soviet Union and Yugoslavia, and personally between Stalin and Tito. The origins of the quarrel are not known for sure, but it is fair to assume they had something to do with the independence of individual communist parties. Also, Tito's party was at this time 'Leftist' in the marxist sense. The Yugoslavs then believed in expanding the communist movement by world revolution. This rang of Trotskyism, to Stalin at least. President Tito was the strongest in character as well as in personal popularity of the east European leaders. He genuinely ruled whereas Gomułka, for instance, did not, his authority being diluted by that of President Bierut, of Jakub Berman, the so-called *éminence grise* of the time, not to mention the Soviet Ambassador Lebedev. Tito was also less vulnerable than most, his country having no frontier with the Soviet Union and being ideal guerrilla country. He decided he was not going to 'play ball'.

The announcement after the third conference in Bucharest expelling Yugoslavia from the Cominform was a surprise to almost everybody. The first report appeared in the Czech Party newspaper *Rude Pravo* on 28 June 1948.* A long *communiqué* called upon the Yugoslavs to 'bring their leaders to see the error of their ways'. The Yugoslav Party had apparently instituted several 'incorrect policies'. It had 'dissolved itself into the non-Party Popular Front'—a scheme for broadening support which was objectionable in Yugoslavia but not, apparently, in other socialist countries where it had been applied. It had refused to ban private agriculture, which involved the buying and selling of land. (So much for Gomułka—his promises, his objections and his future.) In fact, Tito and his colleagues were a 'Turkish, terrorist régime'.

In June Tito had not yet been given up for lost. 'The Cominform,' read the resolution's final paragraph, 'does not doubt that at the heart of the Yugoslav Communist Party there are enough healthy elements, true to Marxism-Leninism, true to the international traditions of the Yugoslav Communist Party, true to the united socialist front. It is the task of these healthy forces . . . to force their present leaders openly and honourably to recognise their error and correct them.'

But this did not happen. In spite of the full force of Soviet propaganda and pressure the Yugoslav communists remained true to Tito. The result was the virtual death of the Cominform and a blow to Stalin's prestige. His reaction was as violent as he

* It appeared the following day in all the main world newspapers.

could make it, short of invasion of Yugoslavia, war and possible American involvement. Within a few weeks the sins of Tito were no longer 'errors' but 'treachery' and 'fascism'. Like a thwarted child Stalin had his propaganda-men think up the most horrible names a communist can imagine. Tito became 'a conscious agent of American imperialism' and 'a follower of Goebbels and Hitler'.

Meanwhile there was the problem of Gomułka. True, there was a split in the Polish communist party, there were differences between the 'Bierut line' and the 'Gomułka line', but they would not have been unresolvable under normal circumstances. But suddenly the Yugoslav affair had made the situation more intense, for it touched the root cause of Stalin's cruelty and destructiveness. No one knows how he reacted to Gomułka's uncooperative attitude of September 1947. Perhaps he did not think it so important at the time. Gomułka was physically in his power and in no position to dominate the Polish party, let alone win a battle of wills against the Soviet party. But then came June 1948, and Gomułka's defiance, small though it was in comparison with Tito's, assumed a greater importance. Stalin, as was his wont, suddenly conceived a great plot being woven against him. The leaders of two east European parties, his creatures, were turning traitor. His three-year-old empire was threatening to crumble about him. There was a need for quick, drastic action. Stalin had said he would lift his little finger and Tito would disappear. But Tito remained. So Stalin was forced to look about for alternative victims. Gomułka was the obvious choice. He was to be the first to 'carry the can' for Tito.

IX: HERESY

It is difficult to know how much Gomułka's heretical actions of the years 1947–49 were attributable to naïveness, and how much to sheer bravery. If he thought he could defy Stalin without putting his liberty and life in danger, he was very naïve. If he realised the danger and acted the way he did in spite of it, he was certainly brave. And he chose a fine time to be defiant. On 3 June, just as the Tito affair was coming to the boil, Gomułka was addressing a closed session of PPR leaders. His subject was the history of the Polish workers' movement. It was one close to his heart for he felt strongly about certain mistaken policies of the PPR's predecessors—the KPP and the SDKPiL.

Gomułka's view was that the main reason why the prewar Polish communists gained so little support was their doubtful attitude to the independence of Poland. It has been shown in a previous chapter how this attitude changed from year to year, how it alternated between the barely loyal and the frankly treasonable. It was this lack of patriotism that Gomułka deplored and which formed the basis for 'Gomułkaism'—a word soon to be used to describe a heresy, later a treasonable heresy, and later still a respectable variant within world communism.

His 3 June speech has never been published. Only a few extracts from it were quoted, with disapproval, by Bolesław Bierut on 31 August 1948, at a Plenum summoned to extirpate the mistaken views of the Secretary-General and to remove him from office.

On 3 June Gomułka said: 'On the matter of the independence of Poland, the Polish Socialist Party showed greater political realism and understood political reality far better than the SDKPiL.' He also said:

'I do not agree with the thesis that the Socialist Party view on independence bankrupted itself. For this raises the question, which view was victorious. . . . The Socialist view of independence was a bourgeois nationalist concept and as such it did not bankrupt itself. It was victorious in the year 1918 [the year Poland gained independence]. The fact that Poland became independent as a result of the Russian revolution and the revolutionary movements in Europe does not change this one bit.'[1]

The consequence of these accurate but embarrassing remarks, delivered at such an inopportune moment for Polish and world communism, was described by Bierut in his long opening speech at the first 'anti-Gomułka' Plenum of 31 August 1948. 'Comrades!' he began, 'for the past three months a state of crisis has existed in the Party leadership which has been harmful and dangerous to the Party.' The reason for the crisis, he said, was the 'mistaken, anti-marxist' position of Gomułka and a group of senior Party members associated with him: Zenon Kliszko, Władysław Bieńkowski, Ignacy Loga-Sowiński, Aleksander Kowalski and, later, Marian Spychalski. Bierut went on: 'A year ago at the first conference of delegates of nine communist parties which brought into existence the Cominform, comrade Gomułka expressed hesitations arising from a failure to understand the international situation of that time. He withdrew from this position only under pressure from other comrades in the Politburo. . . .'[2]

The Szklarska Poręba conference, Bierut announced, was what provided the first warning of heresy in the leadership ranks. He then called Gomułka's 3 June speech 'a conscious and intentional revision of the leninist evaluation of the history of our movement'. It 'showed a lack of political and revolutionary compass', and made it imperative that Gomułka be brought to task. Bierut made no mention at this stage of the Yugoslav issue. The year-long gap between Szklarska Poręba and the August 1948 attack on Gomułka is one of the many indications that Yugoslavia, not the Cominform, was the trigger for the attack. Nor did he mention the Soviet pressure, without which the attack would hardly have been necessary and would probably never have taken place. According to Bierut, the issue was an internal, ideological one. In fact it was largely external, inspired by Stalin's weird ideas of practical politics and his decision to limit the internal independence of the 'satellite' countries.

Gomułka's 3 June speech, said Bierut, had been immediately condemned by the Politburo. Its members expressed the hope that Gomułka would 'by sincere and consistent self-criticism within the Party overcome his mistaken views ... and together with the Central Committee contribute towards a consolidation of ideological and organisational Party unity'. Unfortunately these hopes had not been fulfilled. Gomułka had replied to the Politburo resolution and elaborated his views in greater detail. The reply had been full of 'muddy scholarship' and 'false views' even worse than the 3 June speech. The Politburo then prepared a severe criticism that was delivered to Gomułka orally.

Gomułka momentarily withdrew. He told his colleagues he was ready to resign as Secretary-General of the Party and would not oppose the majority. He did not offer any self-criticism. Instead he told his colleagues he felt unwell and left Warsaw for a rest at Krynica, the health spa in the Beskidy mountains.

Bierut referred to Gomułka's illness with a certain sarcasm. It seemed he was not sure how ill Gomułka really was. Anyway, the July Plenum took place without him. The whole affair was investigated. Telegrams of the Plenum proceedings were sent to him and he was expected to cooperate, if only from a distance, in rooting out the trouble.

Again the Politburo's hopes were dashed. Gomułka sent the July Plenum delegates a letter of support and agreement. But when some of them went to see him in Krynica and talked to him, he seemed to have moderated his views not at all. On 16 August, rested and refreshed, he returned to Warsaw and announced his intention of resuming his work as Secretary-General.

Throughout 18 and 19 August the Politburo members, shocked by such rank ingratitude, again tried to reason with Gomułka. The situation was becoming dangerous. Vague news of the Party crisis was leaking out of the closed Plenums and Politburo sessions. People noticed that Gomułka's office had been empty for most of the summer. Rumours abounded. In a report in *The Times* of London on 11 August an official spokesman described as 'pure nonsense' stories that Gomułka had been arrested, although admitting that differences within the Party did exist. To many, the denial was almost as good as an admission. The whole issue was a threat to the Party's unity, and something had to be done. The leaders remembered what disunity had done to the prewar Party. The KPP's 'factionism' had made the Party introspective and largely ineffective. This chronic illness among Polish progressives had been kept at bay for fifteen years. Clearly it had to be nipped in the bud. This was the view of Bierut and the Stalinist majority.

During these 18–19 August discussions the majority in the PPR gained the upper hand over Gomułka and his followers. Gomułka gave way in the interest of Party unity. He made one final flurry, declaring that 'in the situation that existed it would surely be better for the Party if he [Gomułka] remained its director'. But then he embarked upon the great apology. By 19 August he was beginning to apologise and criticise himself in general terms. This was not at all what the Politburo wanted. They had set their hearts on the Russian legal ideal: a detailed confession, the one essential method of establishing a criminal's guilt. They had prepared a 2,500-word resolution, entitled 'The Rightist-Nationalist Deviation in the Party Leadership and the Means of Overcoming it'. This was presented to Gomułka as a guide. He studied it and said he would abide by it, with the exception of Point 5 of the resolution. He repeated his offer to resign as Secretary-General.

Point 5 of the anti-Gomułka resolution concerned his attitudes and views during the later years of the German occupation, immediately after he was elected Secretary of the Party (23 November 1943). Here are some extracts from Point 5:

'In the period November 1943 to August 1944, the struggle against Nazism reached a decisive stage. The authority of the Polish Workers' Party was growing as the leading factor in the revolutionary programme of national liberation in alliance with the Soviet Union. The National Homeland Council [KRN] was grouping around itself representatives of the most progressive forces in the nation. . . .

'At this difficult time for the Workers' Party leadership certain hesitations became apparent, and later certain mistaken tendencies, which aimed in fact at distorting the form of the National Homeland Council to forming a bloc with the Central Popular Committee [CKL],* and consequently to a withdrawal from the position of leading the working class in the struggle for power.

'These false, capitulationist tendencies were embarked upon first by comrade Bieńkowski, and later among the Party leadership by comrades Loga-Sowiński and Kowalski, after which they were finally supported by the Secretary-General of the Party, comrade Wiesław [Gomułka]. ...'[3]

The whole issue stemmed from Władysław Bieńkowski's article entitled 'Our Standpoint', published in the underground communist journal *Trybuna Wolności* on 1 July 1944. Though four years old, it was resurrected to become the focal point of the ensuing discussions between Gomułka and his opponents. Was Gomułka right to have thought of an alliance, or at least an understanding, with the bourgeois socialists? Bieńkowski had written: 'It is our standpoint that the chief motto of the day is unification, a consolidation of all the forces of the democratic camp. It is not that we want to eliminate any groups at all.' To Bierut, and the new Party leadership that was rapidly forming itself around him, this was disgraceful. By July 1944 it should have been clear to any loyal communist that the KRN must form the nucleus of the future government of an independent Poland. On 22 May 1944, a KRN delegation, led by Edward Osóbka-Morawski and including Marian Spychalski as military representative, had been received by Stalin in the Kremlin—a gesture that was taken by the Polish communists, probably rightly, as a Soviet mandate. Why then should Bieńkowski and Gomułka (who as leader of the Party must have known about the article) talk about 'a consolidation of democratic forces'? The democratic forces were already consolidated. It was time to go on the offensive, not to make concessions. More sinisterly, what was this talk of 'not eliminating any groups at all'? What about the fascists? And what about the parties who collaborated with the fascists? (It had recently become the communist view that they themselves were the only Polish political party innocent in this respect.) Surely fascists and their supporters should always be eliminated

* A socialist political group formed in 1944, allied neither to the 'London' camp nor to the Communist KRN.

without mercy? It was one thing Bierut explained, to support a democratic front during 1942 and 1943, when the communists were quite weak and the end of the war was not yet in sight. But in July 1944, with the Soviet Army only a few days away from Polish territory, with support seemingly ensured from that Army for communist-based authority in Poland, it was out of the question.

The third of Gomułka's sins concerned agriculture. Bierut revealed that Gomułka had 'questioned the correctness of the Cominform resolution on methods for socialist reconstruction of agriculture'. He had opposed collectivisation. He had tried to persuade the Polish delegates at Szklarska Poręba not to vote for this September 1947 resolution before gaining the approval of the Central Committee. Worst of all, in running his Ministry of the Recovered Territories he had favoured the rich farmers—the *'kulaks'* Bierut called them, using the Russian word for 'fist' that was so bandied about in the 1930s. Gomułka had insisted that rich and poor peasant alike pay the same hire charges for the use of state-owned agricultural machinery.

Another accusation was that Gomułka, who had announced in April 1948 the communist PPR's intention of amalgamating with the Polish Socialist Party (PPS), had embarked upon this task too hastily. The amalgamation was never planned to be a complete one. The right wing of the Socialist Party was to be purged and discarded. Gomułka himself had stated this in his 30 April speech. After all, some of the greatest opponents of communist power, such as Zygmunt Zaręmba and the last 'London' Prime Minister Tomasz Arciszewski, had been members of the Socialist Party. So, before 1912, had the pre-war dictator Józef Piłsudski, now branded as a fascist. Clearly the rightists had to go. But Gomułka had brought a moderating influence to bear on some PPR members who wanted too violent a purge. 'The struggle against rightist elements in the PPS,' he said on 30 April, 'is not and can never be a struggle against the PPS. It would be ridiculous to speak of uniting the PPR with the PPS and at the same time to fight the PPS.'[3]

This approach was far too gentle for the liking of the stalinists. Gomułka was accused of cultivating support among the Socialist right-wingers, of 'opportunism'. The implication here was that Gomułka and his PPR 'group' had planned to unite with the right-wing socialists and form a break-away party, thus isolating Bierut and the stalinists.

The final charge was that Gomułka had not been strong enough in his opposition to Tito and the Yugoslav communist party. This charge was probably, as I have claimed in the last chapter, the trigger for the whole anti-Gomułka campaign. It was also the one emphasised in the West. But it was not the charge on which the Polish stalinists based their attack. It may have been reasonable for foreigners—Soviet as well as western—to jump to the conclusion of a link between the two communist party leaders who had provoked the anger of Stalin. But any Pole could see that Tito's standpoint was entirely different from that of Gomułka. Tito had insisted on socialism and *real* independence: administrative, financial and military. Gomułka had not gone anywhere near so far. The military and economic alliance with the Soviet Union has always been the corner-stone of Gomułka's plan for Poland. Gomułka was no Tito. His power inside Poland was nowhere near enough for him to imagine he could take a lone stand. Even if he had been un-disputed ruler of Poland, and even if he had felt so inclined, the thought of defying Stalin to that extent would have been out of the question. Poland, with its long boundary with the Soviet Union, unprotected by any natural obstacle, occupied by units of the Soviet Army and essential to it for its communi-cation with East Germany, could never have done what Yugoslavia did in 1948 and lived to tell the tale. Gomułka's defiance was a partial defiance, hardly to be compared with Tito's. But Stalin was in no mood for such hairsplitting. The point was that Tito was not in his jurisdiction, but Gomułka was.

Gomułka heard the evidence and decided to plead guilty in parts. After Bierut's speech he was allowed to address the Central Committee. He delivered his first, 4,000-word self-criticism in which he admitted all the charges against him except Point 5.[5] He continued a stout defence of his behaviour during the occupation. 'I wish to speak,' he said, 'of my own mistakes committed during the recent past, mistakes which must be measured not only by their own actual content, but also with regard to the fact that I committed them during my tenure of office as Secretary-General of the Party.' It was a strange speech. The tone of it changed again and again. Sometimes it showed the servility normal to opponents of Stalin who suddenly found themselves isolated and accused. For instance: 'The mistakes I have mentioned arise from my strong nationalism, as well as from my unrestrained social-democratic conceptions. I am doing everything I can to liquidate both of these from my system of thought.'

Again, on the question of the history of the workers' movement: 'After a basic rethinking of the historical questions contained in my [3 June] speech, and after familiarising myself in more detail with the literature on the subject, I have come to the conclusion that the explanation of the traditions of the Polish workers' movement provided in my speech was distorted, incomplete and therefore false.'

On Point 5, though, his tune was quite different. 'I do not accept these accusations, comrades,' he said defiantly, 'since I consider they do not correspond with the truth.'

Even on the issues where he admitted he was wrong, Gomułka still did not submit completely. On the agricultural issue, for instance: 'The Politburo has also seen fit to state that I represented a tendency to reach agreement with the *kulaks*, putting off until the distant future the struggle against the capitalist elements in the villages. I admit that I put off until the distant future the matter of collectives, but this in no way involved an attempt to come to terms with the *kulaks*.'

Gomułka went on to analyse his agricultural policy in greater detail. His view was that a collectivisation platform would be 'tactics-wise a mistake, although programme-wise correct'. Deliberately using the word *kollektivizatsia*, which does not exist in Polish except as a russianism, he made plain to the delegates something they all knew but had not yet faced up to—that the Polish people would never swallow the sort of brutal collectivisation imposed upon Russia by Stalin in the early 1930s. Poles had been close to the scene of the crime in those years. They knew what was going on. Many of them had friends and relatives involved in the horrible business. This was why the communists were largely unpopular and feared by the peasants. Gomułka understood these fears, and in the early months after liberation he had gone to some pains to allay them. Other communist leaders had given the same assurances. To have done otherwise would have been 'tactics-wise a mistake'. As he explained to the delegates, in a scarcely veiled attack on their consistency and integrity: 'I wish to state that

on this [agricultural] question there were no basic disagree-
ments between me and the other members of the Politburo
until the time of the Cominform resolution on the Yugoslav
question.'

Gomułka was prepared to recant formally. He was ready to
give way and resign. But he would not make the kind of public
apology and self-abasement stalinists now expected of their
opponents. In his speeches he was hardly ever directly insincere. He seldom said he had changed his mind when he had
not. The apologies he made, on the agricultural question and
on others, were still only half-apologies. The gist of them went
something like this: 'You tell me I'm wrong. I still think I'm
right. But mine isn't the only opinion. Who knows, maybe I
am wrong. Who am I to say I'm right when the Party, the
Party I respect and love, says I'm wrong. I must be wrong. . . .
But I still think I'm right!' No wonder the whole tone of his
speech was self-contradictory and regarded as unsatisfactory
by the stalinists. To their minds a self-criticism was a self-
criticism. There could be no two ways about it.

There was no room in a self-criticism for self-justification.
And Gomułka's sum-up on agriculture was a fine mixture of
these two:

'After rethinking this matter I have come to the conclusion,
to the conviction that although the right conditions for
collective agriculture are far from maturity, and although
much work and effort must be put in to bring them to
maturity, it would nevertheless be wrong to leave the
Party without a definite prospect of transforming individual agriculture into collective agriculture. . . . I
therefore withdraw my reservation with regard to this
part of the Cominform resolution. . . . But I think that any
form of compulsory collectivisation would be harmful to
the very idea of collectives, would cause a drop in agricultural production, and might diminish our base among
the working peasant masses and weaken worker-peasant
union.

Gomułka took a similar two-sided attitude when reviewing
his own general attitude to 'the leading role of the Soviet

Communist Party on the international front of the battle against imperialism', particularly on the Yugoslav question. 'The Yugoslav affair,' he said, 'the conflict that came into existence between the Soviet and Yugoslav communist parties, struck me like lightning out of a clear sky.' One can well believe that this was so. Again Gomułka's explanation has a ring of sincerity about it, unusual in men under such a strain. He went on to defend himself, in part at least, from the charge of anti-Sovietism: 'I have never questioned the right of the Soviet Communist Party, earned by it through revolutionary experience and the building of socialism, to hold the leading role in the international workers' movement. I have no doubts under this heading.'

The greater part of the speech was devoted to Point 5. Here Gomułka at first refused to compromise. Three days earlier, at a Politburo meeting, he had taken his stand on this point. He rejected any idea that Bieńkowski's 1 July 1944 article, and his own policy at the time which was along the same lines, was any attempt to 'sell out' the KRN. After all, he reminded his critics with a tinge of sarcasm, he had been one of the chief founders of the Council. The Workers' Party was the chief member of the Council, and he was the leader of the Workers' Party. He had written the 15 December 1943 manifesto that preceded the formal founding of the Council on 1 January 1944: 'This manifesto follows my ideas most faithfully, since I actually wrote it. The Central leadership of the Party, when confirming it, made only a small number of insignificant corrections.' Was it not ridiculous to accuse him of trying to murder his own creation? The differences between the Council and its 'London' opposite number, the National Unity Council (RJN), were so fundamental that there could not have been any question of a merger between the two. His aim had been merely to woo the *democratic* forces (he meant 'democratic' in the marxist sense, of course) contained in the Central Popular Committee.

Certainly, Gomułka admitted, we had hopes of an agreement with this Committee, consisting as it did mainly of socialists and 'democrats'. But *they* had meanwhile been negotiating with the London Government, trying to rid it of reactionaries and fascists. A waste of time, said Gomułka, and this was the real message behind Bieńkowski's article. There was no point whatever in purging the London Government.

The aim should have been to reconstruct a new government, by extra-constitutional means.

The Polish constitution of April 1935 provided the main difference in law between the London Government and the communists. The London Government had claimed to be the *legal* government of Poland, driven out of the country in September 1939 but still existing and functioning as an administrative body. True, none of its members had been elected by the Polish people, but this was not all that unusual. War and enemy occupation had made elections impossible. Many members of the wartime British government, for instance, were not elected democratically either, nor was de Gaulle's postwar caretaker government.

The KRN enjoyed no such continuity. It had sprung to life spontaneously as a number of political groups among which the communists played the leading role. They had become the Polish government *de facto*, mainly through support from Stalin and the Red Army.

The communists had a ready answer to the charge that they were legally less entitled to political power in Poland than the London Government. They counter-charged that the London Government's authority was based on the constitution of 23 April 1935 and that this was an undemocratic constitution. This constitution had been drafted at the dictation of Józef Piłsudski. Worked out in detail by the lawyer Stanisław Car, it planned for a division of power among six bodies: the President, the Government, the Military, the Sejm (Parliament) the Senate (Upper House) and the judiciary. The main departure from the previous constitution (17 March 1921) was that greater strength was given to the office of President. In 1921, perhaps because of a fear that Piłsudski, recently victorious in the Polish-Soviet war, might become President, the office was made mainly ceremonial and honorary. The President did not even have the right to dissolve Parliament. In 1935 the President could, if necessary, rule by decree. It was, in fact, a political system designed for one man, strikingly similar to the 1958 de Gaulle constitution in France. Ironically, the only enjoyment Piłsudski got from the constitution was that of signing it. He died a few days later, on 12 May 1935.

The point was, the communists had claimed, that this 'April constitution' had never had the support of the Polish people. True enough, after the signing of the constitution and Piłsudski's death, there had been elections. But most of the candidates had been nominated by supporters of the *sanacja*, the Piłsudski line. The elections were boycotted by the political parties, and only 46·5 per cent of the electorate voted.

In the Poland of 1944 Gomułka still hoped for some eventual understanding between his KRN, the leftists of the Peasant Party and the Central Popular Committee (CKL). But he opposed the non-communist view that the Polish government should consist mainly of the London-based politicians, after getting rid of the more reactionary elements. This was what Bieńkowski's article was all about, he said: 'The article tried to convince the CKL and the Peasant Party supporters that reconstruction of the *émigré* government by superficial democratisation was impossible on the basis of the April constitution, that it was necessary it get away from this constitution and to seek extra-constitutional means.'

The April constitution had provided the legal basis for the *émigré* government. Anyone who did recognise the legality of this constitution could not recognise the legality of the *émigré* government.

Gomułka told his critics that the aim behind both Bieńkowski's article and his own policy had been to draw the leftists away from 'London' and towards the KRN. There had never been any intention of moving the KRN in the direction of London:

'In the light of everything I have said, it is quite clear that there was neither in myself nor, as far as I could see, in any of the comrades with whom I worked, any tendency to liquidate the KRN or any movement towards joining the [London] National Unity Council [RJN], as this paragraph of the resolution states. . . .

'For these reasons I cannot agree with Point 5 of the Politburo's resolution, or with any of the accusations made against me that arise from Point 5.

'If, however, the comrades do not share my view with regard to the KRN and the RJN, I will not vote against Point 5, but will abstain on Point 5.'

He admitted that his absence at the July Plenum had done harm to the Party, but pleaded nervous and physical exhaustion. His state of health, he said without much hope of being believed, was also partly the cause of his mistaken and erroneous 3 June speech. He asked to be relieved of his position as Secretary-General of the Party, and of membership of the Politburo. As for the future, he wished to fulfil the Party line and the duty of Party membership in whatever work he might find himself. He ended, again perhaps with a touch of sarcasm, by thanking the delegates for the trust they had placed in him during his tenure of office.

Gomułka's oration was followed by a number of shorter speeches, some defensive, delivered by those comrades linked with Gomułka and about to be censured with him. Aleksander Kowalski criticised Gomułka's defiance on Point 5, though he had the courage to say: 'I had and have much respect for comrade Gomułka.' Kazimierz Mijal expounded the Point 5 issue at greater length, listed and analysed the numerous political groups that existed in Poland towards the end of the war. Strangely, as later events turned out, in 1948 he too was considered a 'Gomułka man'. But he strongly criticised the ex-Secretary's doubtful attitude to the KRN even after its delegation had been received by Stalin. Stalin's approval, said Mijal, showing a touching faith in his hero's infallibility, 'meant the recognition of the KRN by the Soviet government, and therefore a confirmation of the correctness of KRN policies.'

Hilary Minc was the most violent of the accusers. His two main points were Yugoslavia and agriculture. Referring to 'the terrorist dictatorship of Tito and his clique', he attacked Gomułka for suggesting that the Yugoslav leaders might be converted back to the true road. The proper line, said Minc, was to organise the masses against the 'terrorist, anti-communist, anti-Soviet dictatorship of Ranković' (the Yugoslav Minister of the Interior who was at this time successfully combating Soviet infiltration and subversion throughout the country. Eight years later he was dismissed for exceeding his authority).

The next day, 1 September, Gomułka was prevailed upon to make a second statement. He again denied he had held 'liquidatory tendencies' towards the KRN. However, he went on: 'The decision belongs to you, comrades. If you think there are signs of such tendencies contained in my attitude, I shall vote for the resolution and not abstain.'

He was slowly being brought to heel. He had now agreed to

vote for the stalinists' resolution *in toto*. But even this was not
enough. The abuse continued to pour in. Edward Ochab
remarked on the not-very-strange fact that in Silesia, where
Gomułka had recently been so popular, not one voice had in
recent weeks been raised in his defence. 'The people somehow
felt there was something wrong,' he added piously. Marian
Spychalski, as yet not officially identified with the 'Gomułka
group', added his censure to that of such hard-liners as Franciszek Jóźwiak-Witold and Zenon Nowak. A sad tale was told
by Władysław Matwin about the results of Gomułka's 'development of capitalism' in the Western Territories:

> 'Two peasants live next to one another. One has four
> horses, six cows, nine calves and heifers, employs at
> harvest time more than thirty workers and has 50–70
> hectares under plough. And beside him another peasant,
> a former partisan demobilised in 1946, possesses only one
> goat as his whole stock. He has not one horse or cow. He
> and his wife work their four hectares by hand.'

It was enough to bring tears to the eyes of any loyal collective
farmer. On the third day (2 September) Gomułka made his
third and final statement. This time he told the conference he
accepted Point 5 without reservation. 'I am grateful to my
comrades for their speeches and for their criticism,' he told
them. He went on to discuss 'the alien influences that I have
not succeeded in overcoming. Do not imagine, comrades, that
such things can easily be overcome. Do not imagine that such
mistakes can be overcome by uttering a self-criticism. . . .

'Even three days ago, even two days ago I did not appreciate
the importance of your criticism. But now it has penetrated to
my consciousness.'

This was more what the communist dogmatists were used to.
Gomułka's confession was by now almost a *mea culpa*. He had
abased himself before his former friends and colleagues.
Immediately there came a triumphant closing speech from
Bolesław Bierut. He was gracious and condescending: 'Comrades! I wish first of all to refer to comrade Gomułka's speech
and self-criticism. The Politburo has decided that this self-
criticism is sufficient and satisfactory.'

It was all over. On 3 September motions were proposed and carried dismissing Gomułka from the post of Secretary-General and from the Politburo. (He remained in the Central Committee.) His friends Władysław Bieńkowski, Zenon Kliszko, Ignacy Loga-Sowiński and Aleksander Kowalski were censured and reduced in rank. Bolesław Bierut was elected Secretary-General in Gomułka's place.

The abject tone of Gomułka's third statement may conceal, especially from the western reader, the extent of the boldness of his demeanour. To have resisted his political opponents to the extent he did was an immense achievement. He missed no opportunity, even in the midst of confession, to make clear the differences between his view and that of Bierut. He took pains, if only by inference, to put his real beliefs on record, to file them away for future reference. His opponents were right, much of the self-criticism was not self-criticism at all, but an attempt to 'dig himself in' politically. One wonders at Bierut's rashness in agreeing to the publication of the Congress speeches. To a Polish communist with any doubts at all, the printed text was as good as an advertisement for an alternative political programme. And, rashest of all, Gomułka was to be left alive, a dangerous symbol of anti-stalinist freedom and defiance. Gomułka had made his position clear. It was obvious from the order and timing of the speeches that his withdrawal and abasement were made under pressure and hardly valid. The conference had succeeded only superficially. Gomułka and 'Gomułkaism' were scotched in the short term. But that was all. A more lasting result of the three days of accusation and confession was the confirming of Gomułka's reputation as a Polish patriot, a communist perhaps, but one who was not prepared to sacrifice efficiency for the sake of dogma.

Agriculture was the essential issue. Władysław Bieńkowski's article on the KRN, the amalgamation of the two left-wing parties, even the Yugoslav issue—these were far from the thoughts and experience of the average Pole. But agriculture was basic. Gomułka had staked the reputation of himself and his party on the promises he made to the peasant that there would be no collectivisation in Poland on the Russian model. He had done this for two reasons. The first was economic. Polish agriculture could not have been centralised without enormous capital investment in farm machinery and new organisational bodies. But in war-ravaged Poland there simply was not the money available for such investment. The whole Polish countryside was under-equipped. For the moment individual small farmers were able to make do and improvise. But if the collective system was introduced, there was a danger their ingenuity might break down, production might drop and the country might go hungry. The second reason behind Gomułka's stand was probably a purely humane one. As a communist he was a believer in the collective system. But as a peasant he understood, even if he did not agree with, the peasant's attachment to his own piece of land. He knew what had happened in Russia when Stalin had forced collectivisation on the Russian peasant. It had been necessary to 'repress' many millions. He did not want this to happen in Poland. In his fight against Mikołajczyk and the PSL, in his struggle to preserve communist power in Poland, he had shown himself stern, single-minded, ruthless. But there was a limit to his ruthlessness. He would not follow Stalin's example and collectivise by force.

On the fourth day of the Plenum, after Gomułka had apparently been disposed of, there was a long speech by Hilary Minc. He announced that the collective farm system would slowly but surely be established in Poland. It was all to be voluntary, though this hardly reassured the peasants. In theory, the collectivisation of Russian agriculture had also been voluntary. Again it was a matter of timing. On 3 September Gomułka goes. On 4 September collectivisation is introduced. Polish peasants, even those who knew nothing about Party squabbles or Kremlin intrigues, drew the obvious conclusion: when Gomułka returns, collectivisation will stop. It was something for them to look backward to with nostalgia and forward to with hope.

Although Stalin disapproved of and feared Gomułka's political views, it seems he still had a certain admiration for him, a man of ideals and one of the few Polish leaders who was of genuine proletarian origin. In November, Stalin summoned Gomułka to Moscow and invited him to join the Politburo of the future united Party. He even sent a special train to Warsaw for him. Gomułka refused Stalin's hand of reconciliation—a further act of unparalleled defiance.

In the three months from the end of the Plenum to the December unification congress a purge of the Party rank-and-file reduced the membership by 50,000.[6] The weeding-out continued for three years and considerably reduced the Party's numbers. On 15 December 1948 the Polish Workers' Party (PPR) was united with the Polish Socialist Party (PPS) into one organisation, the Polish United Worker's Party (PZPR). This is the party that now rules Poland and is called informally 'the communist party'. The country was gay with flags, public holidays and extra goods in the shops. The press showed the communist and socialist leaders in a state of exalted bonhomie. Bierut, the new communist leader, was depicted again and again shaking hands with the Socialist leader, Józef Cyran-kiewicz. Communists made speeches about their love for the PPS—at least for its left wing. Socialists, anxious to belong, shouted out their love of the communist PPR. Everyone shouted their hatred of the new bogy, nationalism, and of its incarna-tion, Władysław Gomułka. 'Nationalism', said Bierut, 'is the standard of the Arciszewskis, Zarębbas, Mikołajczyks, Bór-Komorowskis, Anderses and others who professionally slander Poland before the world for Judas dollars.'[7]

On 18 December a demonstration was organised in the con-gress hall against Gomułka. Still a member of the Central Committee, he came forward to make a speech. What followed is described by an eye-witness:

'Two things that happened at the Congress will stay for ever in my memory. The first was the announcement of the news that Peking had been captured by the armies of Mao Tse-tung. There was a moment of silence, and then the whole hall audience rose from their seats and burst forth into the strains of the Internationale.

'The second memory was sad, embarrassing and pain-ful. Towards the tribune walked a man, quite uninvited, wearing glasses and stooping. . . . Suddenly there were shouts: "Down with Gomułka"!'[8]

It is said Gomułka then lost his temper and shouted at the Party leaders: 'You've made a rag out of me! What have you done to me? You've ill-treated me!'[9] He accused the Party leaders of organising the demonstration. They denied this. According to Aleksander Zawadski, 'the Congress, the main Party *actif* rose spontaneously in a great manifestation against Gomułka'. His speech was not even reported *verbatim* in the

Party press. It was merely summarised, sarcastically and with bias. He had chosen a difficult subject—the meaning of 'internationalism':

> 'Comrade Gomułka explained his personal theory of the meaning of internationalism. This theory omits the international solidarity of workers of all countries in the struggle for socialism, and confines internationalism to a mutual respect of particular nations for each other— their culture, language, tradition and natural well-being— as well as emphasising particular interests that countries have in common....
>
> 'Towards the end of his speech comrade Gomułka declared that the criticism levelled against him at the August Plenum had been too severe. The speaker rendered a lengthy account of his services to the Polish Workers' Party during the occupation....'[10]

After this it came as a surprise when the 1,200 congress delegates were asked by the Politburo to vote Gomułka to the Central Committee of the new Party. The Party leaders had not yet decided, or been instructed, that he was to be arrested and accused of treason. They may have hoped at this stage that they could gradually fade him away from the scene without too much unpleasantness. True, they had the order from Stalin that 'heads must roll'. But as yet they were taking his words only metaphorically. After all, Gomułka had been demolished *politically*. His opponents had abused him. His supporters had disowned him. One of his closest friends, who was later to become his unofficial deputy, Zenon Kliszko, spoke as follows:

> 'I was one of those who discovered rather later than most that the road along which comrade Gomułka wishes to lead the Party is false and harmful.... Comrade Gomułka has said he has already carried out the necessary self-criticism. I wish to state, as one whose task it was to free himself of the mistakes of right-wing nationalist deviation, that in my search to illumine the sources of my mistakes, and to overcome them, I did not rely on the words of comrade Gomułka. When the Party was engaged in this work, comrade Gomułka was silent....

'I wish to state plainly: the proposition we have heard from the mouth of comrade Gomułka is false and harmful. It is anti-Party [*applause*].'[11]

As Hilary Minc later revealed, 'the comrades had to be persuaded to vote for Gomułka—that's right, they had to be persuaded'.[12] No wonder. They must have been thoroughly confused by the sudden turn of events. To abuse a man and then vote for him seemed a strange way of running an election. But Polish politics were going through a strange phase. They voted for Gomułka, and he became a member of the Central Committee.

A month later (21 January 1949) Gomułka's Ministry of the Recovered Territories was dissolved. He and his deputy Czesław Dubiel ceased to be ministers. He also resigned his vice-Premiership, which went to Aleksander Zawadski. Gomułka was given the modest job of vice-President of the Supreme Control Chamber (Najwyższa Izba Kontroli or NIK), an economic control body subordinate to parliament. Its President, and Gomułka's boss, was Franciszek Jóźwiak-Witold, a staunch conservative and supporter of Bierut. In such a position Gomułka was without political power.

X: STALINISM

The years of Stalinist terror in eastern Europe began in 1949.
Before 1949 there was terror enough, in Poland as in other
satellite countries. But it was terror of a somehow cleaner, more
natural sort. It was the violence that comes with a struggle for
power. In Poland it had been both pro-communist and anti-
communist, a miniature civil war. The special terror westerners
now call 'Stalinism' was another thing altogether. It involves
the oppression, the extermination of the weak by the strong.
It means indiscriminate terror, deliberately haphazard, with
innocent people arrested even when *known* to be innocent.
Stalin knew that violence is best used in an aimless, unjustified
way. Then an atmosphere can be created in which no one
feels safe. Important officials, cabinet ministers, even the
oppressors themselves, can be kept at fever pitch because they
know the blow may soon fall on them. The closer they are to
real power, the more dangerous is their position. So they stay
closer to heel. They try to do their work more efficiently and
to flatter those above them more lavishly.

As ruler of Russia, Stalin saw terror as the traditional,
necessary weapon of the autocrat who wishes to be duly
obeyed. His apologists have compared him to Peter the Great,
his denigrators to Ivan the Terrible. All agree that he became
addicted to terror, as if to a drug. He could not govern without
it.

'Stalinism' is by now an emotive word that conjures up all
manner of unnamed horrors in the mind of the average
westerner. This is why care must be taken in applying it to the
years 1948–53 in Poland. The sufferings of Poland in those
years are not comparable to those of Russia either then or in
the late 1930s. In the Soviet Union millions were arrested and
millions died. Stalin may well have been responsible for more
Russian deaths than Hitler. But in Poland it was a matter of

hundreds rather than millions. There was the same 'spy-mania', the same mutual suspicion and ludicrous accusations. But it was less intense than in the Soviet Union or the other east European countries. Looking back, Poles now say their country was suffering from a disease, but a disease it was already vaccinated against. The worst excesses were somehow avoided.

The terror of stalinist Poland had its compensations. After the wholesale violence of the occupation and the 1945–47 'civil war', it was for most Poles a period of calm and quiet in which the country made economic progress. After the elimination of Mikołajczyk and the legal opposition the government was able to spend more of its energy on rebuilding Poland than on fighting its enemies. There was something of the post-war reconstruction boom that happened elsewhere in Europe. Many thousands of Poles spent years in prison on imaginary charges. But for most people conditions improved. Some communists now look back with nostalgia on the 'order' and 'calm progress' of the time. It is they who are now called 'neo-stalinists'. Many of them are not cruel men. They simply reckon that too much freedom disrupts society and halts progress. They associate stalinism with prosperity. In this they are not entirely inaccurate.

This is in no way to minimise the disastrous effect stalinism had on Poland. Maybe only a few thousand were actually imprisoned. But many more thousands were harassed and bullied by a brutal security police force, dismissed from their jobs or thrown out of the place where they were living. The most educated were the most politically suspect, which is why many of those who suffered were managers, writers, politicians or priests. Not only *people* suffered. Terrible damage was done to Polish literature, journalism, architecture—to every branch of human expression. But the worst casualty was Polish morale. Poland was the only country that fought the Germans from the first day of the Second World War to the last day. It was also the only country unable in any way to enjoy the fruits of victory. They moved straight from war into civil strife and into military occupation by an army most of them regarded as un-friendly. They began to develop a feeling of hopelessness. During the war there was mass murder and a terror a thousand times worse than under stalinism. But at least there was hope. No Pole saw the Nazi occupation as permanent. They knew it could not possibly last. It was simply a question of surviving a few more months and liberation would come. With stalinism there was no such prospect. The western powers had given little help to the non-communist forces in Poland. They had effectively abandoned Poland. There was no hope of Poland being 'liberated' from stalinism. Any change had to come from within Poland, or at least from within the socialist camp. While Stalin was alive this seemed impossible. Poles felt they might have to put up with the oppression indefinitely. This is why many of them suffered mentally under Stalin more than under Hitler.

During 1949 the leaders of the east European countries began to suffer not only criticism and demotion, but also arrest, trial, torture and death. Gomułka was one of the first of these leaders to be criticised. He was one of the last to be arrested. As usual Poland was behind the clock. The atmosphere of terror was a long time in the making. In Hungary and Bulgaria events moved faster. In April 1949 Traicho Kostov, vice-Premier of Bulgaria, was dismissed for allegedly undermining the authority of the Premier, Georgy Dimitrov.* Soon he was under arrest, accused of the most horrible crimes a communist can imagine. He had withheld from the Soviet Union information about the Bulgarian economy. This was economic sabotage. There was worse to come. In 1942 he and a group of communists had been arrested by the Bulgarian authorities of King Boris. Now he was accused of having turned state's evidence against his comrades, all of whom had been executed. He alone had got off with life imprisonment. Armed with this damning information, it was then said, the British Secret Service had blackmailed him and recruited him as an agent. He had been a British spy ever since. Only recently, it was then claimed, he had become a Yugoslav spy. The loose ends were being drawn together with a vengeance. He had apparently plotted with Tito of Yugoslavia to annex Bulgaria to that country as its seventh republic. Meanwhile his former chief Georgy Dimitrov died. But this did not help him. His trial was set down for December 1949.

* It was Georgy Dimitrov who in 1933 was acquitted at the July trial in Berlin of burning the German Reichstag. He was Secretary-General of the Comintern from 1935 to its dissolution in 1943. He was Secretary-General of the Bulgarian Communist Party from 1944 and Premier of Bulgaria from 1946 until his death in 1949.

In Hungary things moved more quickly still. On May Day 1949, Lászlo Rajk, Foreign Minister and a member of the Politburo, delivered an important speech. His position seemed safe enough. He was one of the most important men in Hungary. A few weeks later he was under arrest, and on 16 September he came up for trial in Budapest charged with conspiring with the American Embassy and with Aleksander Ranković, the Yugoslav Minister of the Interior, to spread the Yugoslav heresy throughout Hungary. On 25 September he and two other Hungarians were sentenced to death, and two days later they were executed.

In Poland, by September 1949, two of Gomułka's closest former colleagues were under arrest and charged with espionage. Czesław Dubiel, former vice-Minister of the Western Territories, was accused of working for the Gestapo during the occupation. Bierut announced later that a former Gestapo leader named Heinemeier had denounced him while imprisoned in Poland. He accused Gomułka of 'denying the validity of Heinemeier's evidence on trifling grounds'.

The second victim was Stanisław Lechowicz, who had been the head of a department in Gomułka's ministry until the spring of 1947, when he was transferred to the Ministry of Provisions. He was accused of spying for the *sanacja*, the followers of Józef Piłsudski.

This was the background to the summoning of another anti-Gomułka Plenum on 11 November 1949. The atmosphere was quite different from that of a year ago, when Gomułka was accused merely of mistakes and false concepts. This time the Central Committee was in the grip of a real stalinist spymania. Throughout Poland and eastern Europe spies were being dug up and disposed of. Gomułka was to be accused of lack of vigilance, of allowing spies to infiltrate his ministry. He was also to be held generally responsible, as Secretary-General from 1943 to 1948, for all the disasters that had befallen the Party during those years. Nearly fifty speeches were delivered, all of them abusive of Gomułka. His supporters, the members of his so-called 'group', criticised him with almost as much venom as his opponents. Again, the tone of the debate was set by Bolesław Bierut in his opening oration, 'The Task of the Party in the Struggle for Revolutionary Vigilance against the Background of the Present Situation'.[1] He began with an alarming round-up of world affairs. In England the Labour Government was pushing the country 'deeper and deeper into the corset of American slavery'. The socialist camp was threatened by the diversionary activity of Tito and Rajk. 'Can we say,' came the rhetorical question, 'that we are sufficiently vigilant in the face of attempts to infiltrate enemy agents into our government and state apparatus, and even into our Party?' Clearly, in the light of recent events, the delegates could not say anything of the sort. 'It is a fact,' continued Bierut sensationally and, as it later turned out, erroneously, 'that comrade Nowotko, the first Secretary of the Polish Workers' Party, was murdered by an *agent-provocateur* sent into the Party by the Polish *deuxième bureau*.' There had generally been a tolerant attitude to enemies of the people, to *deuxième bureau* agents like Lechowicz. Bierut then came to the main point at issue:

'Who was most of all responsible for this state of affairs? Comrade Spychalski, as chief of the Intelligence Department of the People's Guard (GL) and later on the People's Army (AL). Comrade Gomułka as Secretary of the Party, with whom comrade Spychalski agreed his various moves, and who himself filled his Ministry of the Western Territories with many men of this type. Comrade Kliszko, who controlled the personnel section of the Party from the liberation until September of last year.'

Of these three 'guilty' men Marian Spychalski was by far the easiest target. He had worked in Intelligence and therefore, as part of his job, had many acquaintances of doubtful reliability. He also had a brother, Józef Spychalski, who had been a career officer before the war. During the war Józef had held high rank in the 'London' Home Army (AK), was sent by the London Government to Poland, caught by the Germans and murdered by them. 'I did not present the Party leadership with the full facts about my brother,' confessed Spychalski. He admitted his behaviour had 'without doubt opened the road to other Piłsudski-ite officers, who chose to see in me a communist they could come to terms with'. He had not taken nearly a strong enough line against these unreliable elements. The most he ever did, he continued significantly, was discuss such matters with Gomułka, his close friend, whom he now realised to be a bad influence in the Party:

'After the Cominform Conference I did not disassociate myself openly enough from comrades Gomułka and Kliszko.... Even after the discovery of comrade Gomułka's anti-Party and anti-Marxist views at the June Plenum, although I did not agree with him, I did not separate myself from him. I expressed my views in a halting fashion. . . .

'Today I see to the full extent how wise, beneficial and far-sighted was the initiative taken by the Soviet Party, led by comrade Stalin, expressed in the Cominform resolution on the Yugoslav affair.'[2]

Jerzy Albrecht, another member of the Gomułka 'group', and himself under fire, delivered the obvious criticism of Spychalski's speech. Why hadn't he said all this a year ago? Had he even today said everything he should have said? Was he keeping anything back? Were there any more guilty secrets? It was a horrible situation. Men were driven to accuse their friends and close associates of collaborating with traitors. Members of Gomułka's 'group' lashed out indiscriminately, imagining that by hurting each other they might save themselves. They were, of course, under great moral and mental pressure and living in a witch-hunt atmosphere. Some of the 'guilty men' were picked out for special treatment. Spychalski was treated worst of all. He was made to humiliate himself quite unnaturally:

'I did not agree with comrade Gomułka. I only say that I was unable to resist him. I gave in to his authority as leader of the Party. . . .

'I have made mistakes, comrades, grave mistakes. I am guilty, extremely guilty. I have done enormous harm to the Party. But I still feel myself to be its faithful member, devoted to it in the past as well as in the present.'

After Gomułka and Spychalski, the man in greatest trouble at the Plenum was Zenon Kliszko. He had from the autumn of 1945 to September 1948 been director of the personnel department of the Central Committee. This meant he had been responsible for many senior appointments, among them those of men now named as traitors. He confessed to a complacent attitude towards the possibility of infiltration into the wartime PPR. 'I gave in to the harmful view,' he said, 'that our Party and its leadership were safe from *agents-provocateurs*, that the arrests, disasters and losses in membership we suffered during the occupation were pure coincidence.' This was, of course, disgraceful, doubly so because it made a distinction between the PPR and the prewar KPP which (according to the prevailing, but false, theory of the time) had been thoroughly infiltrated with enemy agents. (This slander on the prewar Party was only disproved and officially denied in 1956.)[3] Kliszko was also reminded by Stefan Staszewski* of an unguarded remark made in 1946 about the months during the occupation when radio contact with Moscow was lost through the arrest of Finder and Fornalska.[4] Kliszko was alleged to have said it was only in these months that the PPR really became a proper party. Staszewski must have had a superb memory, if he was able to recall such a remark made three years previously. He was not the only communist leader to be searching brains and memories for any dirt that was around and could be thrown.

For all the violence and arrogance of the abuse being thrown at the Gomułka 'group', there was one point on which the delegates were vague. It had not yet been decided whether the group were merely bad communists and disgraceful characters, or whether they were also traitors to the Polish Republic. The delegates used phrases that were ambiguous. They spoke of Gomułka and Spychalski 'allowing traitors to gain high positions'. The question remained, had they done this consciously and treacherously or through ignorance and negligence. Bierut did not answer this question in his opening speech. He had not at this stage decided what was to be done with Gomułka. Clearly Gomułka was to be destroyed, but was the destruction to be merely political or also physical? Staszewski was one of the few delegates to jump the gun and come straight out with an allegation of treason: 'There has been talk here, comrades, of lack of vigilance. But I think there exists a

---

* However, in 1956 Staszewski, then the powerful secretary of the Warsaw Party organisation, was largely responsible for bringing about the October changes. He has since fallen out with Gomułka and is a main target of attacks.

boundary where lack of vigilance ends and where collusion with the class enemy begins. I have the impression that it is somewhere across this boundary that our rightist-nationalist deviationists, led by comrade Gomułka, find themselves.'

Gomułka's speech was far more bold and defiant than those he delivered at the 1948 Plenum. His career was in ruins. He had little to lose (except perhaps his life). Now was the time to return to the attack. His speech was a mixture of confession and justification.[5] For instance, he admitted responsibility for Czesław Dubiel's appointment as vice-Minister. He had not read Dubiel's file and not even noticed he had a doubtful past. He admitted he was blameworthy. The party was in trouble, and he, as its former chief, must bear his share of the responsibility. But he was no more blameworthy than other party leaders. Of his former political allies he attacked only Jerzy Albrecht (who had already attacked him). He claimed that Albrecht was far more responsible for letting Lechowicz into the Party leadership then he was. He had only met Lechowicz after the war was over, and when he came to Warsaw in 1942 Lechowicz was already in the Party. He also denied Roman Zambrowski's allegation that during the war he 'had all the threads in his hands', and therefore must be held responsible for *all* the mistakes that were made. He reminded Zambrowski that he was only elected Party leader in November 1943, by which time the Party machine was in full operation. And even after 1943 it was clearly impossible for him to exercise direct control over the Party. Communication under occupation conditions was difficult and dangerous. Local groups and cells had considerable autonomy. He could not be blamed for everything. He said: 'Do not try to present this matter in such a way that only I, only Gomułka and Spychalski, bear responsibility. Other comrades also bear responsibility.'

The Yugoslav issue was, of course, at the back of the delegates' minds and of the whole affair. Since September 1948 it had been aggravated by the 'discovery' of Titoist agents in high positions in the Hungarian and Bulgarian communist parties. Lászlo Rajk had already been executed as a Titoist agent. A month later (16 December) Traicho Kostov was to follow him to the gallows. It was therefore clear to Gomułka that his standpoint on the Yugoslav issue was no longer an ideological dispute within the Party. It was a matter of his own life or death. This is why he was careful to make his position clear on Tito and Yugoslavia:

'My position and Tito's position were always two different positions. There was never anything basically in common between them, regarding the relationship with the USSR and the Soviet Communist Party. My mistake, comrades, was in imagining that it was all simply a matter of mistakes committed by the Yugoslav Communist Party. I thought that all the Tito clique had done was to make mistakes. But now the situation has changed. It is now a matter not of mistakes, but of something quite different, i.e. diversionary activity by enemy agents.'

Gomułka was quite justified in claiming there was nothing 'Titoist' in his attitude to the Soviet Union. There were similarities in the Tito and Gomułka agricultural policies. Superficially, Gomułka's repeated reference to the 'Polish road to socialism' had a Titoist ring about it. But these were both *internal* matters. Gomułka never imitated Tito in questioning the foreign-policy and military alliance with the Soviet Union. He could therefore quite truthfully disassociate himself from such 'traitorous' ideas. One wonders to what extent Gomułka himself was taken in by the 'spy-mania', whether he ever really believed Tito was an American agent. If he did not, he clearly saw it necessary to pay lip-service to the accusation in order to have a chance of saving his own life. It was a sacrifice of principle which, he hoped, would be justified by later events.

The later part of Gomułka's speech was sad, rather moving, and has the ring of truth about it. He emphasised his great concern for Party unity, his readiness to do almost anything to preserve it. He then answered the accusation that during the previous year he had been too silent. He had said nothing, they claimed, either in reply to the criticism of true communists, or in reply to the support and praise heaped upon him by Titoists and reactionaries, in Poland and abroad. He explained that after the August Plenum he had felt 'crossed out' as a politician, that his opinion was no longer of any worth and therefore not worth uttering. His sentences were jerky and disjointed:

'After all that has happened I desired, I wanted my name to disappear once and for all from the press. This is why

I felt unwilling to write anything. And not only for this reason. Not only. Comrades, I am today talking sincerely and at length because perhaps I am appearing before you for the last time as a member of the Central Committee. I did not want to write because I was afraid of writing, because I had lost that which a man sometimes loses in certain circumstances, when he feels his own guilt and when he feels a state of isolation has been created about him.'

If any of the delegates were moved by these sentences, one who was not was Hilary Minc. He spoke next and attacked Gomułka brutally.[6] His most outrageous accusation was that Gomułka had been responsible for the deaths of his two predecessors as secretary-general of the Party, Nowotko and Finder:

'According to his [Gomułka's] understanding, the arrest of comrade Finder and comrade Fornalska happened by chance. Very well, comrades, but haven't there been rather too many of these coincidences? Pure chance: the murder of the first secretary of the Party [Nowotko], an old and experienced communist. Pure chance: the arrest and murder of the next secretary, an old and tried communist. . . .'

Towards the end of his speech Minc became quite carried away. He compared Gomułka's 'brilliant oratory' today to his silence during the previous year. 'Gomułka has tried to poison the atmosphere of today's Plenum,' he said, 'but he will not succeed.' His closing words were a clear threat: 'We shall create order in our own house. We shall condemn the enemy, without pity, mercy, right to the bitter end.' Towards the end he even stopped giving Gomułka the courtesy 'comrade' before his name. This was the final insult.

After several more speeches in this vein, the Central Committee proceeded to follow Minc's advice. Gomułka, Spychalski and Kliszko were expelled from the Central Committee and forbidden from holding party office. Although this was not announced until years later, they were also expelled from the Party. In their place the Central Committee coopted Konstanty Rokossowski, a Soviet citizen and former Soviet vice-

Minister of Defence who had come to Poland (where he was born) earlier in the year and been appointed Polish Minister of Defence.* This moment—the dismissal of Gomułka and the appointment of the Russian—marked the real beginning of Stalinism in Poland. It seemed symbolic that a Russian had been put in Gomułka's place. An 'inverse relationship' between the two men was created in the minds of Poles. Seven years later this played an important role.

Gomułka returned to his job in the Supreme Control Chamber. A month later (7 December) the trial opened in Sofia of Traicho Kostov. To the amazement of everyone, he pleaded not guilty to the main charges of being a British agent and a Yugoslav agent. He withdrew the written confession he had made while in custody and, presumably, under torture. He was sentenced to death on 14 December and executed two days later.

In 1950 Gomułka was again demoted. He left the Supreme Control Chamber for the insultingly unimportant job of director of the Warsaw Social Insurance Institute. Everywhere he went he had an UB escort. They would deliver him to his office, and come and collect him after the day's work. No longer a party member, politically isolated and completely without power, his name linked directly with those of convicted traitors, it seemed impossible that he should remain long at liberty. He knew that all this time the UB were preparing a case against him on orders from Bierut. In the meanwhile he was to be allowed to carry on working in an unimportant job, under strict security surveillance. When the case was ready, he was to be arrested.

* Rokossowski was born in Poland in 1896, moved in Russia as a young man and joined the Soviet Communist Party in 1919. He suffered in the stalinist purges of the late 1930s, but was reinstated and put in charge of the Byelorussian front towards the end of the Second World War. He commanded the Red Army forces across the Vistula at the time of the Warsaw Uprising.

XI: ARREST

As we have seen, the downfall of Gomułka happened quite gradually. In August 1948 he was accused of 'mistakes and false concepts'. He confessed and was apparently forgiven. In December 1948 he was booed from the floor of his Party's congress and called an arrogant fool. Only then was he forced to resign his vice-Premiership. He was still a member of the Party leadership, the Central Committee. His comrades were abusing him constantly and severely, but he was still officially one of them. There was not yet any mention of treason or criminal action.

The anti-Gromułka campaign was an artificial process set in motion by Stalin as part of his policy of indiscriminate terror. He did this because he believed his empire was about to split up. In Bulgaria, Hungary and, later, Czechoslovakia a number of targets were selected, put on trial and killed in a space of a few months. In Poland Gomułka was the target, but things did not happen as they did elsewhere. His destruction took years, and even when it came it was incomplete.

In other communist countries Stalin's 'orders to destroy' were being carried out at once and without question. In Poland the process was carried part of the way and then resisted, even by 'Stalin's men'—Bierut, Minc, Berman and Radkiewicz. The question remains, why did they do this, and how? They may have been able to suggest to Stalin that the Polish communists had already suffered enough bloodshed—during the purges of the late 1930s. They may have hoped that to disgrace Gomułka and drive him out of political life would be enough for Stalin. They would not have to kill him. This may be because they, unlike their comrades elsewhere in eastern Europe, had had their fill of killing each other.

By 1949 they realised criticism and ridicule would not be enough. They would have to do more. Pressure from the

Soviet Union was increasing. After all, if anyone was guilty of defying Stalin, Gomułka was. Why should he suffer less than Rajk or Kostov, men whose anti-stalinism was extremely vague? Stalin's terror may have been indiscriminate. But this did not mean the truly guilty (in the stalinist sense) could be allowed to go unpunished. Stalin was not as capricious as that.

The November 1949 Plenum provided a transitional stage between 'Gomułka the erroneous' and 'Gomułka the traitor'. The names of Gomułka, Spychalski and Kliszko were *linked* with those of convicted traitors. The Gomułka men were removed from office for allowing traitors to infiltrate the Government and the Party. But had they done this deliberately? Bierut and the men in power were hesitating before taking the plunge.

The details of the decision to arrest Gomułka and charge him with treason are, of course, not officially revealed. It is a painful business that the modern rulers of Poland, Gomułka included, prefer to forget. The main information about the case was revealed in the West by a certain Józef Światło, at the time a colonel in the UB and deputy head of its tenth department. His boss was Roman Romkowski, vice-Minister of State Security, who was reckoned by many to have more power even than his Minister, Stanisław Radkiewicz. Romkowski was later dismissed, arrested and imprisoned on charges of brutality and using 'illegal methods of interrogation'.

Światło's career was probably just as bloodstained as Romkowski's. In December 1953 he defected to the Americans in West Berlin and began to 'reveal all'. Millions of Poles heard what he said. They listened with curiosity and awe, but without sympathy for the speaker. Few doubted he could have stayed so many years in his job in the UB without playing some part in the well-known and confessed excesses of that now extinct organisation. Though they hated what he stood for, they believed what he said.

In 1954 Światło's grisly memoirs were broadcast to Poland by Radio Free Europe, the anti-communist radio station based in Munich. His main target was Bierut, whom he saw as entirely responsible for the terror in Poland that was only then, a year after the death of Stalin, beginning to fade away. The Polish authorities complained noisily, called Światło a traitor and demanded his extradition on charges of murder. But they were not able effectively to challenge the truth of what he was saying and broadcasting. The information he gave about the UB was in great detail. He clearly had the pigeon-hole mind of the successful bureaucrat. He was in a senior position in the UB. He was in a position to know most of what was going on. It seems unlikely that he was foolish enough to lie to his new employers, the Americans. He was interrogated by them for months. If he had made up stories, he would surely have been caught out. Nor is it any more likely that he invented his horrors for their benefit. As all Poles now know, the truth about the UB was quite horrible enough. To exaggerate would have been to gild the lily. It seems likely that what he said was predominantly the truth.

The UB were ordered to prepare a case against Gomułka. They then had a problem. They had to act against a man who for more than a year had been in disgrace. Communist security forces were not normally faced with such a situation. Usually they had the advantage of surprise. They would receive an order and be able to arrest a man out of the blue, before he had time to cover his tracks and prepare his friends, contacts and himself for the coming ordeal. The campaign of abuse against the accused man in the press would come *after* the arrest.

With Gomułka this order was reversed. He had already undergone a year of vilification. All that time his arrest had been confidently expected. If there was anything incriminating against him—and in those hard times there was no one entirely guiltless—there had been plenty of time to destroy it. The UB realised that if they wanted to find dirt, they would have to dig deep. And the case would have to be convincing. Someone of Gomułka's importance could not be condemned on flimsy evidence or behind closed doors. The evidence did not have to be true, it simply had to be convincing and thoroughly damning. Bierut was demanding such evidence. He in turn was being pressed by his Soviet contacts. Therefore the whole burden of the situation fell upon the UB. It was really very embarrassing for them.

Abortive attempts were made to 'get' Gomułka on the usual charge of collaborating with the fascists. They found he knew slightly a woman called Plotnicka, whose husband had been a commander in the prewar police. Also Gomułka had once lived in Zawiercie, near Cracow, in the apartment of some friends and another police officer named Rozbicki used to come and call there. So he once knew two members of the prewar *sanacja* police. Wasn't this incriminating? Not nearly enough, clearly, even to the stalinists' jaundiced eyes. The UB were sent away and told they could do better than that.

In September 1949 the UB were invited by their Hungarian colleagues (the AVO) to send 'observers' to the trial of Lászlo Rajk. Światło and Romkowski travelled to Budapest for the occasion. The inference was obvious. The UB were being given a lesson in how these things ought to be done. 'The "doping" of the Gomułka affair at foreign criminal trials is well known,' wrote Jakub Berman in September 1956 in his declaration of apology.[1] In 1949 he was the Politburo member in charge of security and in 1956 he was made to deliver a 'self-criticism', to explain how it all came about.[2] He blamed it all on a conveniently dead scapegoat, Lavrenti Beria:*

'As is known, pressure from the Beria-ites to mount comrade Gomułka's trial was constantly exerted upon us. The first attempts were made during the Rajk trial in 1949. This was continued in a brutal and provocative manner at the Slansky trial to which, for reasons that became only too obvious, representatives of our Party were invited.'

In 1956 Berman was presenting himself as the injured party, the poor, maligned secret police chief who spent his years of office fighting to protect the innocent. The truth was probably more along the lines of a speech by another Central Committee member, Leon Wudski:

'I remember, comrade Berman, I remember how you spoke after the Rajk trial, how you told us you were going to seek out our "Rajks" here in Poland. This was at a Central Committee meeting where everyone expressed full solidarity with the murderers of Rajk.

'*Comrade Ochab* (interrupting): Your time is nearly up, comrade.'[3]

* Beria was born in 1899 and was made People's Commissar (later Minister) of Internal Affairs in 1938. Like Stalin a Georgian, he is reckoned as largely responsible for the crimes committed in the name of the Soviet state between 1938 and his death, in mysterious circumstances, a few months after Stalin's in 1953.

Berman himself was under particular pressure to act against Poland's 'Rajk traitors'. He was a Jew, and therefore constantly suspected of 'cosmopolitanism' by the Stalinists. According to Berman's 1956 speech, Beria had already begun to prepare the way for his arrest, by linking him with an already convicted American 'spy', Noel Field. Like so many others who have prospered in the unpleasant business of 'security', Berman had to do his job efficiently and ruthlessly, or else suffer the fate of those he was pursuing.

In 1949 he had the difficult task of discovering convincing evidence of treason against Gomułka, a man who was clearly innocent. There were only two satisfactory ways of doing this. Either he must be persuaded to confess (as Rajk had already done) through moral pressure and appeals to 'Party loyalty', or else witnesses must be found to give false evidence. The UB had already failed in a pathetic attempt to link Gomułka with *sanacja* policemen. They now tried to present him as guilty by association.

By the end of 1949 two of Gomułka's senior ex-colleagues were in jail: Czesław Dubiel, his former vice-Minister of the Western Territories, and Lechowicz, a former head of department in that ministry. The UB now became more ambitious and decided to arrest Marian Spychalski, Gomułka's friend who had until 1948 been vice-Minister of Defence.* During the war Spychalski had been chief of the Intelligence Department of the communist People's Army (AL). Part of his job had been to keep tentative contact with the London Government organisations in Poland during the occupation. When the anti-communist forces went underground in 1945, he had maintained these contacts, in the hope of coming to terms with those who were physically resisting communist rule. The UB reckoned that evidence against Spychalski, true or false, would be easy

---

* Spychalski was born in 1906. He qualified as an architect and worked in that field in the prewar years, at the same time contributing to the clandestine left-wing press. He was one of the earliest leaders of the communist anti-Nazi underground in wartime Poland. He joined the PPR on its inception in 1942 and was chief of the intelligence department of the People's Guard (GL), later of the People's Army (AL). From 1944 to 1945 he was Mayor of Warsaw. From 1945 to 1948 he was vice-Minister of Defence. After his imprisonment he was in 1956 appointed Minister of Defence and in 1968 President of Poland.

to find. He had been in many situations which, with a little distortion, could be presented as compromising.

At the November 1949 Plenum the charges against him were made more specific than those against Gomułka. Traitors like Lechowicz and Jaroszewicz, it was claimed, were Spychalski's creatures. He had brought them into the People's Army and promoted them. Many officers who worked closely with Spychalski had already been arrested and condemned. It was made to appear that he had surrounded himself with traitors. Surely this could not be entirely due to lack of vigilance? Surely no one can believe in such a succession of coincidences? Spychalski *must* have known what was going on. This was how the case was presented.

In 1948 Spychalski had been moved from the Ministry of Defence to the Ministry of Building. In May 1950[4] he was in Wrocław, working on a building project, when he was arrested by Józef Światło. There is an air of black comedy about Światło's description of the arrest. Here is a quotation from it, as broadcast to Poland in October 1954:

'I waited for him in his villa in Kaczka Street, Wrocław. The cook and the concierge of the villa were already in my pay. I had also placed two agents in the next-door room. When Spychalski arrived in Wrocław, he came to his villa and found me in his room. His bodyguard stood behind him. When they saw me they knew what was happening. They had been working with me and they knew why I was there. Spychalski had me in front of him and his bodyguard behind him. We knew each other personally. He said hello to me and stretched out his hand. I took his hand, *and I did not let go of it.* My agents frisked him. Spychalski went a little pale. I said to him: "Comrade, let's go to Warsaw."'[5]

What followed was not so funny. Spychalski was confined first of all in a UB villa in Miedzyszyn, and later in the prison at Mokotów. He was interrogated. It was put to him that he was a British spy, that many of his associates were already convicted of espionage, that he must have been an agent, *even if an unwilling agent,* of the imperialists. These were loopholes which, according to the technique of the time, were offered every victim. He was made to feel genuinely guilty, of negligence at the very least. It was then put to him that the guilt could be purged only by a full confession, that in the interest of the Party this confession should be 'expanded'. After all, the spirit of it would be true, if not every little fact. But Spychalski stood remarkably firm. In contrast to his performance at the 1949 Plenum, he refused to incriminate either himself or Gomułka. He was then brutally tortured.

The interrogators derived little profit from their excesses. Only after a year of interrogation was Spychalski ready to be used as a witness in court. Even then the most they could get out of him was an admission of a tenuous link—possibly true, but even if true, hardly treasonable—between himself, Gomułka and a group of AK officers, the chief of which was a certain General Stanisław Tatar. The next stage of the plan was for this group of nine to stand trial for treason, and for it to be shown that Spychalski and Gomułka were involved with them. It was the most spectacular show trial of the stalinist period in Poland.

'The traitors on trial!'—this was the *Trybuna Ludu* headline that announced to Poles on 31 July 1951 the horrible news that 'a miserable mafia of petty merchants in the service of the Anglo-Saxon imperialists were creating diversion in the Polish Army, and selling information about our armed forces to foreign embassies'. The article that followed completely ignored the legal axiom that an accused man is innocent until proved guilty. The guilt of the accused was assumed. They were all to plead guilty and were of secondary importance in the drama. The trial was concerned not so much with national security as with party politics:

'The vile activity of these spies and saboteurs was brought about by the right-wing nationalist policy, whose instrument in the military field was the former vice-Minister of National Defence, Marian Spychalski. . . . Spychalski showed favour to former Piłsudski-ite officers and promoted them to high positions. These were officers well known for their reactionary ideas and for their past careers in the prewar Deuxième Bureau.

'It is no coincidence that the imperialists and the *émigré* London clique put their trust in the right wing of the

Polish Socialist Party, in Gomułkaism and Spychalski-ism, in the hope that Poland, like Titoist Yugoslavia, would fall into their hands.'[6]

As a welcome contrast to such unpleasantness, *Trybuna Ludu* that same day printed an official communiqué congratulating Rudolf Slansky, the Secretary-General of the Czechoslovak Communist Party, on his fiftieth birthday, and wishing him 'many more years of life for the good of the great ideal of socialism'. It is one of those East European ironies that little more than a year later *Trybuna Ludu* was wishing Slansky exactly the opposite. And it got its wish. By the end of 1952 he was dead, hanged for treason. Gomułka and Spychalski were not dead. To be sure, they were in prison, but they had not even been brought to trial. And, as all dictators know, it is safer to kill political opponents than to imprison them. Times change, and new situations can open the strongest prison gates.

From the first day of the Tatar trial the prosecutor spared no pains to involve Spychalski. 'In December 1943,' said Stanisław Tatar in evidence, 'Colonel Józef Spychalski told me he had received a proposition from his brother to join the [communist] People's Guard in a high position.' Józef Spychalski was then commandant of the Cracow district of the Home Army, and clearly it would have been quite treacherous for Marian Spychalski to have allowed such a reactionary to infiltrate the People's Guard. The next day Tatar told of his mysterious trips from London to Poland in 1947, and of meetings with Spychalski. These were, according to the prosecutor, on the instructions of the British Intelligence Service, a certain Colonel Perkins and his deputy, with the unlikely name of 'Pickens'. The prosecutor then announced that Spychalski was under arrest pending investigation, and that he would be giving evidence later in the trial.

The evidence which Spychalski gave on 8 August, as well as being reported in *Trybuna Ludu*, was broadcast on the radio and heard all over Poland. He spoke, by all accounts, like a man in a dream, a well-rehearsed zombie. The prosecutor fed him questions which he answered, using almost the exact words of the prosecutor's question. The first questions concerned Spychalski's alleged plan to infiltrate reactionaries into the Polish Army. The paragraph bore the tendentious heading, 'Spychalski with the agreement of Gomułka admitted the *dwójka* chief Herman into the Polish Army':

'*Prosecutor:* What answer did the witness give Herman to his request to be admitted into the Army?
Witness Spychalski: I told him I would give him an answer within a few days after I had discussed with Gomułka the question of Herman being admitted into the army.
Prosecutor: Did the witness inform Gomułka that Herman had during the occupation been intelligence chief of the 2nd Department of the Home Army High Command?
Witness: I told Gomułka that Herman had been chief of the 2nd Department of the Home Army High Command, and I repeated what Herman had told me.
Prosecutor: Did Gomułka express his agreement to Herman being admitted to the army?
Witness: Gomułka expressed his agreement to this.'

So there it was—a public accusation of Gomułka by one of his closest colleagues, a statement that Gomułka had deliberately, not through lack of vigilance but *deliberately*, tried to bring traitors into high positions in the new, socialist Poland. Later in his evidence Spychalski was forced to incriminate Gomułka again. This time the newspaper heading—a slight distortion of what Spychalski in fact said—was 'Spychalski and Gomułka seek contact with the ringleader of the WiN bandits and promise him immunity'. This concerned a meeting allegedly planned between Spychalski, Gomułka and the leader of WiN, Jan Rzepecki. WiN—as we have seen—was the underground successor to the Home Army, a mass of political groups, united only by their anti-communism, which opposed communist power with violence from the time of the dissolution of the Home Army by Leopold Okulicki on 19 January 1945, for some two or three years, until it was destroyed by the Security Forces. It seems possible, on the face of it, that Gomułka *may* have considered talking to the WiN leadership. The possibility of a negotiated cease-fire and amnesty was always in the air during those difficult months. Gomułka would not have been human if he had not been disgusted by the state Poland was in. It was intolerable that Poles, after losing twenty per cent of their number in the Second World War, should now be killing each other. Some might say that for Gomułka to talk to Rzepecki would be a useful, patriotic act. But this was not the way the prosecutor presented the matter. To him Rzepecki was a reactionary, an enemy of the people, a traitor. To talk to him, let alone to offer him safe conduct, was equally traitorous. Again Spychalski was forced to incriminate Gomułka:

> '*Prosecutor:* Was Herman the initiator of talks with Rzepecki?
> *Witness Spychalski:* Yes
> *Prosecutor:* Did the witness tell Herman immediately that he agreed to the carrying out of talks with Rzepecki?
> *Witness:* I did not agree at once, since I could not give an answer on such a matter. I took the whole matter to Gomułka. I asked him where he stood on it, and whether Herman's proposition could be accepted.'

Later Herman gave Spychalski a document, expressing certain political and military opinions:

> '*Prosecutor:* Did the witness show the document to Gomułka?
> *Witness Spychalski:* The document which Herman had handed to me I presented to Gomułka. . . .'

As each matter was raised, the prosecutor made a point of raising Gomułka's name, of linking him with Spychalski. The upshot of the planned meeting with Rzepecki was, to quote the witness Franciszek Herman, that 'I received instructions to make contact with Rzepecki, to offer him safe-conduct for twenty-four hours for the conduct of talks with vice-Premier Gomułka and with General Spychalski'. The fact that the meeting never took place did not alter the issue. Gomułka and Spychalski had planned a compromise with the enemy, and therefore they were to be regarded as enemies themselves.

Sentences were passed on the accused on 13 August. It is perhaps strange, and certainly one of the peculiarities of Polish stalinism, that there were no death sentences. The three main victims—Stanisław Tatar, Franciszek Herman and Jerzy Kirchmayer—were sentenced to life imprisonment. The others received terms varying from fifteen years to ten years. The final *Trybuna Ludu* editorial on the trial, on 14 August, accused

Gomułka directly of being their accomplice: 'In their vile work the group of spies received support and encouragement from the right-wing nationalist group of Gomułka who is, through Spychalski, directly linked with this diversionary activity.'

Incredibly, Gomułka remained at liberty right up to the day the trial opened. His life was grotesque—the life of a ghost. Avoided by his friends, not mentioned in Poland except abusively in the public press, he was like a man known to be dying of a horrible, incurable disease. The precedent was already set. Lászlo Rajk and Traicho Kostov had already been executed. There can be few who doubted that Gomułka's death would quickly follow. A weaker or a more sensitive man would not have borne the months of waiting. It was common for men in his position to commit suicide. His arrest, when it came, was no surprise. It may even have come as a relief.

Gomułka was arrested on 31 July 1951 in Krynica, a health resort in the Tatra mountains just south-east of Cracow and close to the Czechoslovak border. Again, the deed was done by Józef Światło. Three years after the event he broadcast back to Poland the bizarre account of how he was summoned by First Secretary Bierut and entrusted with the task of arresting Bierut's predecessor:

'Bierut told me there should be no fuss in Krynica. The arrest was to be carried out in such a way that people should not realise what was happening. It was my job to persuade Gomułka to come with me to Warsaw voluntarily. Radkiewicz ordered me to telephone from Cracow immediately after the operation and to report how it had gone. The task was not an easy one. I knew that Gomułka always carried a revolver. So I had to work things out so that, when he saw me, he did not shoot either himself or me. Gomułka had his bodyguard with him in Krynica. They were already in contact with me, for I had been working for some years on the Gomułka case. I had kept close to him, and almost every day I had had to report to Bierut what Gomułka was doing. So I worked things out so that when I came into Gomułka's room, one member of the bodyguard would be by the window and another by the bed. We all drove from Warsaw in three cars the

Władisław Gomułka

Kraj: Galicya.   Okrąg szkolny: *Krośno*

Szkoła wydziałowa męska *wydziałowa* w *Krośnie*

Klasa *pierwsza* szkoły wydziałowej.   L. katalogu klasowego: *12*

Świadectwo szkolne

Władysław Gomułka urodzony dnia *6 lutego* 1905

w *Białobrzegach* w *Galicyi* religii *katolickiej* obrządku

łacińskiego uczęszczał w *drugiem* półroczu roku szkolnego 19__ do klasy

pierwszej szkoły wydziałowej męskiej w *Krośnie*, zacho-

wywał się *chwalebnie*, przykładał się do nauk z pilnością *wytrwałą*

i poczynił w nich następujące postępy:

w nauce religii:	*chwalebny*
w języku polskim z nauką stylu praktycznego:	*chwalebny*
w języku ruskim z nauką stylu praktycznego:	
w języku niemieckim z nauką stylu praktycznego:	*celujący*
w historyi	*chwalebny*
w geografii:	*chwalebny*
w historyi naturalnej:	*chwalebny*
w fizyce i chemii:	
w rachunkach i rachunkowości pojedynczej:	*chwalebny*
w geometryi z rysunkiem geometrycznym:	*chwalebny*
w rysunkach odręcznych:	*zadowalniający*
w kaligrafii	*chwalebny*
w śpiewie	*zadowalniający*
w nauce zręczności	
w gimnastyce	*chwalebny*
w przedmiotach nadobowiązkowych:	

Porządek zewnętrzny ćwiczeń piśmiennych: *bardzo staranny*

Opuścił godzin szkolnych: *15* z tych usprawiedliwił *15*

Na podstawie tych postępów __ uznaje się ucznia tego uzdolnionym do

przejścia do klasy *drugiej szkoły wydziałowej*

W *Krośnie* dnia *30 czerwca* 19*17*

Dyrektor   Nauczyciel religii   Gospodarz klasy

Pieczęć

Gomułka at the age of 17 with his mother, father, brother, and sister

	zachowania się:	pilności:	postępu:	porządku zewnętrznego:
	SKALA		OCENY	
1	chwalebne	wytrwała	celujący	bardzo staranny
2	zadowalające	zadowalająca	chwalebny	staranny
3	odpowiednie	dostateczna	zadowalający	mniej staranny
4	mniej odpowiednie	niejednostajna	dostateczny	niestaranny
5	nieodpowiednie	mała	niedostateczny	niedbały

Facsimile (left and above) of Gomułka's school report, dated June 30, 1917

The house in Krosno (Ulica Mostowa 3) built by Gomułka and his family in 1923. The hut in which Gomułka was born in 1905 formerly stood on this site.

Gomułka with his wife Zofia and son Ryszard in 1934

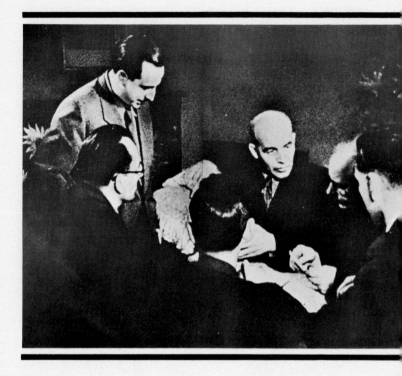

The years of conspiracy. Gomułka with member
of the illegal Central Committe

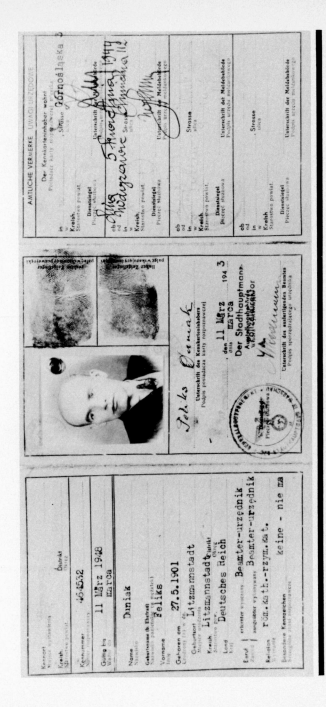

Gomułka's *Kennkarte*, German identity card issued in the pseudonym Feliks
Duniak in 1943

Gomułka during his first term of office

Gomułka casting his vote in the Polish elections of
January 17, 1957

Gomułka addressing a 240,000-strong crowd in
Warsaw's Plac Defilad on October 24, 1956

The saluting base for the First of May parade, 1957. (The street lamp was removed from behind the head of Jozef Cyrankiewicz before this photograph appeared in the Polish press.)

Gomułka is seen here helping Cyrankiewicz to food
at a banquet in Ulan-Bator, Mongolia, in July 1961

Gomułka welcomes Nikita Khrushchev to Polish territory,
July 14, 1959.

A rare picture of Gomułka on holiday with his wife Zofia
and granddaughters Ewunia and Haneczka

Poland

Poland at 1795 Partition ·····   Poland in 1920 ▬▬▬

Copenhagen

Baltic Sea

Riga

l i t h u a n i a

Polotsk

Smolensk

Memel

Kovno (1795)

(1920)

Danzig

Konigsberg

P R U S S I A

Grodno

Minsk

b i e l o r u s s i a

Stettin

Berlin

(1920)

Poznań

R U S S I A

Warsaw

Brest-Litovsk

Dresden

Breslau

(1795)

Lublin

Czartorysk

Kiev

Prague

Cracow

A U S T R I A

Teschen

Lemberg (Lwów)

(1920)

Bar

Vienna

(1795)

Poland

after Nazi-Soviet Occupation 1939 ·····   Poland in 1945 ▬▬▬

S W E D E N

Copenhagen

Baltic Sea

Riga

l i t h u a n i a

Polotsk

Smolensk

Memel (Klaipeda)

Kaliningrad (Konigsberg)

Kaunas (Kovno)

G E R M A N Y

Danzig (Gdańsk)

Elbing

(1945)

Grodno

Szczecin (Stettin)

Minsk

b i e l o r u s s i a

Berlin

(1939)

U. S. S. R.

Poznań

(1939)

P O L A N D

Warsaw

Brest

Dresden

Łódź

Breslau (Wrocław)

Lublin

Rovno

(1945)

Prague

Cracow (Kraków)

Lvov

Kiev

Cieszyn (Teschen)

C Z E C H O S L O V A K I A

Bar

Vienna

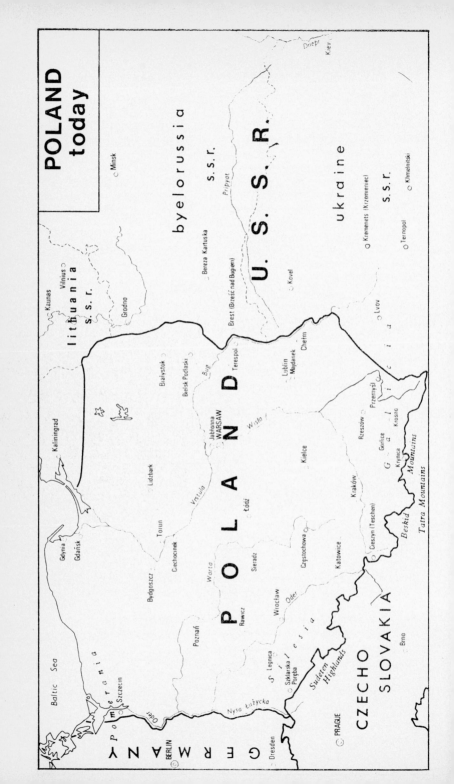

next day after the act of indictment against Tatar had appeared in *Trybuna Ludu*. It was seven o'clock in the morning when I arrived in Krynica. I entered Gomułka's room in the new Health Spa. His wife Zofia was not there. She had gone into town for a moment. Gomułka knew me quite well. So I went in, said good morning, and told him I had come with orders from the Party to take him back to Warsaw with me. Gomułka first of all refused to come. He said he was on holiday and did not want to go to Warsaw. Meanwhile his wife returned and made a bit of a fuss. I tried to calm her down. I explained there was no need for the whole of Krynica to know what was happening. Comrade Gomułka, his wife and I talked from 7 a.m. to 10 a.m., while I tried to persuade them to come to Warsaw voluntarily. In the end Gomułka got dressed, he and his wife Zofia got into one of the cars and we moved off. I then planned the whole journey so as not to arrive in Warsaw during daylight. It would have been neither pleasant nor convenient for me for the whole of Warsaw to see me in the company of the ex-Secretary-General in such circumstances. So I stopped several times along the way. Shortly after leaving Krynica I stopped outside Cracow and sent one of my men into town to telephone Romkowski that the operation had been successful. And we spent some time resting in the Checiny forest near Kielce. I sent my men a little way off, and Gomułka, his wife and I sat by ourselves, talking and eating. We talked about everything except politics.'[7]

One strange thing that comes across in Światło's account is the respect with which Gomułka was treated by his political opponents. Though powerless and politically isolated, he could still inspire disquiet and even fear in Bierut and Minc, who had behind them the full power of the UB. Światło describes how, for his own personal reasons, he was taking his time over the drive to Warsaw. Hours went by, and nothing was heard from him. This provoked 'confusion' among the political leaders.

'Bierut and Minc kept telephoning Romkowski every half hour and asking what was happening. They were worried and frightened. They ordered a radio car to be sent out to make contact with me. I passed this car between Kielce and Radom. I did not stop because I saw no reason to. There was nothing more I could tell them except that the operation had been successful. . . . I reached the city that night and took Gomułka and his wife straight to their prison. Gomułka was to be placed in Miedzyszyn, outside Warsaw, in a special villa belonging to the tenth department of the Ministry of State Security. This villa is just across the street from the American diplomats' club. From the first floor of this club one can even see the courtyard of the villa where Gomułka is. His wife Zofia was accommodated separately, in the next-door house. I was personally responsible for the safety both of him and of his wife.'

Gomułka spent more than three years in this villa. He was treated, by UB standards, quite humanely. His physical sufferings could in no way be compared, for instance, with those of Spychalski, who was detained for far longer, and in Mokotów prison, and for part of the time under torture. It had apparently been decided that Gomułka was not to be tortured. He was to be persuaded to confess by the 'soft' stalinist technique: appeals to party loyalty and solidarity, promises of leniency and moral pressure. His ministerial deputy Dubiel had already confessed to being a Gestapo agent. His close friend and colleague Spychalski had accused him, by implication, of working for the reactionaries. His case had been seized upon delightedly by the anti-communist press. In the West his name was universally linked with that of Tito, known to be in the pay of the imperialists. One can imagine the excruciating *moral* torture of such facts on a man who, however much he disliked the present Polish leadership, believed in communism fervently and loyally.

For the details of Gomułka's treatment in prison, again there is the account of Józef Światło:

'His room has bars on the windows. He receives good food, books and the magazine *Problemy*. He is not allowed to have newspapers. In the wall there is a 'Judas hole' through which a warder watches him all the time. Of course the warders are changed quite often, but there is never one second during which Gomułka is not under observation. His health is not particularly bad. But he does suffer from

stomach aches and from a stiffening in the leg, where he
was shot before the war by the police.'

In the days that followed there was a strange, almost farcical
reversal in the traditional roles of prisoner and gaoler. Those
who had ordered Gomułka's arrest, although they had had
nearly two years to plan it, behaved in a helpless, confused
fashion once their man was under lock and key. The plan was
for some of his senior ex-colleagues to visit him, and to try and
persuade him to 'play ball'. However, according to Światło:

'None of the comrades wanted to go. They said: "It would
be wrong for Bierut to talk to Gomułka. Gomułka despises
Minc. They hate each other. Radkiewicz wouldn't dare
show his face, since Gomułka knows about his disreputable
past. Nor would Jóźwiak. And Chelchowski is too stupid.
The result was that for nearly three months Gomułka
stayed in Miedzyszyn in complete isolation and did not
talk to anybody. In the end the Politburo made a decision.
The vice-Minister of Public Security Romkowski and the
chief of the tenth department Colonel Fejgin were appointed to talk to Gomułka.'

These were two of the most notorious officers in the whole
of the UB. Both of them were, a few years later, convicted by a
Polish court of 'breaches of legality'—a fine euphemism for
sadism and torture—and sentenced to long prison terms. The
Gomułka case cannot have been one of their more delightful
assignments. Ordered to treat their prisoner gently, it would
be interesting to know how they reacted to the prisoner's most
ungentle treatment of them. Gomułka treated the torturers
aggressively. He bullied them. There are rumours that he
assaulted them, that guards ran into the cell with guns asking
permission to shoot Gomułka, that Gomułka screamed at
them; 'Shoot, if you dare, the Secretary-General of the Polish
Workers' Party!' This is the legend. Even if it is not true, the
fact that it exists is equally remarkable. Światło's account is
less melodramatic:

'Gomułka behaved very well in prison under interrogation.
He did not admit anything more than he had admitted
at the Plenum. He did not go one step further than the

self-criticism he had delivered there. The only difference
was that he had now no brakes on him at all. So he accused
Bierut and his clique of everything. He demanded to know
exactly what it was he was accused of. He attacked Bierut
and the Party, accusing them of collaboration with the
Germans during the occupation.'

All this, of course, raises the question, why did the UB stand
for it? It was because in this particular case they were under
direct, close supervision from Bolesław Bierut—President of
the Republic and First Secretary of the Communist Party.
Then why did Bierut stand for it? The obvious answer to
Gomułka's unnatural arrogance was surely to take away his
good food, his books and his comfortable cell; to throw him into
some damp hole in Mokotów prison with his friend Spychalski.
Mightn't that cool his ardour? Then why not apply a little
physical pressure to make him lose his self-respect, make him
feel like a traitor, criminal and enemy of the people? Such
thoughts must have passed through Bierut's mind. Suggestions
to this effect must have been put to Bierut by the more ruthless
members of his government and Soviet advisers. Then why
was their advice rejected?

The most widely believed explanation in Poland today is
that Gomułka and his followers were protected personally by
Bierut. Bierut was one of the very few Polish communists who
was free and at Stalin's mercy during the purge years, and yet
lived to tell the tale. He had been able to observe the arrest
and quasi-judicial murder of his friends and colleagues. It is
suggested that, in 1950, he did not relish a repeat performance.
Communist killing communist (1935–39) was bad enough.
Pole killing Pole (1944–47) was bad enough. But Polish communist killing Polish communist—this had not yet officially
happened. Support for this theory is given by Alicja Wetz, a
Polish communist who later married a French journalist and
emigrated: 'Bierut never wanted Gomułka to stand trial. He
hedged, he temporised, he found pretext after pretext—anything to avoid signing that document. . . . He did not do this
in any way out of sympathy for Gomułka, whose views were
alien to him, but out of pure honesty.'[8]

This is clearly a glamourised opinion of Bierut, whose
'honesty' did not prevent him from allowing thousands of less

important, though equally innocent, Poles to be wrongfully imprisoned and tortured. The best one can say of Bierut is that he was soft-hearted on occasion. He was leader of Poland and he controlled the UB. He was opposed to Gomułka. If he had really wanted to, he could have killed Gomułka. But he didn't. The reason why is another matter.

There is a second theory that Bierut was afraid to put Gomułka on trial, because of what he might say in court. He may have thought Gomułka was too important a prisoner to be quietly disposed of in a secret trial, or murdered in prison. A proper trial would have been necessary with all the trimmings: press transcripts, nation-wide broadcasts and—the dangerous part—foreign correspondents. According to Światło, Bierut *wanted* Gomułka to stand trial: 'They wanted to see him [Gomułka] in the dock. But since they could not break him down, the trial would not have been the trial of Gomułka. It would have been transformed into a public indictment of Bierut and his clique.'

There is a third factor—Bierut's knowledge of Gomułka, of the man's resolution and stubbornness. He may possibly have summed up his man and decided that to torture Gomułka would be a waste of time. Gomułka had already spent some five years of his life in prison and three years in an underground army with a price on his head. Men like him are not easily intimidated. Many of his communist colleagues suffered the worst that either the Gestapo or the NKVD could dispense. He was used to the idea of torture, if not its actual practice. He had literally learnt to live with it. Bierut's only hope was to find good, solid evidence, at least partly true and *based* on fact, that Gomułka had been a right-wing extremist, that his views had become dangerous, that anti-socialist groups had supported him and counted on him, and that Gomułka had used them traitorously to further his own political ends.

The fourth explanation assumes the fact that Bierut and the Stalinists wanted Gomułka to stand trial and were doing their best to find evidence, true or false, that would stick. But such evidence, true or false, was not to be found. Witnesses could not be persuaded to come forward and accuse Gomułka— at least not the sort of witnesses that would cut much ice with the foreign correspondents. Spychalski's ambiguous accusations were not enough. The charges he made against Gomułka amounted, at worst, to mistaken tactics. They were enough—just—to warrant an arrest, but not a trial and an execution.

Why then were there no witnesses? In other east European countries they came forward and lied away the lives of their former colleagues most convincingly. Why not in Poland? Poles now suggest it has something to do with their national character: that they have a simple, inherent loyalty to their friends and allies which they hardly ever violate; that Poland, so frequently disappointed or betrayed by her allies, has become loyalty-mad, and that this is why the techniques imported from Stalin's Russia of mutual blackmail and mutual incrimination were not used in Poland with much success.

The Poland of 1951 had just come through half a century of upheavals unknown in the West for centuries. War (1914), independence (1918), war (1920), *coup d'état* (1926), military dictatorship, war (1939), enemy occupation, Nazi terror, civil war and now Stalinist terror—it is a wonder that any decent politically-minded Pole was able to keep his sanity, let alone his integrity. In Stalinist Poland, as in Stalin's Russia, the authorities could assume with reasonable accuracy that everyone was guilty. Everyone had either gained power or money by doubtful means, everyone at some time or another had betrayed someone, even if that someone was himself, everyone had used violence. This was the state of affairs, and it explains why it was not so illogical for, say, Bierut to summon his security chiefs and to order them to unearth evidence of treason against, say, Gomułka. Why should Gomułka be any different from anybody else? Why should he *not* be guilty? He must have done *something*. Bierut had not reckoned with the modesty of Gomułka's way of life, his indifference to money, his unusual political consistency, and his deep, genuine faith in marxism-leninism. He really was one of the few Polish communists against whom nothing of any substance could be found. His heresies had never been criminal. The violence he condoned had never been anti-communist. Therefore it would have been a mistake to put Gomułka, in his frame of mind at the time, in the dock. The shaky evidence and lying witnesses might have been made to look very foolish.

The Polish people as a whole knew nothing of these events. Gomułka had disappeared from his office in the State Insurance. Hardly anyone knew more than that. It was not until the end of October, three months after the event, that Gomułka's arrest was officially announced. The news was first broadcast on the radio on 31 October. The next day there appeared a small paragraph in *Trybuna Ludu* at the end of a full page of details from Sejm debates. It was headed 'Criminal proceedings against Gomułka and Spychalski', and announced the withdrawal of their parliamentary immunity. Having been elected to the Sejm in 1947 both men were strictly speaking immune from arrest. It was a legal nicety that had not much deterred Bierut and the UB, but the record had to be put straight, even if it was a few months late. The article announced that a Sejm commission had examined the prosecutor's evidence 'in connection with certain activities directed against the state system of People's Poland committed by the above-mentioned deputies, as revealed in the course of the trial of Tatar and others. The Sejm, in accordance with the Commission's recommendations, gave permission for criminal proceedings to be taken against Spychalski and Gomułka.'

XII: DISAPPEARANCE

During 1952 Gomułka was under arrest and it was assumed he would soon stand trial. No very coherent policy was adopted towards this end. According to Światło, he only underwent fifteen working days of interrogation. A campaign of lies in books and the press was maintained against him. In their writings the stalinist leaders in effect committed themselves to a trial. For instance Bierut in his book (presumably ghosted) *About the Party* mentions Tatar and the other 'traitorous' officers and adds:

> 'But it was only because of the protection they received from the right-wing group, the various *deuxième bureau* agents and provocateurs connected with Gomułka and his group that they were able to spy and plot for so many years in the service of imperialism and to the detriment of the Polish people. It is today absolutely clear that it was hypocrisy, dishonesty towards the Party, opportunism, hostility to the USSR and to the building of socialism in Poland which joined Gomułka and Spychalski with the agents of imperialism in Belgrade and Budapest. . . .'[1]

A 1952 biography[2] of Bierut accused Spychalski and, by implication, Gomułka of arranging for the arrest by the Gestapo (14 November 1943) of Pawel Finder, Gomułka's predecessor as secretary of the PPR: 'It is now confirmed that the arrest of Finder, Fornalska, Janek Krasicki and many other Workers' Party leaders was brought about by elements of the London Delegation who collaborated with the Gestapo, by former *deuxième bureau* members whom Spychalski enabled to penetrate the Information Department of the People's Guard headquarters.'

In a later paragraph it was again emphasised that the sins of Gomułka were not mistakes but conscious acts. On the agricultural question, for instance:

'Their policy was to privilege the *kulak* farmers. They strove to dull the struggle of the poor farmers against *kulak* oppression. Everywhere they could, they besmirched the state and party apparatus with enemies. They minimised the Party's role in village life and the role of the USSR as the ideal and example for the victorious building of socialism. Only later did it transpire that these were not accidental slips, but that they arose from the anti-Party, blatantly hostile standpoint of Gomułka and his group. . . . At the basis of the hostile attitude of Gomułka and his group lay his nationalist mistrust of the USSR, his attempt to lead Poland along a separate road towards the building of socialism. Gomułka then drifted into the imperialist camp in the footsteps of Tito and his band of spies.'[3]

Another book full of abuse of Gomułka was written in 1952 by Franciszek Jóźwiak-Witold.* He wrote: 'The Gomułka-controlled Ministry of Western Territories became a refuge for all sorts of *deuxième bureau* and Gestapo agents like Lechowicz, Payor, and agents-provocateurs like Dubiel.'[4] On the Cominform issue: 'Gomułka tried to sabotage the creation of the Cominform. He occupied in this matter a clearly nationalist standpoint, directed against international proletarian solidarity.'[5]

On the Yugoslav issue the stalinist author really loses control of himself. He was outraged by Gomułka's reluctance to condemn Tito as an imperialist spy:

'Even at the August Plenum, after comrade Bierut's deep ideological oration, after the discovery of the murder of

---

* Jóźwiak (his conspiratorial name was Witold) was an early member of the prewar Communist Party, for which he was imprisoned in the *sanacja* camp at Bereza Kartuska. During the occupation he was chief of general staff of the People's Guard (later the People's Army). He was one of the few communists who spent the war years in Poland to associate himself with Bierut's 'Russia' faction in the PPR.

Jowanowicz, after three months of discussion with Gomułka, he still declares in his "self-criticism" on the Yugoslav question: "Comrades, when today I ask myself the question, was there any other way of reacting to the mistaken, nationalist, anti-marxist views and policies of the Communist Party of Yugoslavia, I must confess that I cannot find in myself any definite answer."[6]

Such 'woolly-mindedness' was incomprehensible to the author. He continues: 'When there was no doubt in the mind of any honest marxist that the Tito-Ranković-Djilas-Kardelj clique was a band of traitors, a band of terrorist, anti-communist, anti-Soviet dictators. . . .' Jóźwiak's criticisms dissolve into mere ravings. A few sentences later he calls the Yugoslav Communist Party 'the Gestapo-Tito clique'—on what basis he does not even attempt to define.

With the benefit of fifteen years of hind-sight, it is curious to look back on the author's four Yugoslav arch-enemies—Tito, Ranković, Djilas and Kardelj. Two of them, Djilas and Ranković, were later disgraced, and for exactly opposite reasons. Djilas was dismissed and imprisoned for revisionism, over-liberalism and for publishing anti-marxist books. Ranković, Tito's security chief, was removed by him in 1966 for dogmatism and breaches of legality, for not being liberal enough.

In November 1952 the most notorious of the east European show trials took place—the Slansky affair. Rudolf Slansky, the former secretary-general of the Czechoslovak Communist Party, together with some twenty of his colleagues stood trial in Prague, charged with the usual crimes of the period: espionage, sabotage, treason, betrayal, conspiracy and murder. They were convicted of working for the western imperialists, and on 27 November eleven of them were sentenced to death. Eight of these were Jews. It was a governmental massacre. Among those condemned were Vladimir Clementis, a Slovak, the Foreign Minister, Josef Frank, the deputy Secretary-General of the Communist Party, Bedrich Reicin, deputy Minister of Defence, and Karel Svab, deputy Minister of National Security. They were hanged on 3 December. Three other Jews were sentenced to life imprisonment. 'The time they have already spent in prison will count towards their sentences,' said the judge, presumably without the slightest intention of trying to be funny.[7]

The Polish observers invited to the Slansky trial were left in no doubt. The Gomułka case came up several times in court. The Poles there were being given a lesson, which they were expected to go home and carry out. In his final speech the Czech prosecutor made the position quite clear: 'Thanks to the vigilance of the working masses and the communist parties we have unmasked and rendered harmless the traitorous gangs of László Rajk in Hungary, Traicho Kostov in Bulgaria, Koci Xoxe in Albania, Patrascanu* in Romania and Gomułka in Poland.'[8] Rajk, Kostov, Patrascanu, Xoxe and Slansky were dead. Gomułka was not dead. He was still in his comfortable room in Miedzyszyn. It is extraordinary that the organs of Stalin's violence should have tolerated such a situation. The five who were dead had opposed Stalin hardly, if at all. But Gomułka *had* opposed him. He was the guilty one. It was he who with Tito challenged the dictator in eastern Europe. It was because of him that Stalin began to kill a proportion of his chief lieutenants. And yet he was the one who was still alive.

The day the Slansky sentences were announced was also the tenth anniversary of the death of the first PPR leader Marceli Nowotko (28 November 1942). The communist movement had changed a lot in ten years. In 1942 communists were in mortal combat with the Nazi ideology. In 1952 they had assumed two of the Nazis' worst qualities. They were murderous and they were anti-semitic. The Jews in the Czech trial were humiliated and abused in language no less horrible than that of Dr Goebbels. Zionism had become a crime even worse than imperialism. It was as if Stalin in his last weeks was assuming the mantle of his old enemy Hitler, the only man of the twentieth century who could challenge him for wickedness.

Suddenly the villains of eastern Europe were not the 'reactionaries', but the Zionists, the 'rootless cosmopolitans', the 'bourgeois Jewish imperialists'. In such an atmosphere even *The Times* of London was forced to jump to conclusions. On 1 December it reported a *Rude Pravo* (Prague) article claiming Gomułka would be put on trial 'soon'. The *Times* report went

* The Romanian Party leader Lucretiu Patrascanu was arrested, charged and found guilty of spying for the United States and Great Britain. He was executed on 16 March 1954. He was later rehabilitated and in April 1967 the Minister of the Interior of the time, Alexandru Draghici, was dismissed from all Party posts for rigging this and other trials.

on: 'Like Mr Rudolf Slansky, who held the corresponding post in the Czechoslovak Communist Party, he [Gomułka] is of Jewish origin.' This was not true. Perhaps fortunately for him, Gomułka was in no way a Jew. The English reporter was perhaps confused by the fact that Gomułka's wife Zofia was. In 1952 to have a Jewish wife was bad enough.

Worse was to follow. The machine of Stalin's violence was beginning to go berserk. On 10 January 1953, the *communiqué* was issued in Moscow about the 'Doctors' Plot', the group of doctors, most of them Jews, who were supposed to have planned to kill the leaders of the Soviet government. Many of them were killed. This was to be the last of Stalin's excesses. On 5 March 1953 he died. Władysław Gomułka was still alive.

The effects of Stalin's death were felt more quickly in the Soviet Union itself than in the 'satellite' countries. Those involved in the 'Doctors' Plot' lucky enough to survive until 5 March were quickly released. On 10 July it was announced that Lavrenti Beria, Minister of the Interior and as responsible for Stalin's crimes as Stalin himself, had been arrested as a 'British spy'—the same imaginary crime as Marian Spychalski's. Most of his chief henchmen were shot in the course of that summer. Investigations began into countless cases of 'breach of legality'. The corrective labour camps began to empty. All this was still in 1953.

In the other east European countries Stalinism still had a little momentum left. In Poland there was an intensification in the campaign against the Roman Catholic Church. Many priests and bishops were being arrested. Finally, on 26 September 1953, came the arrest of the Primate of Poland, Cardinal Wyszyński. Three days later *Trybuna Ludu* announced he was not to be allowed to execute the functions of his office. At least he was not locked up in a cell. He was allowed to retire to a monastery. They moved him from one to another, and finally to a monastery at Lidzbark, in north-east Poland.

This was the final fling of Polish stalinism. By 1954 the upheavals that had been taking place in the Soviet Union had filtered westward to the 'People's Democracies'. In Poland 'official circles' began to admit tacitly what the rest of the country already knew: that the security service had for years been abusing its authority, employing illegal and sadistic methods of interrogation, creating for itself a privileged position, a state within a state. Józef Światło was broadcasting details of this from Munich. What he said caused a furore and a scandal. A purge of the UB was already under way, and Światło's broadcasts probably speeded it up. When he defected there was already in progress an investigation into the activity of Józef Rożański, one of the worst of the UB sadists. Investigations soon followed on Światło's direct boss, Anatol Fejgin, and on the deputy minister, Roman Romkowski. In December 1954 the minister himself, Stanisław Radkiewicz, was transferred to a less sensitive area, the Ministry of State Farms—a post from which he was summarily dismissed eighteen months later (20 April 1956).

Gomułka's name had disappeared from the Polish press. His whereabouts were not revealed. It was as if he had never existed. Obviously there were widespread rumours about what had happened to him. People knew his health was not good, and many of them came to the natural assumption that he had died. On 23 May 1953 a short article in *The Times* about Gomułka was sub-headed 'Death in Prison Presumed'. The article announced that 'unconfirmed reports that he [Gomułka] has died in a Warsaw prison have not been denied by the Polish Government'. Unfortunately for Gomułka's sense of humour, *The Times* was not quite sure enough of its facts to run an obituary.

Gomułka was released during September 1954.* But this fact was not announced officially until 7 April 1956, and the rumours continued. Then, in 1954 and 1955 people started to see him around: at his favourite mountain resort of Krynica, at the funeral of his mother Kunegunda Gomułka in Krosno, at the health resort of Ciechocinek. These were only vague impressions, whispered about Poland by people half-ashamed, as if admitting they had seen a ghost, an un-person who had disappeared from the limelight so shatteringly that he really had no right to be seen in public. If no longer a convicted traitor, he was still a convicted heretic, and so could not aspire to political life, let alone to political leadership. He lived quietly, rehabilitating himself as a free man.

* This is the date announced by the Polish Press Agency (PAP) on 20 February 1957. Most other sources claim the date was December 1954. Konrad Syrop in *Spring in October* says it was Christmas Eve, 1954. *Osteuropa Handbuch, Polen* says it was 21 April 1955.

XIII: THE POINT OF RETURN

In communist countries it is more than usually hard for popular opinion to change the form or composition of the government. When change occurs, it is achieved by pressure from within the government, from on top. This has happened frequently in the Soviet Union, most recently in October 1964, when Nikita Khrushchev was eased out of power in a mysterious Kremlin coup. It also happened in January 1968 in Czechoslovakia. Even more rarely do communist governments collapse. The two known examples of this happening—Spain in the late 1930s and Iranian Azerbaijan in 1945—took place, in part at least, because of the withdrawal of Soviet military support and the subsequent military defeat of the communist régimes. But in 1956 two socialist countries, Poland and Hungary, underwent important political change, and in both cases the instigation of the change was public opinion. In Hungary the changes only lasted a few days. In Poland they were less fundamental but lasted longer, and in them Władysław Gomułka played the key role.

With Stalin's death in March 1953, the engine that provided the momentum for the police terror became run down. It did not stop, it reduced power and continued ticking quietly over. The upheavals that took place in Russia in 1953—the death of Beria, his clique and the release of many unjustly sentenced exiles from Siberia—were able to occur without shaking the fundamental structure of Soviet society. Marxism-leninism and stalinism had dominated Russia for decades and would not be put in question because of a few administrative excesses, the like of which had been part of Russian life even under some of the Tsars.

In the satellite countries of eastern Europe, though, the effect of the uncovering of Stalin's crimes was much greater. The crimes were seen in the context of a political system which had ruled them for a mere ten years and which had not yet had time to become more than a small part of living memory. They were therefore less understandable or excusable and caused a greater confusion when knowledge of their full horror became known.

In Poland it was a combination of events: the public admission of faults in the security service, the transfer of Radkiewicz, the Security Minister, to a harmless and less important job in charge of state farms, the sensational broadcasts from the West by former UB Colonel Józef Światło. They triggered off a popular movement for 'democratisation' of political life in which the leading roles were played by the intelligentsia and the students. The security service, under investigation for exceeding its authority, became less active and less terrifying. Writers and journalists who had been hitherto afraid to write the truth began to do so. There was a simultaneous easing of the censorship. Suddenly ideas began to appear in print which had not been heard of for years.

Gomułka, free but not yet rehabilitated or mentioned in the public press, was able to sit back, do nothing, and watch the wind blow in his direction. During 1955 the 'democratisation' campaign in the press gathered momentum, especially in such weekly cultural journals as *Nowa Kultura* (New Culture), *Przegląd Kulturalny* (Cultural Review) and *Po Prostu* (Straightforward), this last specialising in the views of Poland's students. Many of the leading 'agitators' were communist party members. Jan Kott the famous Shakespearean critic, Leszek Kołakowski the philosopher and playwright, Adam Ważyk the poet and the novelist Jerzy Putrament were members of the Party who had in recent years more or less supported communist policy. Now they were leaders of the demand for change. On 21 August 1955 Ważyk's *Poem for Adults* appeared in *Nowa Kultura*, an ingenuous but touching cry from the heart, describing all that Polish communists had hoped for ten years ago and how their hopes had not been fulfilled. On 6 March Jan Kott, also in *Nowa Kultura*, complained 'the writer is paralysed when he knows every word he writes will be scrutinised according to one criterion—whether or not he has exposed himself'. By the end of 1955 the censorship had almost collapsed. In early 1956 there appeared articles with such unheard-of titles as 'Am I a weathercock?',[1] 'Mythology and Truth'[2] and 'Is this the twilight of Marxism?'.[3] On 1 April

1956 *Po Prostu* published an article called 'Behind the Yellow Curtains' which, with *Poem for Adults*, perhaps did most to convince the newspaper-reading public that change must come, and that if it must come, the sooner it came the better. The *Po Prostu* reporter had seen a line of women queueing outside a shop almost empty of things to buy. The Easter transport of meat had not yet arrived. The reporter then noticed a building opposite:

'It has a private parking-space for cars. Several of them are left haphazardly about, all types, Warszawa, Pobieda, Chevrolet, a Cadillac or something, one of those cars where you can't tell the front from the back. In every car is a chauffeur.

'A blue Warszawa, number D 005-817 drives up. A lady in a fur coat, a green handkerchief round her head, gets out and walks towards the door. She opens the door, which is lined with yellow curtains. . . .'

The point is that this *special* shop, curtained off from the public and open only to the families of high officials, contained everything to delight the heart and stomach of the most fastidious Pole. The women queueing in the snow across the road had never seen such a shop. It represented the privilege then given to leading communists, the 'proprietors of People's Poland'. This article was typical of many that condemned the complacent selfishness of some of the pre-1956 communists. Of course, few Poles believed the previous ten years of propaganda that their leaders were like saints, dedicated to work and service to the community. But now at last it was in *print*. It was *admitted* they were concerned also with their own comforts, that they had protected and hidden their privileges from the Polish public by hanging 'yellow curtains' in front of shops crammed with the good things of life.

On 25 February 1956, at the Twentieth Congress of the Soviet Communist Party in Moscow, Nikita Khrushchev delivered his famous speech, soon afterwards 'leaked' to the rest of the world, revealing the crimes of Stalin and attacking his 'cult of personality'. It was a moment of catharsis for the whole of communism. A week earlier on 19 February Poles had been astonished to open their morning party newspaper *Trybuna Ludu* and see prominently displayed on the front page photographs of certain prewar communist leaders, including the 'three Ws', Warski, Walecki and Wera Kostrzewa, hitherto regarded as traitors to the KPP and the Comintern and responsible for its dissolution. Underneath was a special declaration of the communist parties of the Soviet Union, Italy, Bulgaria, Finland and Poland that the KPP was rehabilitated and that the 1938 accusations against it were unjustified. 'The evidence,' said the declaration, 'had been faked by a gang of saboteurs and provocateurs whose real role was only brought to light after the unmasking of Beria.' It followed that all the leading KPP members who had been executed or died in prison in the late 1930s were innocent of their alleged crimes.

If these two bombshells were not enough to disrupt Poland and the Polish Party, a third followed in a matter of days. Bolesław Bierut, Party leader since 1948 and a symbol of the old Stalinist leadership, died on 12 March in Moscow. 'Bolesław Bierut is dead,' said Aleksander Zawadski in a funeral speech, 'but the Polish Workers' Party lives on, united and monolithic.' By now all but the most conservative in the Party could see that such remarks were wishful thinking. The Party had never been so divided. Its leaders were forming themselves into cliques to contest the vacant leadership, to continue or to halt the democratisation, to encourage or to suppress the by now free discussion of current politics. The flood gates were opening.

A brief cease-fire in the battle of wills was observed during Nikita Khrushchev's visit to Warsaw for Bierut's funeral. He stayed for a week, heavily canvassing the candidature of Edward Ochab for the post of First Secretary, and on 21 March Ochab was duly elected. The Russians thought he was 'their man', that he would keep democratisation under control and stabilise the growing political unrest.

To begin with it seemed that this would happen. In the March number of the Party monthly *Nowe Drogi* (New Ways) Jerzy Morawski, known as one of the more liberal young communist leaders, wrote on 'The lessons of the Twentieth Soviet Party Congress' an article fashionably condemning Stalin's excesses: the KPP affair, the Leningrad trials and the doctors' plot. Why did the Party not oppose Stalin's terror earlier, while he was alive? Morawski asked himself the question by then on the lips of many sceptical Poles. His answer was the official Soviet answer: first, no one knew innocent men were suffering; secondly, to oppose Stalin would have been 'to open the gate to the enemy, to clear the way for imperialist aggression, to facilitate such aggression. . . . Was it not better to grit one's teeth and wait for the day when the socialist ideal would triumph?' It was an answer Morawski would never have got away with six months later, especially as his article contained one of the first press references in the new atmosphere to Władysław Gomułka. He wrote: 'Gomułkaism set out the theory of the "Polish road to socialism". It is not so much this slogan which is false as the class content which Gomułkaism put into the slogan—the slowing down of the process of revolutionary change, the freezing of the system of class forces in the villages, the slowing-down of the basic processes of change not only in economics but also in culture, science and education. In essence it meant not a variation on the Soviet system, but its contradiction. Objectively speaking it meant the negation of the road to socialism.'[4]

As far as Gomułka was concerned there were two significant facts about this article. The first was that there was no mention of his alleged treason and betrayal. He was no longer the 'conscious agent of imperialism' that he had been labelled up to the time of Stalin's death.[5] His release had not yet been announced, but clearly his innocence had been tacitly acknowledged in official circles for some time. The second fact is that clearly Morawski did not then envisage Gomułka's return to Party life, let alone into the government. In March 1956 democratisation was in full swing, but it would have to go a long way yet before a declared 'traitor' could have any part to play in it. It is especially strange that such bitter remarks about Gomułka should have come from a man who a few months later emerged as Gomułka's friend and joined him in the inner circle of leadership. It illustrates the prevailing view of the time that Gomułka was too physically ill, had too many enemies and was too generally 'dangerous' to be considered a political force.

On 7 April one of these hurdles was cleared when Ochab made the long-delayed announcement that Gomułka was now free and that his arrest had been unjustified. He said: 'With pain and regret we think of our comrades wrongfully arrested and later completely rehabilitated, but also of the wrongful arrests of men whom we *rightly* fought against as carriers of opportunist and nationalist views, but wrongly accused of diversionary activity, conniving at their arrest . . . giving in to the atmosphere of spy-mania.'[6]

In other words Gomułka's battle for vindication was still only half won. According to Ochab he had been wrongly arrested but rightly opposed. Ochab went on to amplify what he meant. Again he gave the impression that the last thing he foresaw was a return to power by Gomułka. He repeated the *ideological* attack on Gomułka, although he used the mild language of the September 1948 Party congress rather than the frightened, half-crazed invective of November 1949. The fight against Gomuł-ka's deviation, he said, was of great significance. It was during a vital moment for the Party, the socialist reconstruction of agriculture was under way, as was the plan to unify the Workers' and Socialist parties (the PPR and the PPS):

'To this Party line Gomułka opposed a nationalist view of the Polish workers' movement, stating that in the historical argument between the nationalist right wing of the PPS and the SDKPiL [later the Communist Party of Poland], the PPS view was the correct one. He represented a tendency to break with the revolutionary traditions of the KPP and rejected marxism-leninism as the ideological base of the new united party.'

Ochab was still accusing Gomułka of grave offences. To him the rejection of marxism-leninism was the ultimate ideological crime, and to lay it at Gomułka's door after all that had happened seemed to many a perpetuation of the original injustice. Until this accusation was withdrawn there could be no question of Gomułka's readmission to the Party. Considering the free-and-easy atmosphere of the time, Ochab's speech was remarkably conservative. He reminded his audience that Gomułka had 'resisted the policy to relieve poverty in the villages and to restrict *kulak* oppression'. He had quite rightly been politically isolated. He had refused to recant and his attitude had been generally 'anti-Party'. 'At the same time,' he said, 'it must be stated with full emphasis that the arrest of Gomułka in 1951, which took place in the atmosphere created by the Beria terror and the Rajk trial, was wrong and unjustified.'

The Party's recent investigations, he said, had led to Gomułka's rehabilitation from the charges made against him. He had been cleared of these charges and released (he did not say when). But this did not mean the fight against his 'false ideological concepts' was wrong. Still, as Ochab admitted, the rehabilitation process was by no means completed. Some forty or fifty former senior Party men had just been released, and thirty-six of them readmitted to the Party. The Party status of another twenty or so was still under consideration, he said. Perhaps Gomułka was one of these twenty. If so, Ochab seemed to be prejudging the ideological issue against him. Later in his speech he also announced the release of Marian Spychalski, whose case had been coupled with Gomułka's, but he still accused him of breaking Party regulations and 'deceiving' the Party leadership. It seemed he had already decided that however far the 'democratisation' process went, it would never go as far as an alliance, let alone a surrender, to Gomułka and his supporters. Throughout his career Ochab often played the part of middle-man, of 'sitter on the fence', and he must have judged in April 1956 that Gomułka, whom he was later to support so strenuously, would never be tolerated either by the bulk of the present Polish leadership or, more important, by the Soviet leadership whom Gomułka was popularly believed, by Pole and Russian alike, to have opposed. His 6 April speech sounded like an attempt to nip Gomułkaism in the bud, not through malice towards his wronged ex-comrade and comrade-to-be (Ochab still could not speak of Gomułka with the courtesy title 'comrade' before his name), but through sheer practical politics; he was unwilling to attempt the apparent impossible, to resume old quarrels and possibly to provoke unnecessary unpleasantness.

After all, Ochab's speech contained more than enough for his audience to swallow at one dose. It was not an easy or a pleasant moment for him, and it is surprising that his inconsistencies and moments of doubt were so few. Seldom has the leader of any country been forced into such an embarrassing position and made to address his people so abjectly: 'The truth about the mistakes of Joseph Stalin is a bitter fact for us communists to accept, for us who saw in him the ideal of revolutionary virtues. Not in our mouths but in our hearts were born the words of praise for Stalin we once uttered.'

Polish communists were being forced into a strange mixed

attitude of humility and defiance. Their comrades in Russia, being stronger and more firmly entrenched, were able to brazen out the extraordinary situation. Some even took a pride in it. Never, they would claim, has a ruling political group admitted its mistakes so readily and completely. Soviet communists offered their people the most cursory of apologies for the fact that for a quarter of a century they had allowed a man suffering from persecution mania and guilty of mass murder to rule their Party and their country. It was enough, they thought, to express their regret about the millions who were illegally deported to live and work in appalling conditions, about the hundreds of thousands who died. It was not thought necessary to punish all those responsible for the machinery of terror, those supporters and collaborators of Stalin who, if the principles by which Nazis were judged at the Nuremberg trials have any validity, must be held guilty with Stalin for all that happened. Very few indeed of these men, apart from the immediate entourage of Beria, were brought to account. Hardly ever was compensation paid to the victims, even to those publicly rehabilitated after years of torment. Nikita Khrushchev and the new Soviet leadership saw it as their duty to make the formal announcement of their 'mistakes' and to release those innocent prisoners who had managed to survive. Having done that, they felt they had the right to ask the Soviet people to carry on regardless, to continue working for the same marxist-leninist ideas which, until so recently, had produced such appalling abuses of justice. In their view the bad, the millions of victims, had been more than compensated for by the good, the economic and military achievements of the Soviet Union. The plan was for this gigantic 'destalinisation' issue to be mentioned briefly and then considered closed. Thereafter anyone who pursued it too deeply was to be dubbed a wrecker, a stirrer-up of trouble. Russian communists were to claim for themselves the credit for 'exposing' Stalin's excesses, as though before 1956 no one in the world had suspected there was anything wrong.

Polish communists did not dare claim for themselves any such credit. They had followed the Soviet lead in their destalinisation, even if they had carried the process further than their Soviet comrades after the original 'go-ahead'—the death of Stalin itself and the liquidation of the 'Beria clique'. They had not taken the initiative. After the mass deportations of

Poles into eastern Russia in 1939 and 1940, Stalin's homicidal mania had been common knowledge to every Pole except those few communists who preferred to hide their heads in the sand. So by no stretch of the imagination could communists claim to have 'discovered' Stalin's villainy. To make such a claim would be to expose themselves to ridicule as well as to onslaught from the rapidly increasing 'liberal' forces. In this, their hour of trial, Polish communists were as usual behaving with more realism and ordinary human understanding than their mystical, cut-off-from-the-world comrades in Russia. They apologised, and in their momentary loss of confidence they were allowing reformists, revisionists and plain anti-communists to speak their minds and attack them in the press.

It is not known exactly when Ochab and the other leaders first changed their minds about the political future of Gomułka and his supporters; probably it was quite soon after Ochab's 6 April speech. The speech had set in motion a process by which Gomułka was to have power thrust upon him. His release and innocence now declared, there was now no reason why Poles should not exploit the obvious similarity between the new Party 'democratisation' programme and Gomułka's original 'national unity' programme of 1945–47 which was suppressed by the Stalinist leadership in 1948. The issues which in the mid-1940s separated Gomułka from most of his comrades were still mentioned by Ochab on 6 April as his 'mistakes'. But his 'mistaken' opposition to collectivisation and insistence on internal independence from Russia were becoming the central issues of the time. The party line on them was day by day drawing closer and closer to the Gomułka line. Harnessed as they were to the runaway horse of liberalisation, it suddenly dawned on Poles, communist and non-communist alike, that they had a trump card. They had Gomułka. It really was a most amazing piece of luck.

By the end of April a bill had been published and put into effect amnestying almost all the thousands of people still serving terms of imprisonment on trumped-up charges of espionage, sabotage and the like. Stanisław Radkiewicz, the minister responsible for much of the injustice, was dismissed from his demoted position in the Ministry of State Farms. It was announced that two of the worst UB sadists, Roman Romkowski and Anatol Fejgin, were under arrest and would be charged with their crimes. On 7 May Jakub Berman also resigned; he had been the Politburo member in charge of security and, many thought, a more powerful man in Poland than his position would suggest. All through May the prisons poured men back into Polish life, as fast as their cases could be glanced at and their convictions seen as ludicrously unjust. By the beginning of June, 28,000 had been amnestied.*

About this time the first approaches were made to Gomułka. Each group wanted him for its own. The 'liberal' students and intelligentsia saw him as a victim of stalinism, a symbol of resistance against everything they were trying to root out. The ruling 'wait-and-see' group of Ochab, Cyrankiewicz, Zawadski and others now, a few days after Ochab had called him 'anti-Party', became converted to the view that Gomułka could not be dispensed with. His views were by now so close to those of the Party that he must logically be invited to rejoin it. Apart from this, even with Gomułka entirely inactive as he still was, his popularity in Poland was growing so fast that he could no longer be left outside the Party where his influence, once he began to be politically active, might become disastrously subversive. Inside the Party, on the other hand, he could become the basis for a new socialist unity that would embrace a far larger proportion of the Polish people than the Party had ever hitherto managed or hoped to impress.

In the beginning they underestimated Gomułka. They thought they could entice him back into the fold with the offer of a good job, a senior job, but not a dominating job. They had it in mind to make him party secretary of some large provincial area far from Warsaw. Later, according to the reports leaked from the secret talks, they upped the offer to a vice-premiership. Both these jobs would have loaded Gomułka down with work and effectively clipped his wings for any future struggle for power. Gomułka rejected these offers. He had at this stage one basic demand—the right to state his case in an open Party congress, to clear himself of the ideological charges against him which had been on record since September 1948, and which had so recently been repeated by Ochab. It was a demand which the Party leaders felt for a long time they could not accept. It was too great a risk. If he was to clear himself Gomułka would automatically have to present the Party with

* An article in *Time Magazine* (10 December 1956) claims that by that date 36,000 had been released from Polish prisons and 16,000 repatriated from detention in the Soviet Union.

207

his views on the problems of 1948, which were the problems of 1956. He would have to be allowed to present an alternative Party programme, to justify views and actions which in 1948 had been condemned. By doing this he would automatically offer himself for election to the post he had held for five years until 1948, that of First Secretary of the Party.

The 7th Plenum was due to open on 18 July. Attempts were made to bring the Party leaders and Gomułka to agreement so that he could be reinstated in the Party and attend the Plenum, but they failed. 'In spite of my wish,' he said later, 'I was not able to be present at it.'[7] He had also been invited by the Soviet leaders to spend a holiday in the Crimea, but he said no, Ciechocinek was good enough for him.

However, on 28 June the Party leaders again found themselves overtaken by events. On that day the most serious riots of post-war Poland took place in Poznań. Fifty people were killed, two of them UB officials. The causes of the riots were mainly economic, and the ringleaders were workers from the ZISPO factory. On 23 June they had sent a delegation to Warsaw to petition the government.[8] Due to a misunderstanding, their colleagues in Poznań got the impression the delegates had been arrested. They came out into the streets to press their demands, in full view of western journalists and businessmen there to cover the Poznań fair. They invaded a prison, released the inmates and wrecked a radio station which jammed western broadcasts. The police and the military turned out, shots were fired and people were killed. Police arrested 154 men.

On the Poznań riots there was an open difference of opinion between the Soviet and Polish leaderships. On 29 June Premier Cyrankiewicz denounced the rioters, as did a Soviet resolution on 30 June,[9] as inspired by an imperialist plot, American monopoly capital, Radio Free Europe and all the usual bogies. But after a few days of reflection their lines diverged. On 18 July, the first day of the 7th Plenum, Ochab admitted the riots were *not* an imperialist plot and that recently published figures claiming to show how the standard of living had risen were imaginary. From then on the official Polish line was that the rioters were largely justified in taking the action they did. Later he even had the humility to lay part of the blame on himself and his comrades: 'It is a fact that our leadership was unable to protect the country from the tragedy of Poznań, that we were all astounded when the tragedy took place. This means that our awareness of the actual situation, of actual moods in the country was insufficient and superficial.'

The economic basis for the rioters' demands can be illustrated by the following quotation from *Economic Bulletin for Europe*: 'To maintain a family on slightly more than bare subsistence standard needs an income of slightly more than 600 zloty a month per adult member. Two adults and two children need 1,800–2,000 zloty. 1956 statistics show that only 6·4 per cent of employees get 2,000 zloty per month.'[10]

The situation was never quite as bad as this quotation suggests. Most wives went out to work (and still do), and their families had *two* wage packets. And many workers received perks, both official and unofficial: subsidised produce, canteens and other facilities from their place of work. Even so, in 1956 the standard of living, especially in the cities, was alarmingly low, quite low enough to make working men take to the streets to demand their basic economic rights.

This fact was also realised by the judges appointed to try the rioters. Of 154 arrested men only thirty-seven were brought to trial on 8 October and only twenty-three were eventually sent to prison, for quite short terms. A few weeks later all these were released except three who had killed a UB man.

This was the unpromising background to the 7th Plenum, the course of which was complicated by the arrival of the Soviet leader Nikolai Bulganin. On 21 July he made a speech directly contradicting Ochab's conciliatory speech on Poznań three days earlier. In the present Polish situation Bulganin's language sounded old-fashioned and completely out of place. He called for 'a high level of political vigilance' and 'a decisive reinforcement of the organs of the dictatorship of the proletariat'. He attacked 'hostile and opportunist elements exploiting the struggle against the cult of the individual'. In the face of such silliness the best the Polish leaders could do was to pack Bulganin off on a tour of Poland, hope he would not make any more such speeches and themselves try to sort out the mess. But the Marshal's words did not bode well. They served to remind the Poles that direct Soviet intervention could not be ruled out as a simple, if terrible, solution to the impasse.

The 7th Plenum resolutions called for more decentralisation and material incentives in industrial production, for more democratisation and more power to be given to the Sejm, for an end to discrimination against former members of the 'London' Home Army (AK). The Gomułka affair was also discussed and all the charges of heresy made against him were retracted. At last the Party was able to agree upon a course of action. Until then they had been acting in the wake of events, giving way little by little to students, intellectuals and workers, to pressure from below. Now they resolved to take over the helm of democratisation, to race ahead of public opinion and initiate change from above. The key to the Party's success was to be the recruitment of Władysław Gomułka. If necessary he was to be given back the Party leadership he had relinquished eight years ago.

On 5 August there was a brief announcement in *Trybuna Ludu* that Gomułka was readmitted to the Party. His friend Zenon Kliszko was made vice-Minister of Justice. On 24 August a third ex-prisoner of the stalinist years, Wacław Komar, was appointed to the key job of commander of the Internal Security Corps (KWB). On 9 October another of Gomułka's enemies, Hilary Minc, the man who had attacked him so cruelly at the November 1949 Plenum, resigned from the Politburo and as first vice-Premier for Economic Affairs. The way was being cleared.

But there were still two important obstacles. There were Gomułka's enemies in the Polish leadership: Franciszek Mazur (a man of doubtful loyalty to the Polish cause, he was later sent by Gomułka to a diplomatic post in Prague), Zenon Nowak, Wiktor Klosiewicz (the trade-union leader), Franciszek Jóźwiak-Witold (who had been Gomułka's unwilling boss in NIK during 1949 and later wrote a book libelling him disgracefully) and of course Konstanty Rokossowski, the Soviet marshal who was still Polish Minister of Defence. They had become the 'Natolin Group', named after the country house near Warsaw where they used to meet, and they were determined that Gomułka should not dominate the Party. Their plan was to woo the workers with a massive, economically unjustifiable rise in wages, to suppress ruthlessly the truculent intellectuals who, after all, represented only a tiny minority of Poles, and to 'limit' the number of Jews in high places (an unfailing way to gain cheap popularity among the more primitive levels of the

Polish population). These measures would, they felt sure, nip
the revolution in the bud, would satisfy enough people to halt
the momentum of change. There would be a place in this
scheme of things for Gomułka too. They sent one of their
number, Ryszard Strzelecki, to negotiate with him. He could
join them, even at Politburo level, but his views would never
be allowed to dominate. He could be a string to their bow but
nothing more. They were also supported by Bolesław Piasecki,
leader of the anti-Vatican 'Catholic' religious, publishing and
commercial enterprise PAX. On 17 October, just after it was
announced that Gomułka and three of his supporters would
attend the Eighth Plenum due to open on 19 October, he
published in his weekly *Słowo Powszechne* a notorious article
called 'The Instinct of a Statesman' in which he implied that
force might have to be used to settle the crisis. He wrote that 'a
limit must be set to the process of democratisation', otherwise
order might have to be restored 'in conditions reassembling
those of civil war'. Sure enough, within a day a mysterious
coup was planned by the Natolin group. Several hundred
Gomułka supporters were to be arrested, but news of it leaked
out and for a night or two the men threatened did not sleep at
home. At the same time Soviet troops in western Russia moved
towards Poland, while those already in Poland at Legnica and
other large bases near the German border, fortunately some
way from the capital, began to move eastwards. In the Kremlin
there was a 'hawks and doves' situation. The leadership was un-
decided whether or not to invade. Nikita Khrushchev, always
a man of action, saw there was only one way they could make
up their minds, and that was by flying to Warsaw on the day
the Plenum was to open and by settling the matter with the
Poles face to face and, if necessary, army to army.

XIV: OCTOBER

The Polish October, one of the most dramatic political events of this century, is less understood and recorded than it deserves to be. True, it made world headlines for a few days, but after that it was overshadowed by two events more sensational and violent, though perhaps less important in the long term: the Soviet invasion of Hungary and the Anglo-French-Israeli invasion of Egypt. They were two outbursts so shocking that few people realised than in all likelihood Poland was the trigger for them both. If there had been no disturbances in Poland 'Hungary' would not have happened when and how it did. And it may well be that Soviet involvement in Hungary dictated the timing of 'Suez'.

But in mid-October 1956, Poland was the world attraction. An announcement on 17 October that Imre Nagy had been readmitted to the Hungarian Communist Party merited only a small newspaper paragraph. The place where things were happening was Poland. The Central Committee of the Polish communist party was to meet on 19 October for its Eighth Plenum. The communist leaders were resolved, all but a few of them, that Władysław Gomułka would be elected First Secretary and that his political line would in future guide the Party and the Polish state. The general line of the Plenum was thus laid down in advance. The question was, would the Polish communists be allowed to carry out the daring and unusual plan of electing as their leader someone whom a few years earlier they had branded as a traitor and as an imperialist agent.

The night of 18–19 October was one of fear and excitement. As Jan Kott wrote of it a week later: 'It became clear during that feverish night that the real master of the country and Warsaw was the revolutionary working class, that youth had rediscovered a language in common with the workers. . . . The workers of Warsaw mounted guard. They were convinced their voice would be heard in the Central Committee Plenum, and their voice was heard. . . .'[1]

The workers of Warsaw were not the only ones whose voices were heard on 19 October. Early that morning a Soviet airliner appeared over Warsaw and radioed for permission to land. The request took the Poles quite by surprise. The airliner had to circle Warsaw for some time before at last being allowed to land at a small military airport. But the real surprise came when the aeroplane's passengers were revealed. They were Khrushchev, Molotov, Mikoyan, Kaganovich, Marshal Koniev and a dozen other Soviet military and political figures.

Edward Ochab, First Secretary of the communist party, told the assembled Eighth Plenum of this strange visitation in a brief opening speech. He proposed and had carried a motion coopting four new members on to the Central Committee: Gomułka, Zenon Kliszko, Marian Spychalski and Ignacy Loga-Sowiński. He told the assembly that the Soviet visitors 'desired to carry out talks with the Politburo of our Party', and suggested the Plenum adjourn until that evening. The members were restive. 'Why should we have to postpone our discussions until this evening,' one of them asked Ochab. His reply was coolness itself: 'Because of the need to carry out discussions with the Presidium of the Soviet Communist Party which is at present in Warsaw.' One could hardly quarrel with that, especially in the face of such Soviet might, both military and political.

At 11.20 that morning radio programmes were interrupted by a news flash about the co-opting of Gomułka and his three supporters on to the Central Committee. The announcement was repeated every few minutes. Meanwhile the Polish Politburo, plus Gomułka, were on their way to the Belvedere, the residence of the Polish President, to discuss the future of Poland.

Only part of what took place at the talks is on record, the rest is rumour and repeated gossip. But although Poles were in a state of tension, or even fear, they still enjoyed a freedom, unprecedented either before or since in the postwar years, to tell everything they knew or heard to their friends from the West, including western journalists. There are many accounts in print of the twenty-four hours the Russians spent in Warsaw. Doubtless some of them are embellished and over-dramatised because of the genuine drama of the occasion, but they coincide often in such detail that they are probably true in basis.

Khrushchev was behaving with his well-known boorish bluster, shouting at the Poles, accusing them of treachery and of selling their country to American imperialism. He studiously ignored Gomułka who, having as yet no position in the Polish hierarchy, was on the fringe of the group. 'Who is that man?' Khrushchev asked his ambassador Ponomarenko, pointing to Gomułka. 'I am Gomułka,' the man replied, 'and because of you I have just spent three years in prison.' Khrushchev was hardly pleased, especially when Ochab told him this was the man the Poles were proposing to make First Secretary of their Party.

There are on record two restrained official accounts of the discussions. One was told by Gomułka to a private meeting with leading Polish journalists on 29 October.[2] Gomułka said that, in the Russians' view, 'the preparations and changes connected with the Eighth Plenum would lead to a breach of the Warsaw Pact, would lead to a break-off of Soviet-Polish relations'. This extreme Soviet attitude was confirmed, though in less specific terms, by Aleksander Zawadski in his speech to the Eighth Plenum a few hours after the Russians had departed. The Russians had been, he said, deeply disturbed at the way the situation in Poland had developed, at the anti-Soviet propaganda to be found in the Polish press and at the way Polish communists had failed to react against such propaganda. They had brought with them a list of quotations from the Polish press to prove their point.

As the 1968 events in Czechoslovakia have confirmed, Soviet leaders cannot tolerate being criticised by their allies. They are amazingly sensitive to what foreign communists write in their press. While the talks were going on in Warsaw, Moscow *Pravda* was preparing a vituperative piece called 'Anti-socialist articles in the Polish press' which appeared on 20 October. *Pravda* accused the Polish press in general of 'publicly insulting Marx and Lenin' under the pretence of unmasking remnants of the personality cult of Stalin. Two well-known Polish writers, Jerzy Putrament and Zbigniew Florczak were mentioned by name.

Florczak had written: 'Let us get rid of the jargon the communist camp uses in its conversation with the masses. We must put an end to slogans like "Workers of the world, unite", "reactionary", "building socialism". These were battle cries, slogans of armed revolution.'

Jerzy Putrament, a leading novelist and journalist, was supposed to have written that 'our economic system has failed once and for all' and blamed 'the dictatorship of Gosplan' (the organisation that plans the Soviet economy). For this *Pravda* labelled him an 'ignorant scribe' who 'takes his arsenal from the Voice of America'.

It was the Soviet leaders' case that such journalistic heresy was proof of incipient counter-revolution. They complained it was so unfriendly to Russia that it would not be permitted even in some capitalist countries, for example in Finland. Zawadski went on to explain that the Soviet comrades 'were also interested in the construction of our new leadership, to be brought about by the Central Committee's Eighth Plenum. They pointed to the fact that the proposed leadership is now generally known, but that we gave the Soviet comrades no information about it, in spite of the relationship between us.'[3]

In fact throughout much of 19 October it looked as if the Soviet leaders intended to prevent Gomułka's election. It is known there were strong Soviet forces gathered on the Polish borders with East Germany and the Soviet Union, ready to attack if need be. At the same time Soviet units inside Poland were moving from their bases, mostly in the south-west corner of the country, towards Warsaw. Some were already in the outskirts of the capital at Bielany, Łomianki and Jabłonna. Others were stopped on the main road from Poznań by Polish units of the KBW (the 'Internal Security Corps') commanded by the newly appointed Wacław Komar, a former victim of the Stalinist excesses. Members of the Polish air force were constantly aloft reporting on the movement of Soviet troops. Throughout the discussions both delegations were receiving information from their military men, and according to them they would vary the toughness of the line they could adopt. Workers from Warsaw factories (especially the Żerań car works) were being armed and deployed, ready to defend the capital. Of course, Gomułka can have had no illusion about the Poles' ability to defeat the Soviet Army. Poland was as usual in her moments of crisis surrounded, outnumbered and undefendable. But he did know the Russians would think twice before starting what would have amounted to a war against Poland. They knew from experience how Poles can fight even, or perhaps especially, when their cause is hopeless, and how they can inflict great damage on their final conquerors.

Some time during the night of 19–20 October there was a turning point after which the Russians stopped bullying and started to seek an accommodation with the Poles. Reports vary as to what caused the *volte face*. Some say it was a telephone call from Chou En-lai, promising the support of communist China. Kiriluk, the Polish Ambassador in Peking, spent that night closeted with the Chinese leaders and is believed to have persuaded them to intervene. Others say Gomułka threatened to address the Polish people on the radio, tell them what was going on and call on them to fight the Soviet forces. It is this version which sounds the more plausible. It is known that Polish Radio was told to be ready to lay on a broadcast from Gomułka on the night of 19 October, and one can well imagine what the result of such a broadcast would have been. The Soviet leaders would clearly have hated the prospect of a spontaneous outburst of Polish fury and violence, especially while they were themselves in the Polish capital.

In the early hours of 20 October Poles and Russians managed to work out a basis for agreement. The Poles were able to persuade the Soviet leaders that the return of Gomułka would strengthen, not weaken, Polish socialism. (How right they were no one, Pole or Russian, could possibly have guessed.) They reassured the Russians that there would be no more anti-Sovietism in the press and no question of calling for the withdrawal of Soviet troops from Polish soil. In return the Soviets promised them internal independence and to consider the question of financial compensation for the way they had exploited the Polish economy under Stalinism. Gomułka had won, at least for the moment.

At about seven o'clock that morning the Soviet delegation departed. At eleven o'clock the Eighth Plenum reassembled in the hall of the Council of State in Aleje Ujazdowskie and Aleksander Zawadski gave his short account of the all-night meeting. Then it was Gomułka's turn to speak, not only to the hundred or so Central Committee members who were in the hall, but also to millions of Poles. The speech was being broadcast live from the hall.[4] 'When seven years ago,' Gomułka began, 'I addressed the communist party's Central Committee at the November Plenum, I thought it must be for the last time.' It was like a voice from the dead, hardly believable to the listeners anxiously gathered round their radio sets who knew little of the dramatic goings-on of the past twenty-four hours. The whole country was full of rumour. Students from the Warsaw Polytechnic, factory workers and countless other volunteers were deployed about the capital ready to deal with the Soviet tanks which still lurked outside. Gomułka's speech was wonderfully reassuring, both in its content and in the fact that it was taking place at all. Only a few hours earlier the Soviet leaders had taken an interim decision not to invade Poland. As far as most Poles knew, the man on whom they were relying might be under arrest, dead, or simply pushed aside back into political oblivion. But no, there he was addressing the Polish nation and clearly at its head.

Gomułka's speech, about 12,000 words long, raised almost all the difficult issues of Polish politics and provided a satisfactory answer to many of them. On the vital agricultural issue he picked his argument up exactly where he had left it in 1948, quoting to the delegates figures to show how the partial collectivisation of recent years had damaged Polish farm production. The facts were devastating and conclusive:

'If we calculate the value of total production per hectare of agricultural land, we obtain the following picture. Individual farms produce 621·1 złotys, collective farms 517·3 złotys and state farms 393·7 złotys, at constant prices. The difference between individual and collective farms is therefore 16·7 per cent, while individual farms produce 37·2 per cent more than state farms.'

Gomułka made it clear that collectivisation must stop, and even be reversed. This in itself was enough to make him a hero to the vast mass of Polish peasants who had spent the stalinist years struggling to hang on to their own pieces of land in fear of the same thing happening to them as happened to the Soviet peasants in the 1930s.

The gist of Gomułka's message was contained in a series of paragraphs entitled 'The lessons of Poznań'. He said:

'Recently the working class gave a painful lesson to the party leadership and government. The workers of Poznań made use of the strike weapon and came out into the street to demonstrate on that black Thursday in June, calling out in a loud voice, 'Enough! We cannot go on like this! Turn aside from the false road!' . . . The workers of Poznań were not protesting against People's Poland, against socialism, when they came out into their city streets. They were protesting against the evil that has become so widespread in our social system and which touched them so painfully, against distortions of the basic rules of socialism, which is their ideal. . . .

'The clumsy attempt to present the painful Poznań tragedy as the work of imperialist agents and *agents provocateurs* was politically very naïve.'

Gomułka resisted the temptation that was gripping some of his comrades, and did not promise any great immediate rises in workers' incomes. Wage increases would come, he told his audience, only with increases in production. But he did promise a system of incentives which would involve the worker more closely in the profits of his particular enterprise. There would be workers' self-government and self-management. Compulsory deliveries of farm produce would be reduced but not abolished, he told peasants. The deliveries were a form of taxation and, after all, every country has its taxation.

'Our relations with the Soviet Union and its Communist Party' was the next heading—a more sensitive subject where the keen listener could detect a certain dichotomy in Gomułka's thought. On the one hand, he said, 'The Soviet Union was the first state in the world where the socialist revolution triumphed. For the first time in history Lenin and the Bolshevik party assumed the gigantic task of turning the theory of socialism into material and social reality.'

It was impossible for such a communist as Gomułka not to say how he admired the way the Soviet Union had embarked on its great experiment. On the other hand this did not mean the Soviet way was the only way. Again, there was this strange resurrection of what Gomułka had said ten years ago, the political ideas he had canvassed as a tactical measure in his fight against Mikołajczyk and the non-communist opposition. These ideas had for the past eight years been suppressed, but now they were reappearing. People heard Gomułka's words in 1956, realised they were identical to those he had used in 1946 and so assumed they were no longer a tactic. Gomułka had suffered for these opinions, and had emerged out of his suffering still sticking to them. The obvious conclusion was that they were honestly held, that Gomułka could this time be relied upon to live up to the promises he made. 'There can be different types of socialism,' he said. 'It can be the socialism that was created in the Soviet Union, or it can be formed as we see it now in Yugoslavia, or it can be of some other type still. Only by experience and by studying the achievements of the different countries that are building socialism can the best model arise in given circumstances.' Gomułka thus gave Poles the impression that, if he was allowed to rule Poland as he wished, he would create a socialist system different in many respects from that of the Soviet Union, which Poles almost universally disliked.

This impression was confirmed when Gomułka came to discuss the 'cult of personality', the jargon term for stalinism and stalinist excess. It was this system that Poles were trying to get rid of and Gomułka, as one of its victims, was expected to be virulent in his denunciation of it. He did not disappoint his audience:

'The bearer of the personality cult [Stalin] was knowledge-able about everything, knew how to do everything, arranged everything, directed everything and decided about everything in the sphere of his activity. He was the wisest of men, irrespective of what knowledge, what capabilities and what virtues he personally possessed. . . .

'The personality cult system moulded human brains, moulded the thought processes of Party activists and Party members. . . . We have finished with this system, we shall finish with it once and for all.'

He went on to say that although the personality cult arose in the Soviet Union, the blame for it must not be laid entirely at the door of Stalin, the Soviet Union or its communist party. The Poles too had their own police terror. There were elements in the Polish recent past that demanded investigation and, if necessary, eradication. 'The Party must always take care to protect its good name', he said. 'If anyone has knowingly shamed or besmirched its good name, there can be no place for such a person in its ranks.' He promised a commission to investigate those who knowingly charged and convicted men of crimes they did not commit.

At the same time he warned Poles that no one would be allowed to make use of the democratisation process against the state or the socialist system:

'At the head of the democratisation process stands our Party, and our Party alone. . . . We must give a decisive rebuff to all voices and whispers that aim at weakening our friendship with the Soviet Union. . . . If anyone imagines he will be able to sow moods of anti-Sovietism in Poland, he is making a deep mistake. We shall not allow harm to come to the vital interests of the Polish state and of the building of socialism in Poland.'

It was a magnificent speech, a truly revolutionary document which caught the Polish imagination. For eight years Gomułka had been legendary, half-dead figure, seen by many Poles as a vague hope of better things which might perhaps come to pass. But his 20 October speech turned hope into the promise of reality and a legendary figure into a live, powerful hero. Seldom has a ruler been more popular in his own country than Gomułka was in 1956.

There were two more days of speeches, all of them more or less in favour of the Gomułka line. Former anti-Gomułka men like Hilary Minc and Jakub Berman uttered self-criticisms and offered resignations, but some of the other stalinists spoke sullenly and half-heartedly, anxious to jump on the Gomułka band-wagon before it was too late, but on the defence nevertheless. Kazimierz Mijal was openly defiant. Still, after the talks with the Russians Gomułka's election as First Secretary was a foregone conclusion. He was proposed by the Politburo and elected unanimously.

A more difficult decision was whether or not Konstanty Rokossowski, the Minister of Defence imported in 1949 from the Soviet Union, would be included in the new nine-man Politburo. Many of the more conservative Poles claimed his election was essential, otherwise the Soviets would feel insulted and the Polish people would see his exclusion as an anti-Soviet action. But things had gone too far for Rokossowski to be kept. 'It is well known to all,' he had said in his speech on 20 October, 'that the life of the country is continuing along its normal course.' It was a ludicrous remark in the circumstances, and after it the delegates were disinclined to believe him when he claimed to have known nothing about the anti-Gomułka coup of two days ago. Although himself by no means a conventional Stalinist (he suffered in the 'repressions' of the late 1930s and and had been assigned to Warsaw in 1949 as a sort of honourable exile), he had become a symbol of Russian oppression in the minds of Poles. Therefore he had to go. His supporters were able to secure his nomination to the Politburo, but they could not stop him coming bottom of the ballot with only 23 votes out of a possible 75. He was tenth out of ten, and since the Politburo was to be a nine-man body, he was not elected.

After the result was announced Gomułka was at pains to reassure the more Soviet-minded delegates. The voting in no way represented a lack of confidence in Rokossowski, he told them. Many of Gomułka's supporters in the full flush of victory felt that he need not have pacified his conservative opponents so blatantly. A few days later, though, they were to realise that his remarks were an act of moderation and magnanimity that paid great dividends, and perhaps prevented Poland from falling once again into danger.

The three-day Plenum was an undreamt-of triumph for Gomułka. Although only one of his 'fellow-martyrs' of the Stalinist years, Ignacy Loga-Sowiński, was elected to the Politburo with him, he now enjoyed the support of a good majority of its members. Ochab, Cyrankiewicz, Morawski, Rapacki and Zawadski were now committed Gomułka men, and were to remain so for many years. Great was the rejoicing throughout Poland on the evening of 21 October, when it was realised how fully Gomułka had won. The Party newspaper *Trybuna Ludu* even dared to take Moscow's *Pravda* to task for its abusive article, accusing it of using 'language that cannot be used in honest discussion within the Party' and referring to the 'understandable anger of honest patriots and the broad masses of the Polish working people'. Freedom was heady stuff, and the Poles probably did not realise how close they were to being carried away into disaster.

The hours of euphoria were few. On 23 October, two days after Gomułka's return to power, there were mass demonstrations in the streets of Budapest in sympathy with the Poles. Hungarian students laid flowers on the grave of Józef Bem, the Polish general who fought with Kossuth in the 1848–49 Hungarian Revolution. By 24 October the uprising now known as 'Hungary' was in full swing. Imre Nagy, readmitted to the communist party only a week before, was appointed Prime Minister. It was this day on which it fell to Gomułka's lot to address a mass meeting in Warsaw's huge Plac Defilad, in front of the 'Palace of Culture', stalinist Russia's monstrous gift to the Polish people. His audience numbered between 300,000 and 400,000, and at times it was touch and go whether or not he would keep the crowd under control. True, much of what he said was grist to the crowd's mill. For example:

'During the past years much evil, injustice and painful disappointment have been our lot. The ideas of socialism, steeped in the spirit of human freedom and respect for citizen's rights, have in practice been deeply stained and distorted. . . . I believe deeply that these years have moved into the irrevocable past. . . . Only by moving consistently along the road of democratisation and by tearing up by the roots all the evil of the past period shall we come to construct a model of socialism that best suits the needs of our people. . . . Our recent meeting with a delegation of the Soviet Communist Party enabled our Soviet comrades to become better orientated on the political situation in Poland. . . . It depends only upon us whether and for how long Soviet specialists and military advisers are essential in our armed forces.'[5]

Remarks like these were greeted with prolonged, ear-shattering applause. It was a scene unprecedented in recent Polish history either before or since—the hero in the midst of his admirers. Gomułka was on the crest of the wave. In that moment he reached such a height that, even if he were to fall immediately afterwards, his place in history was assured.

Such enthusiasm did he arouse that he was able to make his audience swallow the occasional bitter pill as well as all the jam. There was a definite lull in the applause as he told them that Soviet troops were to remain stationed on Polish soil, a necessity that was 'directly connected with the presence of Soviet forces in the German Democratic Republic'. He went on: 'So long as there remain bases of the Atlantic Pact in West Germany, so long as there is a new Wehrmacht arming itself there, setting its chauvinism and revanchism against our frontiers, the presence of the Soviet Army in Germany is in accordance with our highest state interests.'

It was the germ of an argument that was in future years to justify much of Gomułka's policy and action. The fact was that the integrity of the Polish state was still, in theory, threatened by West German claims to Pomerania, Silesia and East Prussia—areas which had only since the war formed part of Poland. The Polish frontiers were still not recognised by the United States or Great Britain. It seemed to Gomułka and, even in 1956, to many millions of other Poles that this represented a hostile attitude. What could be worse than to deny a country her territorial integrity? It was as if NATO still hoped to be able to justify a future invasion of Poland. Therefore the Americans, the British and especially the West Germans still had to be regarded as the enemies of Poland.

The great crowd of almost half-a-million broke away from Warsaw's Plac Defilad. Most of them went home. Gomułka had concluded his oration with the appeal: 'Enough demonstrations and debating! It is time to return to everyday work. . . .' Most of the audience were prepared to obey him. Some, though, surged along Marszałkowska Street towards the Soviet Embassy. Their spirits were aroused and they wanted to vent their spleen on something, if only on the twenty-foot high wall that surrounds the great building at the bottom of Ujazdowskie. But Warsaw was slowly returning to order and normality. A fleet of cars drew across the road, almost blocking it, and a number of Party activists jumped out. They managed to divert the crowd as much by argument and appeals to reason and moderation as by physical pressure.

The Poles, both communist and non-communist, were thrilled at the news of the Hungarian uprising and supported it by any means they could. Collection boxes were placed in the streets of Polish towns, quite unguarded, and passers-by put money in them to provide food and medical supplies for Hungary, which were flown there by aeroplane on 29 October. Other Polish supplies for Hungary were dispatched by train, only to be refused transit across Czechoslovakia by the government of Antonin Novotny. A few train loads were actually escorted across Czechoslovakia by the forcible efforts of Polish paratroop units—an admirable, though shockingly illegal measure that damaged Polish-Czech relations for some time to come. It was incidents like these that gave rise to the oft-quoted saying about October 1956 that 'the Hungarians behaved like Poles, the Poles like Czechs, and the Czechs behaved like the swine they are'. It was a vicious, partly-justified gibe that was to sound very out-of-place twelve years later when the situations of the three countries were entirely reversed.

On 28 October Gomułka and Cyrankiewicz sent a message of support to Imre Nagy and Janos Kadar, First Secretary of the Hungarian Communist Party. It began 'Hungarian brethren! Cease from shedding the blood of your brothers', and went on to support Nagy and his movement unequivocally.

'We know the programme of the Hungarian Government of National Unity, a programme of socialist democracy, of better living standards, of creating workers' councils with full national sovereignty, *of withdrawal of Soviet troops from Hungary* [author's italics] and a friendship with the Soviet Union based on the Leninist principles of equality.

'We are far from wishing to interfere in your internal affairs, but we think that this programme follows the interest of the Hungarian people and of the whole camp of peace. . . . You and we are on the same side. . . .'[6]

On the same day, 28 October, an article appeared in the Yugoslav Party daily *Borba* under the title 'A strengthening of socialism in Poland' identifying Tito and the Yugoslav Party with the new socialist democracy, which seemed to be tearing the Soviet empire apart. In Poland, also on 28 October, two leading communists were sent to the monastery where the Primate, Cardinal Wyszyński, had been kept in detention since 1953. They brought him back to Warsaw in triumph. It was an exciting day for east Europe, and a terrifying one for the Kremlin.

The next day, 29 October, Gomułka addressed members of the Polish press, men who had been in great part responsible for bringing him to power eight days earlier. While he left them still hopeful that the new, liberal attitude to journalism would be allowed to continue, he sounded notes of warning and appeals to self-discipline. It was the day that Soviet troops were preparing to leave Budapest. Nagy seemed to have won but Gomułka was cautious in his reference to the Hungarian situation. 'The Hungarians,' he said, 'are in a different geographical situation, and quite simply live under different conditions. The interests of our state dictate to us other necessities and other methods of behaviour.' It never occurred to Gomułka to copy the policies of Imre Nagy, even when he approved of them for Hungary and it looked as though Nagy was going to win. Furthermore, while Gomułka was speaking, the Israeli army was beginning its attack upon Egypt.

Soviet troops were actually moving out of Budapest and towards the Soviet frontier when, at 4.30 on the afternoon of 30 October, the British Prime Minister Anthony Eden stood up in the House of Commons to announce an ultimatum to Egypt and Israel. Unless the warring armies desisted immediately, he said, the British and French armed forces might move into the area to 'protect' and 'police' the canal. It was an announcement that baffled almost everyone who heard it. In east Europe it seemed strangely unimportant and irrelevant, and received scant attention in the press. But the next day, unbelievably, the British and French air forces were bombing Egyptian airfields. By then the Soviet leaders may have been forgiven for thinking that not only their 'empire' of socialist countries was slipping away from them. Their power and influence over world affairs was being ignored and spurned, first by the Poles, then by the Hungarians, and now by the British, French and Israelis. The Russian bear was being baited, and in such circumstances he is liable to react violently.

It would appear that before the Anglo-French attack the Moscow 'doves' held the upper hand and the Kremlin leaders were resolved on taking a soft line over Hungary. There is evidence for this in the withdrawal of Soviet troops from Hungary that was taking place during the last days of October. Still, this could have been a ruse to lull the Hungarians and world opinion into a sense of false security. The real evidence is a statement the Soviet government issued on 30 October, the actual day of Eden's ultimatum, which was as reasonable and moderate as one could possibly wish. Relations between the Soviet Union and the other socialist countries would, it said, be built in future 'only on the basis of full equality, territorial integrity, independence and sovereignty and non-interference in internal affairs'. It admitted that in the past there had been a number of 'difficulties, unfulfilled tasks and pure mistakes . . . that violated the principle of equality in relations between socialist states'. The statement went on:

'Because any further stay of Soviet armed detachments in Hungary may lead to an even tenser situation, the Soviet government has ordered its military leadership to withdraw Soviet armed detachments from Budapest for as long as the Hungarian government thinks fit.

'At the same time the Soviet government expresses its readiness to enter into appropriate discussions with the government of the Hungarian People's Republic, as well as with the other signatories to the Warsaw treaty, on the question of whether Soviet troops should remain on Hungarian territory.'[7]

As we now know, a day or two after issuing this statement, the Soviet government went back on it and sent its armies to crush Hungary. Was it mere coincidence that the change of mind in the Kremlin took place just after the Anglo-French attack? Would the Soviet army have moved back into Hungary if the British and French armies had not moved into Egypt? It is hard to believe the two events were not connected. Alternatively, did the Soviet involvement in Hungary and Poland select the timing for the Suez invasion in the first place? These secrets, like so many, are locked away in government files to which few have access, and those few who are in the know are silent as the grave. What is undeniable is that many Hungarians believe that the Anglo-French invasion is one of the reasons why their country is not free today. And there are many Poles who think the same invasion put in jeopardy their newly-won, if temporary, freedom under Władysław Gomułka.

By 2 November British and French bombs had already destroyed the Egyptian air force. But the question of Hungary was still not resolved. It was on this day that Imre Nagy renounced the Warsaw Pact, the action believed to be the main reason why the Soviets intervened. But on 2 November Gomułka and the Polish leadership were still, both privately and publicly, on the side of Nagy. The Polish communist party's Central Committee, which Gomułka now led, issued a further appeal to its Hungarian comrades referring to 'the tragic consequences of the policies of the former Hungarian leadership which, instead of obeying the will of the majority, called in Soviet forces'. The defence of people's power, it said, 'can be maintained by the internal forces of the Hungarian people . . . and not by intervention from without'. This was to be the last time Gomułka and his men came out in favour of the Nagy leadership. After 2 November Nagy's policies, the rejection of the Warsaw pact and the establishment of a coalition government, became unacceptable even to Gomułka.

At dawn on 4 November the Soviet Army attacked Budapest in great strength and it was suddenly clear that the Hungarian experiment had failed. Gomułka wasted no time in publicly dissociating himself from Nagy, although not in terms that indicated that he approved of the Soviet invasion. In a speech on 4 November to the Party *actif* he promised that in future the government and the Party would tell the people the truth. He added: 'We must speak the truth today also, so that Poland may never stand in the situation in which Hungary stands.' It was perhaps only on this day that Poles actually realised what a hair's-breadth escape they had had from war, massacre and subjection.

In Poland 4 November (a Sunday) was remarkable for Cardinal Wyszyński's first sermon after his release from detention. His words, pronounced while Hungarians were actually fighting and dying in their battles with the Russian tanks, seemed singularly apt. 'Poles know how to die magnificently,' Wyszyński told his congregation. 'But, beloved, Poles need to know how to work magnificently. A man dies but once and is quickly covered in glory. But he gives long years in trouble, hardship, pain and suffering. This is a greater heroism.'[8]

They were strange words to hear from the lips of a Polish leader (for such the Polish primate always was and is). For centuries Poles had prided themselves on making the grand gesture in the face of foreign oppression. The Kościuszko Uprising of 1794, the November Uprising of 1830 and the January Uprising of 1863 had been glorious, if finally futile, attempts to overthrow the rule of Tsarist Russia. It was a tradition that was continued into recent history with the vain, valiant attempts to ward off the Germans in September 1939 and especially during the Warsaw Uprising (August 1944). Now in 1956 it stuck in the throats of many Poles to remain idle while the Hungarians, many of whom had supported the Poles during the 1944 Uprising, bore the brunt of the age-old anti-Russian battle. It was a measure of Gomułka's sudden influence and the trust he had instilled into Poles that even the hotheads among them kept themselves under control. Later on there was the occasional anti-Soviet outburst, such as the 10 December attack on the Soviet consulate in Szczecin, but it was not enough to provoke a 'Hungarian' solution. During November 1956 many Poles, while sympathetic and shocked at what had happened in Hungary, were congratulating themselves on their *raison d'état*, their good sense and uncharacteristic moderation.

The next day, 5 November, Imre Nagy was overthrown and taken into an arrest from which he never emerged. At the same time British and French forces were landing at Port Said, still doggedly pursuing their half-hearted, sad attempt to topple President Nasser. It was a miserable day for the world. Only in Poland did there seem that some scrap of brightness survived. It seemed to the world, even to the Poles, that in Poland justice had come out on top—in the shape of Władysław Gomułka.

XV: POWER

It is all very well being carried shoulder high to power by the mob. Eighty per cent popular support is an ideal few national leaders have been able to achieve this century. Winston Churchill (Great Britain, 1940), Władysław Gomułka (Poland, October 1956), Imre Nagy (Hungary, 1–4 November 1956) and Alexander Dubček (Czechoslovakia, 1968) managed the ideal, but very few others. None of these attained his popularity by natural electoral means. It depended on an atmosphere of crisis and on the build-up of a myth around a certain man. It is heady stuff, being ruled by a hero, especially one who has suffered for his political beliefs. It is easy to make such a man into something more than human, especially if his move from obscurity to leadership has been sudden and accompanied by the threat of violence.

But once the threat is removed, the idol is killed, or the moment of glory is past, the myth collapses and the demigod becomes human again. Normal 'anti-boss' resentments, suppressed only rarely in moments of patriotism and stress, are quick to reassert themselves and can destroy effortlessly what has been built up over a lifetime. The higher they rise the farther they fall—in politics, more than in any other profession except sport.

On 24 October 1956 Władysław Gomułka had ruled Poland for three days (from 1945 to 1948 he had been only one of many rulers), and he was on the crest of the wave. But though his support among the Polish people was vast, his power in the Polish government was still open to question. He had been in office a mere ten days when the Soviet Army in Budapest demonstrated to him how easily his power and his life could be taken away from him if a group of people in Moscow so decided. For some years he was not his own master, having the difficult task of trying to satisfy both his creators (the Polish people) and his potential dethroners (the Soviet leaders).

The days that followed 'Hungary' were anxious ones for the Poles. It seemed logical that, having crushed Nazism, Moscow might complete the job they had begun so ruthlessly and crush Gomułkaism. These fears were partly dispelled when, on 14 November, a group of Soviet military advisers to the Polish army were awarded Polish decorations and departed quietly home. Their leader, Marshal Rokossowski, who had spent the last fortnight 'on leave', went with them.

One of Gomułka's closest friends, Marian Spychalski, had already been appointed his deputy instead of the 'hard-liner' Witaszewski, and he was quickly appointed Minister in Rokossowski's place—a post he held until 1968 when he became President of Poland.

Great effort was made to minimise the scandal caused by the Russian Marshal's hasty departure. All available formal Polish honours were heaped upon him. He was given a 'government certificate'[1] listing the great services he had rendered the Polish state and a letter signed by Gomułka, Cyrankiewicz and Zawadski expressing 'our appreciation and thanks for your devoted work in the post of Minister of National Defence'. On 19 November *Pravda* announced that he had been relieved of the Polish post 'at his own request' and appointed a Soviet Deputy-Minister of Defence.

A Polish delegation left for the Soviet Union, also on 14 November, including Gomułka, Cyrankiewicz and Zawadski. After four days they were able to announce complete agreement on the future of Polish-Soviet relations: mutual friendship, continued military alliance and Soviet military presence in Poland, but complete internal Polish sovereignty and the payment of financial compensation for the way Poland had been exploited in the past.* On 18 November a great crowd gathered at Terespol on the Polish-Soviet frontier to welcome back the train containing Gomułka and the other delegates. At Warsaw's Dworzec Główny (Main Railway Station) Gomułka made a short speech. 'Comrades and citizens!' he said, 'the discrepancy between words and deeds which occurred frequently in Polish-Soviet relations in the past, has now been liquidated.' Poles were relieved to see their new leader back home, there being precedents for communist

---

* Polish-Soviet trade during the years of Stalin is now described by Poles, jokingly but ruefully, thus: 'The agreement was we send them our corn and they take our coal'.

leaders not returning from difficult 'consultations' with their Soviet counterparts.

The success of the talks was another early feather in Gomułka's cap. He could point to the agreement, which was quite favourable to Poland, and let his countrymen see that only a Polish *communist* government was capable of achieving it. 'Who did this thing?' he asked a meeting of local party secretaries on 29 November. 'We did it! No one else. We did it!' More and more non-communists were supporting Gomułka as the only possible, reasonable leader. And he needed the help of such men. To maintain his unnatural great popularity was hardly possible. 'Hungary', a world tragedy such as occurs perhaps once in a decade, took place during his first month in office. Since he disapproved of the 'reactionary' line taken by Imre Nagy two days before his destruction, Gomułka was unable to dissociate himself publicly from the Soviet Army's punitive action. But he could not approve it either.

Leading Polish communists, like almost all Poles, detested what the Soviets had done. This is clear from an account of the period written by the British Labour Member of Parliament Konni Zilliacus, who was invited to Poland immediately after the Gomułka takeover, exonerated of the charges made against him in the Stalinist trials and fêted by the new Polish 'democratic' socialist leadership.[2] Zilliacus tells how his Polish hosts felt strongly about the Soviet assault, that it was the worst thing that could have happened. 'Soviet intervention is a dishonour to communism everywhere,' they told him. Clearly this was Gomułka's personal view also. On 21 November the Polish delegation to the United Nations abstained on a motion asking the Hungarian government to admit UN observers to their territory. It was one of very few occasions when the Soviet bloc has failed to vote together as a single body, and an early superficial sign that Gomułka's Poland might not necessarily remain wholeheartedly within the Soviet alliance. On the strength of such signs the United States government decided to treat Poland as a nation semi-independent of the Soviet communists, to grant her aid and substantial credits.

Most Poles understood Gomułka's dilemma over Hungary and were prepared to forgive him the compromise attitude he took. From their point of view as well as the Russians' he was still on probation, depending for his survival on victory in a national election set down for 20 January 1957. But his electoral campaign was able to generate its own momentum. Poles saw there was no question but that they must vote for Gomułka. Therefore he felt able to allow comparatively free elections. They were quite unlike the first, notorious elections of exactly ten years earlier. The voters were allowed a genuine choice of 717 candidates for 459 seats. Only 51 per cent of these candidates were communist party members, the others being supporters of Gomułkaite socialism but members of other political groups such as the United Peasant Party (the ZSL), the Democratic Party (the SD) and certain Catholic groups. Gomułka could hardly avoid winning the elections formally, but anything other than massive support might well have destroyed him. The candidates he supported were listed at the top of each ballot paper and the voter's only recourse was to cross out the name of any candidate he did not like. In an eve-of-poll broadcast speech Gomułka appealed to the electorate not to cross out any of the names. His plea was eloquent and, in the circumstances, thoroughly reasonable: 'An appeal to cross communist party candidates off the ballot paper means more than a simple appeal to cross out socialism. Crossing out our party's candidates means crossing out the independence of our country, crossing out Poland from the map of European states.'[3]

The Polish press was still quite free, being censored mainly by the self-control of journalists and their common sense in the given situation. How free they were can be gauged from an article that appeared in *Po Prostu* on election morning, i.e. the same day that Gomułka's speech appeared in the Party's *Trybuna Ludu*: 'The *majority* of the candidates on the National Front list are supporters of the Polish October programme. It is *to the best* of these that we offer our confidence.' [Author's italics.]

Po Prostu was already cautious in its support of the Gomułka line, far more so than many blatant anti-communists. The western 'opposition' Radio Free Europe, as well as the Catholic Church, advised Poles to vote exactly as Gomułka outlined. 20 January 1957 was an extraordinary day for Poland. Priests led their congregations into the voting booths to support Gomułka, a communist and an atheist. Radio Free Europe was advised by many reasoning non-communists that they might as well pack up and discontinue their services, that their mission to restore freedom to Poland was over and won, because Gomułka was 'a Pole first and a communist second'. Voices of doubt and caution, like that of *Po Prostu*, were few indeed.

It was not so much a general election as a plebiscite, on the lines of the 'oui' or 'non' elections of de Gaulle's France. As such it was another great win for Gomułka, who personally polled 99·4 per cent of the votes in his Warsaw constituency. His communist-dominated National Front bloc received massive support. Significantly, the non-Party candidates did best of all, polling an average of 94·3 per cent of the available votes. On this basis the communist party candidates came bottom, though still with a high average of 88 per cent. There were no opposition candidates.

After such a wonderful, explosive episode, Gomułka's life could hardly avoid turning into an anti-climax. Having regained his freedom and won power he found his movement and action restricted by the necessities of high office in a country which has little room for political manœuvre. His life became guided by circumstance and therefore biographically less interesting.

Gomułka had promised in his 20 October speech that collective farms would be allowed to 'decide for themselves the question of whether or not they should dissolve'. He was as good as his word, and many reluctant collective farmers took him up on it. By 1956 8·6 per cent of Polish agricultural land had been collectivised, and there was a target of 25–30 per cent to be achieved by 1960. But by mid-1957 more than eighty per cent of this collective land was back to individual cultivation.[4] 8,280 of the 9,790 collective farms were disbanded.

A new 'liberal' line was adopted towards craftsmen, tailors, shopkeepers and other 'private enterprise' practitioners. Again, this was a reversion to the policy of ten years earlier, before the rise of Bierut and Polish stalinism, when private enterprise was recognised as having a part to play in a socialist economy. An article in *Trybuna Ludu* (15 November 1956) called 'The new prerogatives of private trade' declared that permits for such trade, hitherto issued only year by year, would be given for indefinite periods. Credit and raw materials were to be provided for craftsmen and for individuals who wished to construct their own houses. In February 1957 Stefan Jędrychowski reassured craftsmen that they would not be driven out of business by crippling taxes and petty regulations, as had happened in the past. On 9 January 1957 Gomułka was asked at a pre-election meeting whether or not private initiative was going to last. He replied:

'The change in our policy towards trades is not a momentary one. This new policy shows all the signs of being lasting. Well-developed trades are not only no threat to a socialist economy, they can provide a useful completion to it. This is why we support and shall continue to support the growth of trades and small private enterprises. . . . The policy of liquidating all small private enterprises did not help the construction of socialism in Poland, it hindered it.'

Unlike most communists, Gomułka seems genuinely to believe that there is nothing wrong with a limited private-initiative sector in a socialist economy. He made no apology for the sector's restoration in 1956, a step which more dogmatic socialists would regard as reactionary and ideologically incorrect. He did not regard it as a necessary 'one step backwards', as Lenin saw a similar move in Soviet Russia—his New Economic Policy of 1921–28. On the contrary, he took pride in its development. Maybe in the years that followed shopkeepers, restaurant owners and craftsmen did begin to have some troubles over taxation, supplies and unnecessary regulations, but this did not prevent their becoming far and away the richest section of Polish society. As Gomułka said on 6 February 1961, addressing the congress of the Democratic Party, the political group that still represents the interests of the private sector:

'We now have in our country, in towns and villages, about 147,000 craftsmen's shops which employ, including their owners, about 240,000 people. . . . The number of craftsmen's shops and the number of people employed in them has grown considerably during the past five-year plan. The number of institutions is up by 53 per cent and the number of employed by 76 per cent. This position is still unsatisfactory, however, especially as regards skilled-craft services. The lack of such men is felt painfully by the whole of society.'[5]

Some might see a contradiction in this picture of a communist leader calling for the growth and improvement of his country's private initiative. But Gomułka believes the Polish economy needs a limited private sector. Recent visitors to Poland are often surprised to see how many shops and stalls there are in private hands. Prices are higher than in the state shops, but those who can afford it usually prefer to go to a private trader, whose interest it is to provide better quality, variety and service. Doctors, dentists and even school teachers also have the occasional private client. State health and educational services, while good, are capable of improvement, and those with money will naturally try to find and buy such improvement. In 1968 the private sector employed about 400,000 people, many more than in 1957, and there was still no sign of any abolition of this sector of the economy. Poland is still a much less 'socialist' country than, for instance, Czechoslovakia where the private sector hardly exists.

Before 1956 the 'yellow curtain' shops gave a privileged service to those in high official positions. One of Gomułka's first acts was to close them. Himself a man of sober tastes and modest habits, he had little use for communists who pined after the good things of life. Before 1956 communists had lived like a new Polish aristocracy, and it is one of Gomułka's more endearing features that he has no use for such hypocrisy. But he did not carry his dislike of capitalist 'goodies' to any extreme. He has allowed shops to exist where they can be bought freely, with only one difficulty—all prices are marked in dollars and payment must be made in that currency. The existence of these foreign-currency shops serves several purposes. Poles are encouraged to send money to their relatives in Poland. This is then spent in the shops, becomes the property of the exchequer and can be spent on medicines, machinery or anything else the state regards as important. Before the existence of the shops Poles, especially Polish peasants, would store their dollars under the bed. The money would lie idle, gathering dust but no interest, useless both to the citizen and to the state.

The vast number of Poles now in emigration—an estimated one-third of all Poles live outside Poland—also enabled the new Polish government to restore a limited freedom of travel. Before 1956 to apply for a passport was to ask for the moon. All Poles, except for a handful of the privileged, were literally imprisoned inside their country. The barrier was the Polish frontier control. After 1956 passports were being given to almost all who applied for them, and the barrier became largely a financial one. The Polish złoty is unconvertible outside the Soviet bloc. The Polish traveller is allowed to buy only five dollars in Poland to take with him abroad. He has to find some means of finance. This can be literary or other foreign earnings, but it is usually an *émigré* relative.

Gomułkaism has restored links between Poles at home and abroad. Before 1956 such links were a matter for suspicion. People were dismissed from their jobs, or even arrested and imprisoned, merely for writing letters to *émigré* Poles. It is now as usual for *émigrés* to visit Poland as for Poles who live at home to travel abroad. Only those *émigrés* most hostile to communist power are excluded. Some *émigré* parents even send their children to youth camps in Poland, where they can learn about their country of origin and avoid losing their national identity.

Perhaps Gomułka's greatest achievement was his abolition of the cruder forms of police terror. A victim of this terror himself and brought to power by an anti-terror movement partly for this reason, Gomułka could hardly avoid continuing the assault on the security services that was already in full swing when he came to power. The abuse of power by the UB had been monstrous, and its abolition was one of the platforms on which Gomułka had been elected. On 4 November he had said in his address to the Party *actif*:

> 'We intend as soon as possible to reorganise the work of the public security apparatus. The competence of the security organs will be contracted and confined to fighting espionage, terror and other hostile activity directed against people's power and the interests of the state. The security apparatus will be subordinated to the Ministry of Internal Affairs. The Committee for Public Security [the UB] will therefore be liquidated.'[6]

Gomułka did what he promised. By early January 1957 the UB was no more. For a year or so it had been lying low, harmless and under fire, but still in existence and ready to reappear with all its old ferocity as soon as the fashionable liberal madness was past. The UB's liquidation was an administrative act that meant little in the short term. The tortures and rank injustices had ended before Gomułka's ascendancy. Everyone knew that the end of the UB did not mean the end of totalitarianism and the obsession with security that goes with it.

Thick, detailed files would still be kept on any Pole with any education or official position. Telephones would still be tapped and agents would still be infiltrated into every student, intellectual, economic or commercial body. The transfer of the security forces to a new ministry would change none of this. But it did mean that the scope and power given to these forces, though wide by western standards, would be limited and kept within some sort of legal framework. In practice, the average Pole was no longer terrified of them. He realised the police were unlikely to ring his doorbell at 5 a.m., arrest him and imprison him because of some chance remark to a friend or some anonymous letter to an official body. On 5 June 1957 Gomułka was able to announce that 5,800 prisoners had been freed following the 'amnesty' for political prisoners of 27 April 1956.[7] Another 770 were completely rehabilitated.

It was only in 1968 that the security service gained a new lease of life and was able to capitalise on the many internal troubles of that year. It was then that certain groups of Poles, particularly students, intellectuals or Poles of Jewish origin, began to feel once again the heavy hand of police oppression. Even then the onslaught was mild indeed compared with that of the stalinist years. Westerners who visit Poland for the first time are often staggered by the frank way Poles will speak of the communist leaders, and attack aspects of their policies that displease them. Foreigners would find themselves seized upon and made the receptacle for every possible complaint and tale of woe. It was not a practice indulged in by employees of the state, of course, but it was widespread among the ordinary Poles.

There was no more jamming of the Voice of America, the BBC or Radio Free Europe. Jamming had never been fully effective anyway, and the new 'enlightened' Polish leaders were determined to answer anti-communist propaganda 'with argument rather than by noise'. Poland was the first socialist country to take this step. They even began to allow a limited number of foreign periodicals into the country, only to ban them once again in the 1960s.

Before 1956 foreign literature had been carefully selected before being offered in Polish translation. To qualify, foreign writers had to fall into one of two categories: either dead and established as 'classics', or alive and favourably inclined towards communism. A western writer's claim for the attention of the Polish reader had to be investigated and proved, and the onus of proof was on the writer to show his 'positive attitude' to the new order. Under Gomułka the onus of proof was shifted on to the excluding censor. Anything that was not *anticommunist* was now eligible and publishable. The result was like a great cultural flower suddenly bursting into bloom. Dozens of foreign names began to appear on the bookshop shelves, names famous all over the world but quite unknown in Poland: Kafka, Steinbeck, Eliot, Faulkner, Mailer—even Simenon and Agatha Christie. Bans were maintained only on such, from the communist point of view, extreme cases as George Orwell and Ian Fleming.

Likewise the door was opened to western films and theatre. Visits to Poland by western theatre companies and orchestras became quite frequent, and the best foreign films usually appeared, even though it might be as much as a year after their general release in the West. As with travel, the main difficulty was no longer official barriers but finance. There simply were not the dollars to pay for, say, an American film when the country needed a piece of American machinery much more. But then the US government made a wise decision in allowing Poland to buy quantities of books, films and other 'cultural goods' with Polish *złoty* currency.

The sudden bloom of western culture was soon followed by a bloom in the culture of Poland. The plays of Mrożek and Różewicz, the novels of Andrzejewski, the poetry of Zbigniew Herbert and especially the films of Munk and Wajda were appearing widely throughout central Europe, including West Germany, and even to some extent in the Anglo-Saxon world. Perhaps for the first time in her history Poland was, in certain fields, giving the world a cultural lead. The film is the verbal art-form that can most easily break the language barrier, and Polish films were blazing a path for Poland into the mainstream of world intellectual attention.

In the beginning the 'Polish experiment' seemed to be going so well that Gomułka gained the support of many noncommunists. Many students of east Europe in the West were taking the view that Gomułkaism meant the end of communism and of Poland's satellite status. Many thousands of *émigrés* who had feared to return to Poland in 1945 did not fear to do so in the months that followed October 1956. Democratic socialists from the West visited Poland and came home excited by what had happened and curious as to what was going to happen. The fact of the Hungarian tragedy satisfied such men that, with the best non-communist will in the world, Gomułka could not possibly have achieved more in 1956 than he did. Democratic socialists like Konni Zilliacus were assuaged by such Gomułkaite pronouncements as Julian Hochfeld's 'Letter to a Labour Party comrade':

'. . . Our history has not yet allowed us to break with what in your history were the pioneering days of the Elizabethan adventurers, the fanaticism of Cromwell's republicans with their horrifying cruelty at times to opponents and criminals. We must pass through this stage at lightning speed and catch up with history, which has not been kind to us, whereas your way is to move forward calmly with your famous British phlegm.'[8]

In the early years of Gomułkaism many Polish communists were thus eager to broaden their support and attract sympathisers from the world labour movement. Men like Adam Schaff, a leading economist and one of Gomułka's new 'bright boys', were at pains to justify their country's authoritarian system which had hitherto been taken as the norm. In 1961 Schaff wrote:

'So long as the enemies of freedom exist, so long as they struggle effectively against it, various restrictions on their freedom, depending on conditions and situation, are a necessity accepted by socialist humanism precisely because it is a militant humanism. There is, however, one proviso: one should never exaggerate in this respect or do more than necessary.'[9]

Gomułka had allowed Poland freedom of speech, but this did not mean there was to be freedom of written expression. Even during the first days after 20 October 1956, there was a voluntary censorship and a particular embargo on articles attacking the Soviet Union. The 20 October *Pravda* article on Poland was one of the last occasions when the Poles retaliated in print. On

16 February 1957 Jerzy Morawski criticised another *Pravda* article, which had described the new Polish farming system as a hotbed of *kulak* (privately owned) speculative and capitalistic heresy. But most Polish journalists, knowing how touchy the Russians are and how they hate criticism, were ready to forgo attacking them. It was a small price to pay for internal independence.

But then it became clear that Gomułka, far from abolishing the official censorship, intended to strengthen it. Being a communist he saw his country's press as one of the weapons which, as ruler, he had a right to control. To allow the press to criticise his new, none-too-stable régime seemed as illogical as self-mutilation. He did not want merely to tame the press, he wanted to harness it.

Early in 1957 Gomułka, having failed to trim the sails of *Trybuna Ludu*, the official communist party newspaper, sacked almost the whole editorial board. In May 1957 an attack began on *Po Prostu*, the student and intellectual weekly that had campaigned and supported Gomułka so staunchly during 1956. Its editor Eligiusz Lasota was dismissed. At the end of June it was forced to close 'for the summer'. On 7 September a number were prepared for press and printed, only to be confiscated before distribution. In October *Po Prostu* was finally banned and closed down, and for days there were student riots in Warsaw.

The fact was that Gomułka had found himself in power with a wide political support which he was now intent on narrowing. So long as he was a martyr and in opposition he had naturally attracted the support of progressive 'rebel' communists like Lasota, Jan Kott, Leszek Kołakowski, Jerzy Andrzejewski and Adam Ważyk—all of them connected with *Po Prostu*. But once rebels come to power, they tend to lose their unorthodoxy. They will then seek to unload their rebellious friends, men who were once necessary and useful, but who cannot be expected to form part of orderly revolutionary government.

Like all communists Gomułka was a frequent user of labels and catch-phrases. However vague and disorganised may be the danger to their entrenched position, the marxists have a word for it. In the case of the *Po Prostu* men the word was 'revisionist'. The label came to be applied to the Party's left wing, to those whose views and activity went beyond the limits laid down by Gomułka. For the Party's right wing, the 'conservative' stalinists, Gomułka was to decide a similar limit of activity and an appropriate label. They were the 'dogmatists'. The Polish communist, from being the freest in the socialist world, found himself being confined to an ever-narrowing political field. To avoid becoming either a revisionist or a dogmatist became a complicated political exercise.

By a quick, if shallow, piece of political thinking, Gomułka began to link revisionism and dogmatism, the two extremes, and to attack them both simultaneously. His theory was that the 'liberal' revisionists, men whose thought was close to that of western socialists, who believed in democracy within the Party and a greater freedom of the press and of inter-Party discussion, had emerged only because of the stalinist past and the injustices that went with it. Revisionism was an unnatural product of dogmatism, and the two must be fought against as a single enemy. It was Gomułka's first great over-simplification, a device he was to use again and again in his speeches during 1957 and 1958. For instance, in his speech to the Party's Tenth Plenum (5 October 1957) he said:

'Influenza, even in its most serious form, cannot be cured by contacting tuberculosis. Dogmatism cannot be cured by revisionism. Revisionist tuberculosis can only strengthen the dogmatist influenza. . . . The revisionist wing must be cut out of the Party. . . . We shall destroy with equal firmness all organised or individual forms of anti-Party activity launched from a position of dogmatism.'[10]

Gomułka began his purge, but it was not a purge in the old sense of the term. When Gomułka set out to 'destroy', he meant politically, not physically. He did not arrest or liquidate his political opponents, it was enough to remove them from the Party. According to Richard F. Staar, 200,000 Party members were affected and the total membership was reduced to just over a million.[11]

Although on the face of it the purge was directed equally against dogmatist and revisionist, it was the latter that suffered the more, if only because they were more numerous and therefore the greater threat. Gomułka had been carried to power on a wave of liberalism and progressive socialism. For some months the wave had swept him along with it. After all, he had been out of politics for many years; he could not immediately take up the reins of power and create his new socialism without resistance from those who disagreed with him.

By the end of the 1950s Gomułka was beginning to enlist the aid of his old enemies, the Stalinist dogmatists, against his old friends who had placed such trust in him in 1956. In September 1959 Colonel Pawel Monat, a senior Polish intelligence officer, defected to the West. His defection, just as Colonel Światło's had done in 1954, triggered off important political changes. Hard men like Eugeniusz Szyr and Tadeusz Gede were brought back into the government. So was Kazimierz Witaszewski, Rokossowski's former deputy who was believed to have played a part in the abortive anti-Gomułka coup of 18 October 1956. He became director of personnel to the Party's Central Committee, a key post which enabled him to take into government employ men of his own way of thinking. Also in 1959 two of Gomułka's early 'liberal' supporters were dismissed: Władysław Bieńkowski from his post as Minister of Education and Jerzy Morawski from the Politburo. Morawski became Ambassador to London and Bieńkowski was put in charge of Poland's parks and forests, a job known widely and aptly as 'Minister of Fresh Air'.

Then in 1964 Gomułka's equilibrium was disturbed by a strange political event, hardly recorded in the western press. In January 1964 Gomułka and Khrushchev met in the north-east corner of Poland at Lańsk. Khrushchev announced that he would shortly go to Bonn to seek some sort of a German–Soviet rapprochement, a lessening of emphasis in the anti-West German campaign which was and is the pillar of the east European countries' foreign policies. Gomułka's reaction to this idea was one of terror. He took the view, simplified perhaps but hard to challenge, that when Russians and Germans agree, Poles suffer, and he would not sanction the tiniest approach to Bonn. The two men quarrelled and for the most of 1964 Gomułka felt that his foreign policy, and for that matter the fate of Poland, was hanging in the balance.

For a country as strategically indefensible as Poland is, thought Gomułka, there can be only one foreign policy: to keep the two great neighbours, eastern and western, apart and at daggers drawn. After all, Poland owed her very existence after a hundred years of extinction to the military collapse of *both Germany and Russia* in 1918. For Poland this was an amazing stroke of luck. It happened to have been in the victorious Allies' interest to create Poland out of the ashes of war to be a buffer state, a stabilising influence in eastern Europe. True, Poland endured for a mere twenty-one years before being destroyed again, but then by another amazing coincidence she was again able to endure war, partition and occupation, to rise from the dead.

To have Poland as a buffer state was now in Russia's interest, and Stalin saw to it that Poland's territory expanded deep into the former Germany, thus making any future Polish–German alliance impossible. But in the short term the position was excellent from the Polish point of view also. The new 1945 Poland was more compact, richer and militarily more viable than her between-the-wars predecessor. She now possessed wide access to the sea and a nationally homogeneous population. Most importantly, owing to the division of Germany *she* now had a buffer state—East Germany. From the Polish point of view East Germany is a vital wedge between her and the larger German state which, of course, has still not accepted the territorial losses imposed on her in 1945.

It is Gomułka's view that the present division of eastern and central Europe is, from the Polish point of view, ideal. He sees the situation as almost incapable of improvement, and so anything which tends to upset the *status quo* must be resisted at all cost. To challenge the division of Germany or the division of Europe, he feels, would be to threaten Poland's existence as a separate state. In 1964 and again in 1968 there were such challenges, and in both cases Gomułka's reaction was a violent one.

That summer Khrushchev's son-in-law Aleksey Adzhubey, editor of *Izvestiya* and the Russian leader's unofficial personal ambassador, visited Bonn and produced broad hints of an ease-up in the Soviet anti-German hostility, perhaps on the conditions originally suggested by Stalin in 1952—German neutralisation in exchange for reunification. In his cups Adzhubey was heard to whisper that Walter Ulbricht (the East German leader) had cancer and was not long for this world, that his successors might not be so dogmatic and hard to deal with. In those days West Germans had hopes of better things to come from their separated brethren. If only a freer atmosphere, which they termed 'Polish conditions', should prevail in East Germany, some dialogue might be possible.

In September 1964 Gomułka took the unusual step of

addressing the Writers' Congress in Lublin. His speech there was not reported, but it is known that he expressed strongly his view that if peace were to be maintained, a Soviet–German rapprochement was out of the question. After his speech the Soviet delegation, lead by the prominent writer Konstantin Simonov, was in a quandary. They knew which way the wind was then blowing in Moscow, and there was even talk that they might have to leave the Congress. A few days later though, something strange happened in Moscow and Nikita Khrushchev was manœuvred into resigning on 15 October. Various reasons are given for his downfall—his humiliation over Cuba, his failure to mend the Sino–Soviet split, his unpolished and sometimes unsober way of conducting public affairs—but there is reason to believe that his proposed new policy towards Germany, which was reversed as soon as he and Adzhubey left the political scene, was an important factor.

The whole affair shook the Polish leader horribly. He saw it as a confirmation of his worst fears. Poland had had a hair's-breadth escape from becoming yet again a matter of Russian–German bargaining. Gomułka had long ago discarded what he thought were the over-liberal ideas of the Polish 'October' and late 1950s. He had managed almost to stabilise the Polish political scene, to narrow it at the edges but still to leave it the freest and most lively in eastern Europe. But after the experience of 1964 he began to turn into that epitome of conservatives, the man who is frightened of political change.

This is probably the main reason why the late 1960s have been disappointing years for Poland. Gomułka's former flexibility, his lack of Marxist dogma, became hardened by his obsession with preserving the integrity of the Polish state, both her existence as a separate political unit and her western frontiers. His motives were patriotic enough—even his worst enemies would not challenge his honesty, his basic belief in the immediacy of the danger of West German 'revanchism'—but his preoccupation with Poland's very existence was hardening his attitudes to other less basic aspects of Polish life, especially cultural life. His movements became restricted by the awful responsibility he possessed, his unorthodoxy and flashes of character dulled by the need to conserve, to protect mere existence. Gomułka's greatest complaint against his political opponents is that they take Poland's existence and integrity for granted, that they act as if Poland were a self-sufficient island. He sees such men as totally unrealistic and does not hesitate to accuse them of being ready to sacrifice Poland's vital interests for the sake of such luxuries as freedom of expression.

It was not that Poland suffered tragedy and disaster. The years that followed 1956 have been some of the most stable and least violent of Poland's history. It was just that there was one pin-prick after the other, against the Church, against the intellectuals, against many of the principles and ideals which Poles had agitated for and been ready to fight and die for in 1956. Gomułka and his former intellectual supporters—men like Jan Kott, Leszek Kołakowski, Eligiusz Lasota, Gustav Gottesman, Wiktor Woroszylski, Adam Ważyk and Jerzy Andrzejewski—were soon at loggerheads when it became clear that their ideas about the future of Poland had very little in common. The status of east European writers was and is much higher than that of those who live in the West. East Europeans have a basic respect for the written word—a fact which gives writers who have access to print a great influence over the population. This is one reason why communist politicians take such pains to control their writers. Gomułka saw such men as Kołakowski—a professor of philosophy, journalist and playwright—as a definite political force which might, if allowed to expand too far, become a danger to him. He has little sympathy with the intellectual style of marxism, and he was determined that his Party should not fall under the control of men like Kołakowski, whom he would refer to spitefully as 'our young theoretician'. Sure enough, in November 1966 Kołakowski was expelled from the Party and in 1969 he left Poland to work at McGill University in Canada.

A country's cultural climate is its window on the world and is often taken as a yardstick for judging a whole society. Of course this is wrong. Poland does not consist of intellectuals, it is a country of workers and peasants many of whom care little whether this or that play is banned, or this or that writer expelled from the Party. The reasons why they too feel the recent stagnation of Gomułka's rule are quite different.

Wages in Poland are still very low, even by east European standards. Working on a purchasing-power rate of 100 złoty to the pound sterling, one finds that in 1968 the average monthly wage was £21. The legal minimum monthly wage was £8 10s, although there were only a few hundred thousand on this miserable pittance. The highest salaries were earned by factory managers, and the highest in the country was the £240 (24,000 złoty) a month drawn by the director of the Huta Lenina complex near Cracow. But this salary is so exceptional that its holder is by local standards a millionaire. Even ministers in the government do not normally receive more than about £60 a month. The only big money-spinners are those in the private initiative sector, especially those who run small factory workshops or shops, and the large-scale farmers or market gardeners. White-collar officials can never hope to match such earnings. Even when promoted, officials find that their wages are only marginally increased, and so many of them prefer to lead quiet, unambitious lives.

Given the fact that most Polish married women go out to work and bring in a second wage packet, the low Polish salaries are above subsistence level. Such basic essentials as food and rent are cheap enough, but the problem comes when a Pole aspires towards luxuries—a car, for example. A new Polish-made car costs 150,000 złoty, the equivalent of six years' work for an average wage earner, and is therefore an unattainable dream to all but the rich few. Polish workers are well informed about conditions in the West and they know how easy it is for, say, a German to own his own car. Poles find it hard to understand a world in which the Germans, a defeated nation, live better and have more political freedom than themselves, who were on the side which won the last war. Of course money is not the only criterion. A Pole will choose his job not so much for its salary as for its perks—free car, free accommodation, foreign travel, subsidised restaurants or clubs—which are often more valuable. Generally speaking, Poles are less money-conscious than westerners, there is so much in their country that money cannot buy. Many too will seek promotion out of professional interest and self-satisfaction, not in order to improve their living standard. But Poles, even Polish communists, are human beings and there are few indeed selfless enough to work out of pure marxist idealism, to find work its own reward.

Centuries of bitter history have made Poles a cynical people, and twenty-five years of socialism have not been enough to dispel this cynicism. Poles tend to live for the moment, to regard the future as a doubtful entity they may not live to see. This is an understandable attitude after a war in which twenty per cent of the population were killed, and one which socialism has changed hardly at all. There is still little of the team spirit, dedication to the community and desire to serve humanity that existed in large measure in between-the-wars Soviet Russia. Poles have not yet learnt to despise money and the bourgeois values, and they are only too ready to complain about their low standard of living, to compare it unfavourably with that of western Europe. Of course the citizen blames his rulers when things go badly and ignores them when things go well, and recently Poles have been becoming more and more inclined to blame Gomułka for their country's slow economic progress.

Poles who work on the land are richer than most. Polish ham, butter, eggs and bacon are excellent and widely exported. Clearly the authorities are unwilling to do anything to put at risk the wealth that the peasants provide. Even if the peasants could be persuaded to collectivise voluntarily, which at present they could not be, Polish agriculture is still not sufficiently mechanised to work efficiently under the collective system. Farmers' carts and machinery are still largely horse-drawn (in 1968 there were about 2,700,000 horses in Poland). At night time the country's roads are still cluttered with horse-drawn cartloads of vegetables moving at snail's pace, without lights and dangerously invisible, into town for the early morning market. This is why at the present stage the family agricultural unit has been found more productive. It is more adaptable. Doubtless Gomułka's long-term intention is to collectivise, as has been done with some success in East Germany and in Czechoslovakia, but he is realistic enough to see that Poland still lags behind these two countries, which were well industrialised even before the Second World War, and cannot therefore follow their example for the moment. To do so would be unwise from the point of view of both politics and productivity.

Individual farms are limited in size (they cannot be larger than fifty hectares), and the average farm is about five hectares (12·3 acres). Obviously farmers have little of the sophisticated machinery that is usual in Western Europe. They cannot afford it, nor would it be economical. To remedy this the government buys heavy machinery, keeps it in depots and hires it out to peasants. Alternatively it helps peasants to club together to buy machinery and share the use of it. But peasants are often unwilling to join these clubs. They see them as the thin edge of the wedge, the germ of future collectives, part of a subtle scheme to seduce them.

They complain of being overtaxed, undersupplied and hamstrung by bureaucracy. They have difficulty in getting permits to build on their land or to get proper materials. A peasant's land is often scattered over a wide area—one strip here, one strip there—and his efforts to amalgamate his holding by purchase or exchange of land are often frustrated by officials. But for the present Gomułka makes few demands on the peasants. Although few are communists, many still admire him for the stand he took in their defence in 1947, and again in 1956. They are grateful to him for giving them back their land. It is among the peasantry that Gomułka's popularity has been least eroded since 1956.

The Polish countryside is one of the most religious areas of Europe. The Roman Catholic Church is supported by almost all villagers, many of whose beliefs would be considered reactionary and dogmatic even in Rome. Twenty-five years of socialism have done little to uproot the Catholic religion—on the contrary, there are more priests in Poland now than there were before the Second World War. The Church in Poland has many rights which are not enjoyed by, say, the Orthodox Church in the Soviet Union. It has its own university in Lublin, the right to publish and to propagate the faith (in Russia it is only the right to private worship which is protected) and even (in 1969) a total of thirteen members* of the Sejm, although most of these are not on good terms with Cardinal Wyszyński and the hierarchy. There are even Catholic chaplains in the Polish armed forces.

For Gomułka, an atheist, to have to rule a predominantly religious country is yet another harrowing problem. In 1956 he and the Cardinal were on good terms. Both men had suffered imprisonment in the preceding year, and to secure the Cardinal's release from detention was one of Gomułka's first political acts. In return the Cardinal helped Gomułka to consolidate his rule and to restrain irresponsible elements who

---

* In 1969 there were five deputies of the 'Znak' group, lead by Stanisław Stomma, five deputies of the 'Pax' group, lead by Bolesław Piasecki, and three deputies of the Christain Social Fellowship, lead by Jan Frankowski. Of these only one or two members of the 'Znak' group were on good terms with the Primate of Poland, Cardinal Wyszyński.

might have led Poland into disaster. The two men's characters are in many ways similar, both are men of power, resolution, strength and stubbornness. When their views conflict it is like a meeting between an irresistible force and an immovable object. The honeymoon period was short, and after the euphoric days of 1956 points of conflict were quick to arise. There were difficulties over religious instruction in the schools, the payment of priests for such instruction, taxation of Church property, the building of churches in newly populated areas, and especially over the long pilgrimages on foot made by some of the more intense Catholics. Perhaps the main problem concerns the right or non-right of religious leaders, especially the Primate, to speak on political issues. The government view was put to the author in 1969 by Dr Skarżynski, Director of the Religious Affairs Office (Urząd do Spraw Wyznań):

> 'As a religious leader the Primate has the right to speak freely on religious matters. He may also, as a private individual, speak on political matters, provided that he obeys the law. What he may not do is to speak on political matters in his capacity as religious leader. This we will not tolerate.'

The state is prepared to make full use of the sanctions at its disposal to try to enforce this view. Several times the Primate has been refused his passport and has been unable to attend conclaves in Rome, because the authorities took exception to the political content of his sermons. Similarly, when the Pope expressed the wish to come to Poland for the Millennium celebrations in 1966, he was refused an entry visa. Poland still has no diplomatic relations with the Vatican, and will refuse them until the Vatican recognises the present frontiers of Poland. In 1969 the only Polish diplomat in the Vatican was Kazimierz Papée, chargé d'affaires for the prewar Government.

It has been the Government's policy to dilute the Primate's great status and authority by allowing splinter groups within the Church to form and to be active. It is these anti-Wyszyński Catholics who mainly control the Catholic press and publishing houses. It is a struggle, though, which concerns mainly the upper layer of Polish Catholic life. The Catholic from the villages does not concern himself with such sectarianism. Traditionally the Primate is a leader of the people, and as such he is heard and obeyed. Traditionally, too, the Virgin Mary is Queen of Poland, and every year thousands of believers journey hundreds of kilometres *on foot* to her shrine at Częstochowa.

Gomułka could perhaps destroy the Church in Poland if he was prepared to use severe repressive measures, if he was prepared to confiscate Church property, imprison priests, close monasteries, ban religious publications and exclude believers from public life. Such methods were used in the Soviet Union and have successfully intimidated the hierarchy into collaboration with the atheist government. But since 1956 there has been little of such crude brutality in Poland. Relations between Church and state are uneasy, but at least they exist. There is still a 'Mixed Commission' of three men on each side which discusses burning problems, and leading Catholics are still ready to criticise the Government, albeit from a standpoint of total loyalty to socialist People's Poland. For instance Konstanty Lubiński, a 'Znak' Member of Parliament, told the author in 1969:

> 'There are three obsessive themes running through Gomułka's politics. The first is agriculture. He is constantly at pains to reassure the peasants that they will keep their land, for this generation at least, and he will allow no talk of collectivisation. The second is Germany. He will consider no compromise over the frontiers with Germany, nor will he seek any improvement in West German–Polish relations so long as they lay claim to part of our territory. With these two "obsessions" I am in agreement. His third "obsession" concerns the governing role of the communist party, and with this policy I am not in agreement. He is extremely reluctant to give key jobs in administration to non-party men. (By "party" I mean the three main political parties in Poland: the communists, the Peasant Party and the Democratic Front. The differences between these parties are very slight.) Poland possesses a wealth of superb men, entirely loyal to the present system, who nevertheless do not wish to enter politics by joining a party. To deprive these non-party men of the chance of attaining high office is, in my opinion, a mistake.'

I have quoted these remarks to show that, even in 1969, there was *some* room for argument in Polish political life. Critics of the Gomułka line were still prepared to speak up, provided only that they did not challenge certain basic principles of Gomułkaism—the socialist order, the alliance with the Soviet Union, the verbal confrontation with West Germany. Leading Poles, even senior officials, could still be found who criticised Gomułka's direction of affairs—his reluctance to change his personnel, his proneness to fly into furies and treat subordinates in an arbitrary way.

Gomułka's internal policies were becoming noticeably less flexible. He had now ruled Poland for a decade and was accepted by Poland's communists as their natural leader, the builder of the Polish road to socialism. His prestige was based not only on his performance during October 1956, but also on his activities and writings during the early years of the Polish Workers' Party, while Poland was still under enemy occupation. After all, it was Gomułka who had written the manifesto of the new Polish communism, 'What we are fighting for', back in March 1943, who had fought the Nazis with guns and grenades, the British and Americans with passion and oratory, the Polish anti-communists with organisation and terror, who had suffered under stalinism and returned to power as the embodiment of the new post-Stalin movement. He was rightly accepted by most communists as the father of his Party, by many non-communists as the father of socialist Poland. Poles have longer memories about their country than the average western journalist. When in the late 1960s westerners finally realised that Gomułka was no liberal reformer, they turned on him as the betrayer of their unjustified hopes and illusions. But there were still Poles who, taking not a journalist's view but a twenty-five-year view of Gomułka's career, saw him as a great man.

In 1969, though, such men were undoubtedly the exception. Poland had just endured a terrible year, and as leader Gomułka was of course taking the blame for it. The more he gained the confidence of the Russians and of the convinced communists, the more he was alienating himself from the vast majority of Poles, perhaps as many as ninety per cent, who are not marxists.

In 1956 Gomułka had momentarily restored Polish unity. While reaffirming his sincere marxist beliefs he had promised a place in the administration of his country to men who, while agreeing to differ with him politically, appreciated the inevitability of a communist government in Poland and were prepared to work for it so long as it upheld certain principles of legality and personal freedom. But as these principles were eroded, so Gomułka was losing the non-communist support he once enjoyed. In the same way the more established and power-ful he became, the less inclined he was to tolerate such Poles who were merely 'not against him', whose politics and beliefs he did not share and who, he thought, were subtly sabotaging his directives somewhere along the chain of command, pre-venting his policies from full implementation and therefore hindering Poland's development. As he grew older he was losing his former width of vision. Disappointed by Poland's slow economic progress he was becoming withdrawn into himself and dependent on an inner circle of confidants to keep him informed and to advise him. Such men soon discovered that their survival depended on keeping their ruler in a good temper. Like so many communist rulers he became infected by the obligatory mood of optimism that surrounded him, until he began to believe that things were well with his country and to distrust those colleagues who brought bad news. He began to develop whims and quirks. Men who caught his eye would be suddenly pulled from oblivion and placed in some top adminis-trative post in Warsaw, then just as suddenly dismissed. Gomułka had once impressed people by his great enthusiasm, passion and sincerity, but as his power increased, these fiery qualities were degenerating into ordinary capriciousness.

Gomułka had begun his reign by curbing his security police, the organisation he had called in 1946 'the strongest arm of people's power', but in the early 1960s he was learning that a socialist leader with such scant active support from the popula-tion was hardly able to govern without a strong and active internal security service. In the late 1950s he had disposed of his opponents, right wing and left wing, by posting them abroad, criticising them in his speeches and occasionally removing them from their jobs. But in the 1960s the political groups were becoming more numerous and varied. There was a 'liberal' movement centred around the University of War-saw. Its members were not politically united, but they did make speeches and write pamphlets, the distribution of which is a criminal offence. In November 1966 Leszek Kołakowski, one of the leaders of this group, was expelled from the Party, and further expulsions soon followed. Also in 1966 two young lecturers, Jacek Kuroń and Karol Modzelewski, were arrested and sentenced to terms of imprisonment. Also imprisoned were the leaders of a small 'Trotskyist' group, Hass, Badoski and

Śmiech. In February 1966 light relief was provided by the flight to Albania of Kazimierz Mijal, the leader of the pro-Chinese faction in the Party. He disguised himself to look like an Albanian trade delegate and got through Polish immigration control by using the man's passport, given to Mijal for this purpose by the Albanian ambassador.

There was, of course, no question of a return to the excesses of stalinism. Politically motivated arrests were few and isolated. Each one was an event in itself and had some basis in law, albeit a harsh law. The accused would be charged under the 'Shorter Criminal Code', introduced in the stalinist years to curb political opposition, with such crimes as 'distributing printed material harmful to People's Poland', 'possessing a printing press' or even 'slandering the Polish people'. In prison they were treated humanely, allowed books, visits from relatives, even to buy food in the prison shop. There was none of the torture there had been in Stalin's day. Arrest became Gomułka's ultimate weapon to be used on Poles who really defied him. For the rest there were sanctions less drastic but usually just as effective: no man likes to have his passport refused or his career damaged, and the communist authorities were in a position to do this to almost anyone they disliked.

Liberal-minded Poles and westerners were gradually and ruefully forced to realise that they had misjudged Gomułka. Noting his liberal attitudes on the agricultural and internal-independence issues they had written him down as a liberal and canvassed his return to office in the mid-1950s. Too late did they appreciate that on most other issues he was inclined to be unreasonable and unmovable—in fact thoroughly illiberal. By the early 1960s the myth of Gomułka 'the Pole first and the communist second' was entirely exploded. On his sixtieth birthday (6 February 1965) one of the rare profiles of Gomułka appeared, in the weekly *Polityka*. The editor Mieczysław Rakowski, who knows Gomułka well, wrote: 'What nonsense it was for western journalists to write him [Gomułka] up as a national communist, to try to pass him off as an opponent of the Soviet Union, as a communist who rejects the experience of other parties or wishes to withdraw our party from the international communist movement.'

Rakowski's article went on in a vein that was becoming more and more usual: 'When I reflect on the First Secretary's policies in this respect I come to the conclusion that he acts infallibly.' It was an unconscious reflection of a mood many leading Polish communists were beginning to feel, that Gomułka's directives were unchallengeable, that the man was not to be argued with.

In decision-making and administration Gomułka was demanding a finger in every pie. As a subordinate leader (1945–48) and as a prisoner (1951–54) his chief attribute had been stubbornness. Now that he was his country's undoubted ruler his stubbornness was turned into a sort of arrogance, the self-satisfied feeling of a ruler who knows that his people cannot vote him out of office even if they want to, that barring accidents he will be able to continue as ruler for decades.

At the same time not even his worst enemies would complain of any lack of modesty in his private life or of his standard of living. In his early years as ruler he lived with his wife Zofia in a small flat in Saska Kępa, on the wrong side of the Vistula. He ran an ordinary Warszawa car and his wife was often seen queueing at an ordinary shop for the family provisions. Later he moved to a small block of six flats in Aleje na Skarpie, near the Sejm building. His son Ryszard (who worked for a couple of years in England for the Associated Electrical Industries) lived in the same block with his wife and daughters, Ewa and Anna.

Poles are apt to remark acidly that 'there are no funny stories about Gomułka'. He is not the sort of politician who is easily cartooned or satirised. His character is so un-flamboyant, his faults so un-carnal. This is why even among anti-communists he has few deadly enemies. It is hard to hate a man of such asceticism and such passionate sincerity. Grudging admiration can be detected even in the broadcasts of the anti-communist Radio Free Europe. For example Colonel Władysław Tykociński, who defected to the West in May 1965, tells us that:

'The general opinion is that Gomułka is personally an honest man. And indeed he is honest in the sense that he does not abuse his power for personal aims. He does not seek publicity and, compared to the other Party leaders, he lives in relative modesty. I remember how Gomułka returned from Belgrade indignant at the Byzantine luxury in which Tito and the Yugoslav dignitaries live. He threw down with anger a gold cigarette case studded with diamonds that Tito had given him as a present. I personally think that Gomułka's indignation was genuine.'[12]

Tykociński goes on to qualify these words of praise: 'But this honesty that is talked about is very peculiar and narrow. It does not prevent Gomułka from resorting to lies, tricks and treachery in the struggle against the internal and external enemy. It does not prevent him from approving the ignoble and criminal methods of the Bezpieka [security police].'

For an autocratic leader he carries his dislike of material privilege to unusual lengths. According to Hansjakob Stehle: 'when a grandchild [of Gomułka's] was expected and transport was needed quickly, his son asked his father for a car to take his wife to the clinic. "Official cars are not for private use," barked Gomułka over the telephone.'[13]

It is understandable paradox that the more autocratic Gomułka has become, the more he has shied away from the personal publicity on which most autocrats thrive. Perhaps he realises he has assumed some of the characteristics of a Stalin-like 'personality cult', and therefore withdraws from personal publicity as a sort of over-compensation. He does not usually approve of journalists who try to analyse and humanise him. An exception to this rule was a famous interview he gave to Iveragh McDonald, Foreign Editor of *The Times*, who wrote: 'All the time, throughout the six hours, we were sitting in leather armchairs around a small octogonal table, occasionally sipping coffee or nibbling biscuits. Mr Gomułka would take a cigarette, break it in three and put each little bit in turn into a holder.'[14]

This was the first of very few interviews Gomułka gave to the western press. Unlike most Polish communists he shuns the company of westerners who, he feels, do not understand the problems of Poland. He tends to find western journalistic methods naïve or offensive. He does not know the West. Almost the only occasion when he has visited it was in September 1960, when he addressed the United Nations in New York and took time off to visit his sister Józefa, whom he had not seen for years. Nor does Gomułka usually receive western ambassadors or attend diplomatic receptions. Having no high position in the government (as opposed to the Party) hierarchy, he can leave matters of etiquette and ceremonial to his perpetual Prime Minister Józef Cyrankiewicz and to successive Presidents of Poland (Zawadski, Ochab and Spychalski). His life is one of constant, unremitting work relieved only by family life, the occasional holiday in southern Poland and a regular early-morning swim in the baths at the Palace of Culture.

To write a *personal* biography of Gomułka would be an impossible task. He takes such pains to hide his real self from the people he rules, trying instead to project himself as a faceless symbol of socialist Poland, an example to other Poles, most of whom are so unlike him in character. Hard-working, a fervent communist, with no detectable worldly vices, he gives himself with almost saint-like devotion to his task of changing the Polish character, so unlike his own, and leading the Polish people as gently as possible (but by force if necessary) along the road he is convinced it is in their best interest to follow.

XVI: HIS DARKEST YEAR

The year 1968 was Gomułka's historic Waterloo. If one had judged him before 1968 one might have concluded with a picture of a man who devoted his life to Poland and to socialism, who was always a patriot and briefly a hero, who did not live up to the hopes and expectations placed in him when he was made leader, but who nevertheless did his country proud by heading its transformation from intolerable stalinism to a socialism in which most decent men could lead decent, happy lives. If in later years he brought Poland to stagnation and depression, at least he kept her out of tragedy and managed to preserve her limited freedom. The years of Gomułka have been Poland's freest since before the Second World War. This basically positive evaluation of Gomułka was justifiable at the end of 1967, but not at the end of 1968.

Of course Poles were over-optimistic. They had been led by Gomułka out of hell and imagined he would lead them into paradise. When this did not happen they were disappointed and sometimes so ungrateful they forgot what he had done. Even in 1967 there could be no doubt that Gomułka had brought immense improvement to Polish life.

Gomułka did not initiate the 'liberal' anti-Stalinist movement of 1955–56. The initiators were the Polish people themselves; Gomułka was merely thrust into the movement sometime around the middle of 1956, then carried to the head of it by the momentum of his previous career as Stalin's opponent and victim. He was chosen as communist leader without being required to make one single political speech or to expand his plans for the future. He had become a myth, an idea in the minds of politically active Poles intent on reform, who did not take the man's strength of purpose and rigid ideas sufficiently into account.

Although the movement was originally not Gomułka's, it

became his by adoption. And this was only just. If Gomułka had not been available, if he had not been able to stand as leader in October 1956, the movement would either have collapsed or been crushed by Soviet tanks. The views of the Polish people and the Soviet communist party seemed then quite irreconcilable. The machine of reform and newly-won freedom had run away with itself and would have met disaster if Gomułka had not been there to curb it. It was an amazing coincidence. He was the only man with the tiniest chance of satisfying both the runaway reformers and the anxious Soviet leaders. This he was able to do—although it was touch and go—and Poland was spared a foreign invasion.

The 1956 movement originally belonged to men who in their optimism and their enthusiasm for freedom, underestimated the ruthlessness of the Soviet communists and brought Poland to the brink of military disaster. Gomułka was the last resort of both sides in the struggle. When he came to power he assumed a grand programme of reform, with some of whose points he did not agree. After all, he did not design the programme, he was merely handed it, together with his country's leadership, and asked to salvage it. He succeeded in the main task and went on to modify the points of reform he disliked. Of course he was then accused of betraying his mandate, but he could always answer such critics by pointing out that without him the programme of reform and Polish internal independence would have ceased to exist.

The year 1968 was one of tragedy for both Poland and Gomułka. It was not the sort of tragedy Poles are used to enduring. *Their* country was not invaded, occupied or destroyed. By now accustomed to their role as the political underdog, the injured innocent, Poles find it difficult to see themselves as the prejudiced aggressor. The point was that during 1968 Poland and Gomułka suffered a *moral* tragedy, a disaster which was self-inflicted and therefore in some ways more damaging than any they had known before.

In 1968 there were a mere 30,000 Jews in Poland, a tiny remnant of a pre-war 3,000,000-strong community all but annihilated by the Nazis. Most of the survivors did so because they lived the war years outside Poland, often in the Soviet Union. Naturally enough, those Jews who had moved themselves to Russia tended to be those most inclined towards communism.

After the war there were few restrictions on Polish Jews who wished to emigrate to Palestine and Israel. After the horrors European Jewry had just endured, the survivors were only too pleased to leave the guilty continent for their new home on the Fertile Crescent. Indeed it is hard to imagine what would have made a Polish Jew want to stay in the new Poland if it was not an identification or sympathy with communism. The result was, firstly, that most of the surviving Jews who stayed in Poland were communists, secondly, that very many of the post-war communist rulers of Poland were Jews. There was a particularly large Jewish element in the Polish security service (the UB), perhaps as much as fifty per cent.

Since the defeat of Nazism the Jewish question played little part in Western European politics, but in 1968 it was still very much a living issue in Poland. It is not that Poles are naturally any more prejudiced than other nations, it is simply that, for various valid historical reasons, many of them associate the Jews with stalinist communism, the doctrine which caused Poland so much harm between the years 1939 and 1953.

It was, of course, not the first time that the Jews have been used as a whipping boy by a group of ambitious politicians intent on achieving power. In the mid-1960s Mieczysław Moczar was a middle-rank Party leader known mainly for his role in the wartime underground, as described by him in a book and later in a film. In September 1948 he had been identified with Gomułka's heresy and, in the words of the post-Congress resolution, 'allowed to remain in the ranks of the Central Committee only through regard to the services rendered by him during the partisan struggle'. In 1967 he began a well-organised bid for power, using as his two main weapons an admirable campaign to unite the pro- and anti-communist wartime underground movements and a deplorable campaign to investigate and purge Poland's Jews.

When war broke out between Arab and Israeli in June 1967 the members of the Soviet bloc sided with the Arabs and branded the Israelis as aggressors. The Polish government, though, carried the anti-Israeli campaign much further and eventually turned it into an attack on so-called 'Zionist elements' in Poland. How many Zionists there actually were in Poland is hard to estimate. Since 1956 any Jew who wanted to leave Poland for Israel had been allowed to do so. Logically, therefore, if a Jew by 1968 had not taken this opportunity, he was surely a Pole first and a Jew second, and therefore not a Zionist. But doubtless Jews everywhere felt sympathy and admiration for the Israeli effort in 1967. Jewish officers in the Polish armed forces were said to have given parties to drink the health of General Moshe Dayan, and there were cases of Jews going to the Israeli Embassy to express their solidarity, and even to volunteer to join the Israeli Army. The Jewish minority in Poland was small. These demonstrations could hardly be called a threat to Poland's security, but unfortunately there were senior officials in the government who saw that political capital might be gained by provoking a witch-hunt, by carrying out a purge of Poland's Jews, all of whom were by now under suspicion of 'Zionism'.

The spearhead of the anti-Zionist campaign was the Polish security service which, early in 1968, flung itself with gusto into the task of unmasking the Zionist menace. Two policemen-journalists, Tadeusz Walichnowski and Ryszard Gontarz, became specialists in the field. Gontarz would arrive at a newspaper editor's office with an anti-Zionist article, which he would request the editor to publish. The editor would not be quite sure whether the request was made in Gontarz's capacity as a journalist, or as policeman. The result was that the piece was usually accepted, and writings appeared which were a disgrace to Poland. Tadeusz Walichnowski's speciality was the short book, hastily researched and luridly printed, exposing the world Zionist conspiracy, its close connection with Hitlerism, Stalinism, West German revanchism and American imperialism, its hostility to socialist Poland. One of his books, called *Zionist Activists and Organisations*, begins with the words:

'The activities of Zionist organisation concern not only their own aims, but also the foreign interests of the western powers, particularly the USA. In the interest of the imperialist countries Zionist organisations carry out propaganda against the USSR and other socialist countries and sow political subversion. The aim of these organisations is to recruit for these activities all the Jews of the world.'[1]

In another pamphlet, *The Mechanism of Zionist Propaganda*, Walichnowski condemned *en masse* those Polish Jews who had emigrated to Israel after the war. 'Jewish émigrés from Poland now in Israel,' he wrote, 'number about 350,000. They fully supported the Israeli government's stand in its aggression against the Arab countries.' He continued:

'The Jewish émigrés from Poland have taken a firm stand on a position of Jewish chauvinism, of active anti-communism. They have fully supported the reactionary, pro-imperialist, neo-colonialist policies of the Israeli government. It is worth remembering that Jews from Poland, especially of the post-war emigration, occupy many important positions in the Israeli state apparatus, in the political parties, in economic life, etc. It is sufficient to point out that in the present Israeli parliament twenty-seven per cent of the members are Jews from Poland.'[2]

Having accused Polish Jews of anti-communism, Walichnowski next accused them of stalinism. In his book *Israeli Aggression* he wrote:

'The Israeli campaign was conducted by men, many of whom committed breaches of legality against Poles during the past period [i.e. the Stalinist period]. Having left Poland after 1956 they then arranged things so as to take part in aggression against the Arab countries. There are many of these officers, well known for their particular brutality during the past period, who are now behaving just as brutally as they did in Poland towards the Arab civilian population of the occupied areas.'[3]

Another of Walichnowski's books, *Israel, West Germany and Poland*, aims to show how leading Jews collaborated with the Nazis during the Second World War, and how Israel was now collaborating with West Germany to make trouble for Poland. Seemingly innocent photographs of German and Israeli leaders chatting together illustrated an alarming chronicle of German–Israeli anti-Polish machinations. A particularly nauseating series of four photographs, designed to prove Jewish–Nazi wartime collaboration, was captioned as follows: '1. The Warsaw Ghetto police prepare the Jewish people for transportation to Treblinka; 2. A death-transport of aged cripples, guarded by the SS and the volunteer Jewish police in the Warsaw Ghetto in 1942; 3. A round-up in the Warsaw ghetto in 1942, conducted with the cooperation of the volunteer Jewish police; 4. A souvenir photograph of a Jewish policeman together with an SS-man during the liquidation of the Warsaw Ghetto in 1942.'

These are a few samples of the sort of propaganda widely printed in Polish books and newspapers during the early months of 1968. Anxious to avoid if possible the charge of anti-semitism, the propagandists would announce that they had nothing against Jews as such, only against the Zionists. Some may even have seen the distinction as a valid one, but it was a nuance few Poles were able to appreciate. One could not be a Zionist unless one was a Jew. But the Jews were so few (no more than 30,000) and the supposed Zionist threat so enormous that in practice it became necessary to put almost all Jews to the question. They were summoned and asked their attitude to the Arab–Israeli war. Any answer less than an outright con-demnation of Israel was taken as proof of doubtful loyalty and resulted in demotion or dismissal. Since in Poland living accommodation and job often go together, many Jews found themselves not only dismissed but also thrown out of their apartments. 'Down with reactionary Zionism' became the slogan of the day. The problem was that few Poles had ever met a Zionist or knew what Zionism was. However much the Polish authorities might protest or differentiate, the simple fact was that the campaign became in practice an attack on Poland's Jews.

In March 1968 there took place the most violent civil dis-turbances since 1956. Alexander Dubček's 'palace revolution' two months earlier and his 'progressive' movement in Czecho-slovakia caught the imagination of Poland's youth. The spark was provided by the banning of a production of *Forefathers*, a play by the national poet Adam Mickiewicz, which was held to be anti-Russian. Only in eastern Europe, perhaps, could the banning of a play have provoked such violence and dis-order. It was not a 1956 situation. Dubček's movement was not enough to fire the Polish nation, the workers and peasants as well as the students and intellectuals. Polish students carried through the streets the slogan 'Poland is waiting for her Dubček'—in Polish it makes a pleasant rhyme thus: '*Polska czeka / na swego Dubczeka*'—and in essence the Polish students' demands were the same as the Czechoslovak people's, political reform and cultural freedom, but there were big differences in the two countries' situations. In Czechoslovakia the explosive force, pent up through years of stagnation and neo-Stalinism under President Antonin Novotny, consisted of the entire nation and was therefore quite uncontainable. In Poland the force was diluted by twelve years of relative freedom under Gomułka. Polish workers were in a more conservative mood than they had been in 1956, than their Czechoslovak comrades were in 1968. They did not actively support the students' demands for an end to censorship and for wider freedom of political discussion. The students were joined only by the intelligentsia, not by the workers, and so they became an isolated group which the authorities were able to suppress.

For a few days, though, it was touch and go, with thousands of students marching through the streets of the main towns and shock troops being flown from place to place to disperse them. The students employed the 'occupation strike', a weapon of protest used with success by pre-war communists, among others by Gomułka. Simultaneously the device was also being used in western Europe, where it was known as the 'sit in', and this lead newspaper reporters to make the obvious, though quite ill-founded, comparison between protest in eastern Europe and in the West.

The young Polish demonstrators, by and large, were not attempting to challenge Poland's socialist system. Everyone, even the most passionate anti-communist, accepted that to do so would be futile, dangerous, suicidal even. The students' demands were moderate, far more so than those of their fellows in Paris, Chicago, London or Berlin. They did not set out to commit violence or to destroy property, let alone to seize power. Perhaps the strangest thing about them is that they provoked such a panicky reaction from the authorities. It was a reminder to the world that in spite of twelve years of seeming stability under Gomułka, in spite of the universally accepted immutability of Poland's political system, Poland's rulers were still insecure, nervous men, ready to see the tiniest show of opposition as a threat not only to their authority but also to Poland's existence. Where Poles differed was in their evaluation of this threat. How much reform could Poland afford to make before provoking Russian intervention? It was a question which, with Gomułka in power, did not arise, although Polish officials when talking to liberal westerners would use the Russian threat to justify the repression.

The more dogmatic of Poland's rulers were quick to find links between the students and the 'Zionist fifth column', to label the protest as a Zionist plot. It was true that many of the leading protesters were of Jewish origin, the sons of former important Stalinist officials, and in the panicky atmosphere of the moment it was enough basis for some to draw wildly exaggerated conclusions. The Minister of the Interior Mieczysław Moczar was exploiting the crisis to build up his own authority and to make himself indispensable, while the First Secretary Władysław Gomułka was being torn apart by the two extremes.

Gomułka is no anti-semite. On the contrary his wife Zofia is Jewish, and there is evidence that veiled in the anti-Zionist campaign there was also an attack on him. Although he ruled Poland at the time of the anti-Zionism and must therefore bear some responsibility for the campaign, his part in it was half-hearted and on the whole restraining. In February 1969 a member of the Party Secretariat told the author that 'not all the manifestations of the anti-Zionist campaign were supported by Gomułka'. He was dragged along by events, by a situation he did not entirely control.

In a speech on 19 June 1967, a few days after the Arab–Israeli ceasefire, Gomułka said, 'A Pole may only have one fatherland—People's Poland.' The crisis was not yet under way, and one leading writer was able to joke, 'I agree, but why does the one fatherland have to be Egypt?' But during March 1968 the country was in such a serious state that jokes were out of the question. On 19 March, a few days after students sitting in at the University of Warsaw had been violently dispersed by a force of 146 policemen and 'activist workers',[4] Gomułka addressed an audience of 3,000 Party men in Warsaw's Congress Hall (the 'Sala Kongresowa', part of the Palace of Culture). The speech was broadcast on radio and television and was heard by many millions of Poles. He spoke for two hours, clearly under great emotional pressure, fighting not only for his own job as leader, but also, as he saw the situation, in order to stop Poland from disintegrating. The hall was festooned with banners, with such slogans as 'Down with the Zionists, agents of imperialism', 'Long live Polish–Soviet friendship' and 'We demand the unmasking and punishment of the political trouble-makers'. The speech was constantly interrupted by shouts from the floor, some encouraging, some challenging. As he mounted the rostrum he received a three-minute ovation before he began: 'Dear and respected comrades! Important events have taken place in our country during the past ten days. A significant part of the student youth of Warsaw and of other academic centres has been deceived and misled by forces contrary to socialism.'

This doubtful statement set the tone for a great oration, perhaps the most important he has ever made apart from his return-to-power speech of 20 October 1956. A comparison of the two speeches shows to what extent the wheel had turned full circle. The former fiery reformer, arguing logically and calmly for a Polish 'new deal', was now the ruler at bay, lashing out with great uncoordinated strokes at every enemy who came within range. One such was Pawel Jasienica, a well-known writer who had supported the students, whom Gomułka cruelly accused of betrayal. Arrested by the security police in 1949, Gomułka announced to millions of Poles, Jasienica bought his own life by denouncing his friends in the anti-communist underground. Another enemy was Janusz Szpotański, already serving three years' imprisonment for writing and distributing what Gomułka called 'a reactionary slander that spread sadistic poison of hatred for our Party and our state authorities'. It was, in fact, a comic opera recorded on tape satirising Gomułka and other prominent Poles which Szpotański had been in the habit of taking into Warsaw bars and playing to drinkers for the price of a glass of vodka. Him Gomułka accused of possessing 'the morality of a pimp'.

Gomułka spent the greater part of his speech exaggerating the anti-communist nature of the demonstrations, tarring moderate reformers with the same brush as the few extremists who were pressing for a complete break with Russia and Russian socialism. To him there was little difference between a reformer and a wrecker. It was a tactic he had used back in 1946 in his struggle against Mikołajczyk. Now, twenty-two years later, his oratory which in 1956 had been so hopeful and constructive was reverting to the exaggerated crisis-talk of the post-war period.

On the other hand what really marked the speech was a brave attempt to limit the anti-Zionist campaign. Towards the end of his speech he asked, 'Are there in Poland any Jewish nationalists, exponents of the Zionist ideology? Certainly there are. But it would be a misunderstanding if anyone were to wish to see in Zionism a danger to socialism in Poland, to Poland's social and political system.' And this was the whole point.

Zionism, if it existed at all in Poland, was the thought of a tiny group of people, a few hundred at the most. To make of this small group a national bogy, to launch a nation-wide campaign against it, was a piece of unnatural, provocative politics. Gomułka's statement on 19 March reduced the campaign's potency. Gomułka had gone along with the campaign up to a certain point, but he was now setting a limit. If Mieczysław Moczar and his men wanted to continue their purges beyond this limit, they would have to reckon with Gomułka as an opponent.

The Polish press reacted to Gomułka's speech in a similarly hysterical tone. For the next week newspaper headlines were the same; accounts of the thousands of telegrams of support flooding into Gomułka's office from all over Poland. 'We are with you, Comrade Wiesław', was the usual message, although others demanded 'punishment for the trouble-makers' and that the Party be 'purged of Zionists'. 'We want only to work in peace', was the message of one pious proletarian group. Another headline announced that 'The young people of Białystok demand the punishment of Paweł Jasienica'. The Party was announcing to the world how strong it was, which meant it felt itself weak and threatened.

It is hard, of course, to guess at the inner secrets of the Polish Party leadership, but it would seem that there was a stage during the summer of 1968 when Gomułka's power was in the balance. The Party's Fifth Congress was scheduled to open on 11 November, and all political groups were preparing for a lively debate and an even livelier vote. It is not that there was to be any question of Gomułka's re-election as First Secretary, his prestige and position as founder-in-chief were too great for him to be brutally voted out of office. The question was whether after November he was to be ruler in name or in deed, whether he was to rule a court or a kingdom. His challengers adopted a classic communist technique. Instead of attacking the ruler directly they attacked his juniors, his known favourite supporters. Men like Mieczysław Rakowski, the editor of *Polityka*, and Jerzy Morawski, the former Politburo member who was then Ambassador in London, were subjected to criticism which they only just managed to survive. In June Andrzej Werblan, a Central Committee member and leading ideologist, wrote a long exposé of the Jewish question in *Literary Monthly* (*Miesięcznik Literacki*) which was a direct challenge to what Gomułka had said on 19 March. As for the November Congress, three targets were set up for attack during the crucial Central Committee vote: Artur Starewicz, Eugeniusz Szyr and Stefan Jędrychowski. Szyr and Starewicz were both close to Gomułka and of Jewish origin. A vote against them would imply that Gomułka was 'soft' on the Zionists. Jędrychowski was adopted as symbol for attacks on Gomułka's economic and personnel policies. Many communists, and not only Moczarites, felt Gomułka was being too conservative in his choice of key officials. When he won office in 1956 he had adopted a policy of 'no revenge'. He had dismissed hardly any of the key officials who had been appointed in the Stalinist period. There had been no system of recruitment other than through personal influence, no system of retirement other than through dismissal or death. Once appointed to a top job a Polish official had tended to stay indefinitely. The fact that many such officials were of Jewish origin was seen by Gomułka's opponents as a further justification for the anti-Zionist campaign.

Starewicz was defeated at the preliminary election of Congress delegates in Zielona Góra. It was only by Gomułka's intervention that he was able to find a safe seat in the Cracow area and attend the Congress at all. Gomułka himself was forced to change his electoral area. Addressing a meeting at the Zerań car works in a suburb of Warsaw which he usually represented, he was asked by a questioner, either someone very naïve or very provocative, 'What is your attitude to mixed marriages between Poles and Jews?' Gomułka, who has a Jewish wife, took this as a personal insult and stormed out of the meeting. All in all 1968 was a terrible year for him, and in August it was further complicated by another great event, the invasion of Czechoslovakia. Morally and historically it was a tragedy for Gomułka, although in the short term it assisted him politically.

The 1968 Czechoslovak 'progressive' movement was in many ways similar to the Polish liberalisation of 1956. There was the same sudden popular enthusiasm for the communist party which seemed to have reformed itself, and for a communist leader who seemed to have become a hero. Gomułka and Dubček were both communists of long standing, both had fathers who emigrated to the United States. Both were born shortly after their families re-emigrated back to eastern Europe. During 1968 Dubček was subjected to the same heavy-handed

Soviet pressure that Gomułka suffered during the night of 19–20 October 1956, and during the weeks that followed. Surely Gomułka must have felt some sympathy with his young comrade at this hour of trial? It appears he felt none whatever.

A close colleague of Gomułka's told the author in 1969 that Gomułka never hesitated in urging his Soviet allies to invade. He had convinced himself that socialism in Czechoslovakia was in danger of breaking down, that the reform movement had run away with itself, that the Communist Party had lost control, and most importantly, that the country was becoming infiltrated by West Germany. He foresaw the creation of, at best, a neutral power vacuum, at worst, a hostile German-dominated regime along Poland's southern border. In a speech delivered shortly after the invasion (8 September) he said, 'There was more than enough proof to demonstrate the rapid development of the counter-revolutionary process in Czechoslovakia. . . . If an enemy places dynamite under our homes, under the community of socialist countries, it is our patriotic and internationalist duty to stop him by whatever measures are necessary.'

Likewise in a speech delivered on 31 August Premier Cyrankiewicz declared that 'this counter-revolution was directed both against Czechoslovakia and against all the socialist states, since in fact it sought to wrest Czechoslovakia from the socialist camp, from the Warsaw Pact, and to change the alignment of forces in Europe'. This was in the face of repeated announcements by Dubček and the other leaders, in fact of all politically aware and realistic Czechoslovaks, that there was no question either of a withdrawal from the Warsaw Pact or of any close economic or political ties with West Germany. Once more the Polish leaders were exaggerating the threat to their country in order to justify the use of violent repression.

Gomułka's decision to invade in August 1968 was perhaps the most dismal of his career. Throughout the crisis he was an undoubted hard-liner, continually pressing the Russians to take action. At this point it is worth recalling how in November 1956, when Gomułka was hero of the world, the villain of the world was the Hungarian Janos Kadar, who had just been treacherously installed by the Russians as ruler amid the carnage of unsuccessful revolution. Such is the irony of history that twelve years later it was Janos Kadar who urged moderation on the Soviet leaders. The puppet became the defender of sovereignty, while Gomułka the hero became the prejudiced aggressor. And it seemed like a fateful coincidence that their victim in 1968 was Czechoslovakia, the country which in 1956 had served as a brutal, unsympathetic wedge between a wonderful Polish–Hungarian solidarity.

During July Gomułka played host to the other four Warsaw Pact delegations who drafted a letter to the Czechoslovaks ordering them to desist. He was present at the Bratislava agreement of 3 August which followed the Czech–Soviet discussions in eastern Slovakia. The days of the Cierna talks he had spent a few miles away, just across the frontier in the Ukraine. Every evening after the talks a train would bring the Soviet delegates back across the border to confer with Gomułka and Russia's other chief allies: Ulbricht of East Germany, Kadar of Hungary and Zhivkov of Bulgaria. He agreed to the Polish Army forming part of a joint Warsaw Pact force to be held in readiness in case the decision was taken to invade. He agreed to an influx of Soviet units into southern Poland, to the use of Poland as a base for harassing the Czechoslovak leaders during summer manœuvres. He agreed that Poland, which has a long frontier with Czechoslovakia, much longer than the Soviet Union's, would provide the main base for the invasion. There is no question that he acted thus under compulsion. He could if he wished have stuck to his original principles of sovereignty and independence between communist parties and refused to join in the Soviet attack. He could not, of course, have prevented the invasion, but he could have told the Russians to go ahead and do their own dirty work without his assistance. But he did not, he helped the invading armies in every way he could.

It was exactly thirty years since Poland had last invaded Czechoslovakia. Shortly after the Munich Agreement (30 September 1938) Poland had seized the Cieszyn (Teschen) area and tried to persuade Hitler to agree to Polish annexation of Slovakia. Seldom in history have Poland and Czechoslovakia been on the same side, which may explain why, several months after the invasion, few Poles could be found to express much sympathy for the brutally wronged Czechs and Slovaks.

There were only two redeeming features about Gomułka's decision. The first was that it was honestly taken in what Gomułka believed was the best interest of Poland. Sadly, he was misinformed or else self-deceived about the real intentions of the Czechoslovak communists, which is why he did the deed. Of course, to mean well is no excuse. Some of the worst tyrants of history have meant well. But at least the image of Gomułka the 'honest man' was not contradicted. The second redeeming feature is that, in 1968 as in previous years, there were limits to Gomułka's destructiveness. He had no intention of putting the clock back to the Novotny era. On 8 September he spoke of Dubček acting 'in the haste of the just renewal which started last January after a delay of many years'. On 7 October in his speech to the Katowice Conference he said, 'We do not intend to defend, nor do we want to reactivate the policy conducted by the previous Czechoslovak leadership.' It was as if he was assuming his old middle-of-the-road stance between dogmatist and revisionist. In this same speech he made what seemed a statesmanlike call for a wider discussion of the differences between Czechoslovakia and her occupying 'allies'. 'Such controversial issues must be the subject of public inter-party discussion,' he said. 'It would be particularly useful if the Czech Party leaders would allow its press organs to reprint our statements. We on our part are ready to present in our press extracts from their press about the stand our Czech and Slovak comrades take on various problems. In this way the discussion could bring good results, both for communists in Czechoslovakia and for members of our Party.'

Gomułka sees no inconsistency between what he did in 1956 and what he did in 1968. 'We too had errors in our Party line,' he said on 7 October 1968. 'Then we had our year 1956. In our country too the reactionaries wanted to exploit the situation. But the Party was tightly holding the rudder of the country. It was itself eliminating the mistakes, and no one was imposing any policy upon it.' In Gomułka's mind the problem boiled down to one of power and control. In October 1956 he promised the Russians he would control a dangerous situation. They believed him, and how right they were. Twelve years later the boot was on the other foot. This time Gomułka was one of the sceptics, and Dubček was unable to satisfy his doubts.

The August invasion clinched the November Congress for Gomułka. Former waverers became convinced that now was not the time for drastic changes in the Polish power structure. The Russian leaders were in a strange unpredictable mood. Gomułka was now, extraordinarily, one of the few foreigners they trusted. They offered him their support, and this was enough to quieten the cries for change. Supporters of Moczar in particular saw that the time was not ripe for their hero's advancement. His brand of hard-line nationalism had an independent ring about it, and many thought he might try a more eccentric foreign policy, to lead Poland away from Russia, perhaps in a similar direction to that of Nikolai Ceausescu in Rumania. In November 1968 in Poland such ideas were out of the question.

Economic reform was the main topic of discussion at the Congress, and clearly it is this, not political reform, which is seen as the key to progress. In Warsaw early in 1969 Party officials described to the author future plans to shorten the cycle of industrial investment, to step up the production of consumer goods, to rationalise industry by permitting direct inter-factory link-ups. There was to be a blitz on car production, and a movement towards achieving convertibility of the złoty within the socialist bloc. It is issues like these that Polish communists regarded as important. By economic progress they would redeem Poland from the tragedies of 1968. Gomułka believes in doing first things first: consolidating Poland's frontiers and her very existence as a separate state, building up her agriculture and industry. He is impatient with those who feel Poland does not live by bread alone, who press for political reform and cultural freedom when—in his view—Poland cannot afford such luxuries.

When it came to the crucial Central Committee vote Gomułka's challengers were unable to defeat their three 'targets', but they relegated them to the last three places on the elected list. Of 1,693 delegate votes Szyr received 1,003, Starewicz 1,058 and Jędrychowski 1,076. Thus more than 600 delegates crossed out the three symbolic names on the ballot paper. Only seven delegates crossed out Gomułka's name. (These figures were given to the author in conversation by a member of the Central Committee.) Gomułka's men won by a clear majority, but it was far from unanimity, which is usually the aim in communist elections. Six hundred delegates were prepared to stand up and be counted, and to express their dissatisfaction, which proved that as late as November 1968 the opposition could not be as weak as all that. Mieczysław Moczar did not achieve his coveted membership of the Politburo, but he did become a deputy member, as well as a member of the Party's nine-man Secretariat. As a political force he was scotched, but hardly destroyed.

In January 1969 there were mild upheavals in the security ministry, resulting in the dismissal of the two most rampant anti-Zionists, Gontarz and Walichnowski. In February the Writers' Union met in Bydgoszcz and in spite of Gomułka's virulent attacks on individual writers during 1968, in spite of the numerous writers who had recently resigned or been expelled from the Party, there were no expulsions from the Union. People were beginning to relax and things to return to what in eastern Europe passes for normal. Gomułka was still there, his authority shaken, his historical image besmirched, but his power undiminished. The general feeling was that he would continue in office only until 1972. Even so he will have ruled Poland for sixteen years, while poor Dubček, dismissed on 17 April 1969, could only rule for sixteen months.

If the year 1968 achieved one thing, it was to end once and for all the legend of 'Gomułka the liberal'. But although it did this one service to truth, 1968 was a terrible year for Poland. It left Poland in the dock of world opinion, accused of anti-semitism, anti-Czech chauvinism, hysteria and immaturity. From being in 1956 the epitome of man's will to survive and remain free, she had become once again a mere reflection of Soviet orthodoxy. Her leader, once a man of triumph, promise and enigma, had become, whether willingly or unwillingly, a supporter of violence and aggression. It is sad to write thus of a man who is honest, brave and according to his lights patriotic. He is not a genuine villain, any more than he was a genuine hero in 1956. He is a victim of east European politics, so strange and violent to the western eye, which so often produces rulers who are men of extremes. And Gomułka is still less of an extremist than many who have reached the top in his profession. It was not his fault that 1968 happened and turned him from a falling but still living hero into an aggressor, jumping to the tune of the Soviet leaders, men who once plotted his death. It is unfair of chance to have cast him in the role of political cannibal, destroyer of his own creation—communist sovereignty. For Gomułka pioneered national independence and freedom of speech under communism, even though he ended by stamping them out both at home and in Czechoslovakia. Dubček was Gomułka's successor. Dubček was to an extent relying on the Polish experience of the mid-1950s when he began to draft his 'action programme' in 1968. Gomułka made the programme a possibility within the communist framework. He created the 'Polish variant'—a new marxist-leninist term used to describe a communist country different internally from the Soviet Union but entirely loyal to it and therefore to be tolerated by the Soviet leadership.

Gomułka can hardly complain about the ways of chance. If 1968 was a piece of shocking bad luck, 1956 was a million-to-one success. His stubbornness, bravery and mild unorthodoxy of 1945–48 made him a martyr in 1951 and a hero in 1956. These were roles of high drama to which Gomułka could not under normal circumstances have aspired. He is no genius, nor are his academic talents outstanding. It is not usually such men as Gomułka who challenge a world-wide ideology and who change it even while they are submitting to it. As for Czechoslovakia— perhaps it takes a Gomułka to catch a Gomułka. Converts tend to be the most fervent of orthodox worshippers, to resent and attack those who suffer the doubts and hesitations they have now overcome.

Gomułka had power thrust upon him. His greatness was that he helped make viable a form of communism which both his people and the Soviet leaders were able to find generally tolerable. His weakness was in his stubbornness and lack of flexibility—qualities which are admirable when a statesman is in opposition but not when he is in government—and in his prejudices and obsessions which lead him to make decisions in good faith that to the objective eye seem cruel and criminal. But no eye is entirely objective, and it will be many years before such a controversial man as Gomułka can be fairly judged. His achievements, both good and bad, have been so momentous. There is as yet no set of scales capacious enough to weigh him and work out his balance.

NOTES

CHAPTER II: EDUCATION AND AGITATION

1. A short pamphlet entitled '*Władysław Gomułka-Wiesław, Dzieje, Walki i Myśli*' (*Władysław Gomułka-Wiesław, his Activities, Struggles and Thoughts*), Łódź, 1947.

2. It is published in *The Communist Party of Poland in Defence of Polish Independence* (*K.P.P. w Obronie Niepodległości Polski*), Książka i Wiedza, Warsaw, 1954, p. 59.

3. See *Communist Affairs*, September 1965, p. 20. This and the following number of *Communist Affairs* contain two short biographical articles about Gomułka.

4. So claims Gomułka's 1947 biography, '*Władysław Golmułka-Wiesław, Dzieje, Walki i Myśli*'.

5. Writing in *Communist Affairs*, September 1965.

6. According to Hansjakob Stehle, *The Independent Satellite*, p. 24.

7. See Józef Kowalski, *Trudne Lata* (*Difficult Years*), p. 66.

8. See Ludwik Hass (ed.), *P.P.S.-Lewica, 1926–1931* (*The Polish Socialist Party, Left, 1926–1931*), p. 244.

9. See *ibid.*, p. 259.

10. See Kowalski, *Difficult Years*, p. 252–3.

11. Hansjakob Stehle, *The Independent Satellite*, p. 24.

12. Volume 51, pp. 84–5.

13. Henryk Rechowicz, *Ludzie P.P.R.* (*People of the Polish Workers' Party*), p. 30.

14. Issue of 10 December 1956. See also *Life*, 26 July 1956

CHAPTER III: THE COMMUNIST PARTY OF POLAND

1. These figures are quoted in Richard F. Staar, *Poland 1944–62*, p. 72, who quotes Jan Alfred Reguła (*Historia Komunistycznej Partii Polski*) (*History of the Communist Party of Poland*), p. 259, who quotes a KPP Central Committee brochure.

2. See Jan Kwiatkowski, *Komuniści w Polsce* (*Communists in Poland*), p. 21 and elsewhere.

3. Quoted in Jan Kwiatkowski, *Communists in Poland*, p. 14.

4. See Jan Alfred Reguła, *History of the Communist Party of Poland*, p. 105. He quotes the pamphlet *Sprawa polska na V Kongresie Kominternu* (*The Polish Affair discussed at the Fifth Komintern Congress*), p. 19.

5. *Ibid.*, p. 109, quoting Komintern pamphlet, p. 29.

6. *Ibid.*, p. 167.

7. See the communist periodical, *Nowy Przegląd* (*New Review*), August–September 1926, pp. 116–17, and elsewhere.

8. *Projekt Programu K.K.P.* (*Projected programme of the communist party of Poland*), p. 284.

9. See *Nowy Przegląd*, January–February 1933, p. 112, quoted by Reguła (*op. cit.*), p. 287.

10. Quoted from an article by Tadeusz Daniszewski, 'Droga Walki K.K.P.' ('*The Struggle of the Communist Party of Poland*'), which appeared in the November 1948 number of the communist ideological monthly, *Nowe Drogi* (*New Ways*), p. 144.

11. In his article on the Communist Party of Poland, contained in the Polish *Wielka Encyklopedia Powszechna* (*Great Universal Encyclopaedia*).

12. In his article on the *Communist Party of Poland* (*op. cit.*).

CHAPTER IV: THE 'IMPERIALIST' WAR

1. See *Polski Ruch Robotniczy w Okresie Wojny i Okupacji Hitlerowskiej* (*The Polish Workers' Movement During the War and the Nazi Occupation*), edited by Marian Malinowski and others, p. 59.

2. These figures were quoted by Gomułka in his speech that marked the twentieth anniversary of the foundation of the Polish Workers' Party. See Władysław Gomułka, *Przemówienia* (*Speeches*) *1962*, p. 16.

3. For the text of the 'secret protocol' see p. 78 of *Nazi–Soviet Relations 1939–41*, a collection of documents from the archives of German Foreign Office, published in Washington in 1948.

4. The text of the note appears in the Moscow daily *Izvestiya*, 18 September 1939.

5. The timing of the evacuation is thus pinpointed by Kowalski (*op. cit.*), p. 10.

6. He is Marian Malinowski, whose articles in the weekly *Polityka*, Nos. 40–4, 1957, are quoted in many places in this chapter.

7. For instance, by Stanisław Mikołajczyk in *The Pattern of Soviet Domination*, p. 15.

8. See *Polish Workers' Movement During the War and the Nazi Occupation*, p. 98.

9. The transcript of a document claiming to be the text of the order for these arrests appeared on page 248 of *Biała Księga* (*White Book*), published in Paris by Instytut Literacki.

10. The article appeared in the Moscow periodical *Communist International*, number 8–9, 1939, pp. 23–6.

11. See articles by Marian Malinowski which appeared in *Polityka* during October 1957.

12. So claims the Polish émigré historian Władysław Pobóg-Malinowski in his *Najnowsza Historia Polityczna Polski* (*Modern Political History of Poland*), Part III, 1939–45, p. 400.

13. See Stanisław Zabiełło, *Sprawa Polska Podczas II wojny światowej w świetle pamiętników* (*The Polish Question During the Second World War in the Light of Memoirs*), Warsaw 1958, page 246.

14. Anders's unusual wartime experiences are described in his book, *Bez ostatniego rozdziału* (*Without a Final Chapter*), 'Veritas', London, 1949.

15. This is described on p. 155 of *The Polish Workers' Movement During the War and the Nazi Occupation* (*op. cit.*).

16. See p. 178 of Ambassador Kot's book *Listy z Rosji do gen. Sikorskiego*, (*Letters from Russia to General Sikorski*, London, 1955).

17. See Władysław Góra, *P.P.R. w Walce o Niepodległość i Władzę Ludu* (*The Polish Workers' Party in the Struggle for Independence and People's Power*), p. 32, for this and subsequent telegram.

18. See Władysław Gomułka, *Przemówienia 1962* (*Speeches*), p. 27.

CHAPTER V: THE UNDERGROUND LIMELIGHT

1. Władysław Gomułka, *Artykuły i Przemówienia* (*Articles and Speeches*) *1943–45*, p. 565.

2. From a transcript of one of Światło's broadcasts on Radio Free Europe, Munich, during 1954.

3. See Władysław Gomułka, *Przemówienia* (*Speeches*), *1962*, p. 26.

4. The text appears in Władysław Gomułka, *Artykuły i Przemówienia 1943–45*, as Gomulka's first piece of published writing.

5. *Ibid.*, p. 13.

6. *Ibid.*, p. 15.

7. See *The Polish Workers' Movement During the War and the Nazi Occupation* (*op. cit.*), p. 265.

8. *Ibid.*, p. 306.

9. Quoted by Marian Malinowski in his article in *Polityka*, number 40, 1957.

10. Quoted from the 1 June 1943 number of *Okólnik*, as reprinted in Volume 2 of *The Polish Workers' Party's Conspiritorial Journalism (Publicystyka Konspiracyjna PPR)* 1942–45.

11. Figures quoted from *The Polish Workers' Party in the Struggle for Independence and People's Power (op. cit.)*, p. 165. A useful table outlining the fluctuating numbers of Polish communist party membership appears on p. 167 of Richard F. Staar's *Poland, 1944–62*.

12. According to the speech by Zenon Kliszko to the communist party Plenum in November 1949, as published in *Nowe Drogi*.

13. See Winston Churchill's account of the Teheran Conference in his book, *The Second World War*, Part 5, *Closing the Ring*, p. 357.

14. The text appears in Władysław Gomułka *Artykuły i Przemówiena (Articles and Speeches)*, *1943–45*, p. 34.

15. *Ibid.*, p. 61.

CHAPTER VI: ASPIRING TO THE SUPREME POWER

1. Włodzimierz T. Kowalski, *Walka Dyplomatyczna o Miejsce Polski w Europie, 1939–45*, p. 389.

2. Quoted by Kowalski, *ibid.*, p. 390.

3. Władysław Gomułka, *Artykuły i Przemówienia (Articles and Speeches)*, *1943–45*, p. 61.

4. *Ibid.*

5. *Ibid.*

6. See E. J. Różek, *Allied Wartime Diplomacy*, New York, 1958, pp. 237 ff.

7. See Winston Churchill, *The Second World War*, Volume 6, *Triumph and Tragedy*, p. 116.

8. Quoted by Mikołajczyk in his book *The Pattern of Soviet Domination*, p. 83.

9. An interesting discussion on this point is contained in Alexander Werth's *Russia at War, 1941–45*.

10. He is Norbert Kołomejczyk, writing in his book *The Polish Workers' Party. 1944–45 (PPR 1944–45)*, p. 27.

11. Foreign Minister Tadeusz Romer's account is quoted extensively by Włodzimierz T. Kowalski (*op. cit.*).

12. *Ibid.*, p. 451.

13. *Ibid.*, p. 457.

14. The text of the interview appears in Władysław Gomułka, *Articles and Speeches 1943–45*, p. 141.

15. See Winston Churchill, *The Second World War*, Volume 6, *Triumph and Tragedy*, p. 290.

16. The London-published *Polish Daily* (*Dziennik Polski*), 6 January 1945.

17. Quoted by Winston Churchill, *op. cit.*, p. 292.

18. *Ibid.*, p. 332.

19. *Ibid.*, p. 338.

20. *Ibid.*, p. 351.

21. *Ibid.*, p. 351.

22. The article, by W. Fordoński, appeared on 21 October 1944.

23. Speech to Central Committee Plenum on 6 October. See *Articles and Speeches*, p. 201.

24. See *Zarys Historii Polskiego Ruchu Robotniczego* (*Outline of the History of the Polish Workers' Movement*), *1944–47*, edited by Władysław Góra and others, p. 129.

25. See Winston Churchill, *op. cit.*, p. 385, for text of this note despatched on 7 April 1945.

26. See *Articles and Speeches*, p. 249.

CHAPTER VII: NATIONAL UNITY?

1. In his article 'The One-Season Prima Donna', which appeared in the Warsaw communist daily *Głos Ludu* (*Voice of the People*) 14 January 1947.

2. *Ibid.*

3. The text of this speech was printed in the weekly *Polityka* on 19 July 1958, and later published in *Articles and Speeches*, p. 293.

4. See Winston Churchill, *op. cit.*, p. 528.

5. It was H. Kołodziejski. See article by Jerzy Borejsza (*op. cit.*).

CHAPTER VIII: CO-VICE-PREMIER

1. See Stanisław Mikołajczyk, *The Pattern of Soviet Domination*, p. 152.

2. See Stefan Korboński, *Warsaw in Chains*, p. 24.

3. See Marian Turski, *Operacja Terminal* (*Operation Terminal*), p. 189, published by the Ministry of Defence, Warsaw, in 1966.

4. See Winston Churchill, *The Second World War*, Volume 6, *Triumph and Tragedy*, p. 575.

5. Reprinted in *Articles and Speeches, 1943–45*, p. 339.

6. Reprinted in *Articles and Speeches, 1943–45*, p. 428.

7. *Ibid.*, p. 444.

8. Quoted from Gomułka's speech, *ibid.*, p. 451.

9. See Władysław Gomułka, *Ku nowej Polsce* (*Towards a New Poland*), p. 142.

10. Quoted from his 7 December speech. See *Articles and Speeches, 1943–45*, p. 509.

11. *Ibid.*, p. 485.

12. See Władysław Gomułka, *W walce o Demokrację Ludową* (*In the Struggle for People's Democracy*), p. 305.

13. See his speech on 13 January 1946, at the opening of the Peasant Party Congress, published in *Głos Ludu* the following day and in *Articles and Speeches, 1946–48*, p. 9.

14. See *Zarys Historii Polskiego Ruchu Robotniczego* (*Outline of the History of the Polish Workers' Movement 1944–47*), p. 155.

15. See *Articles and Speeches, 1946–48*, p. 94.

16. See Staniłsaw Mikołajczyk, *op. cit.*, p. 166.

17. See *Articles and Speeches, 1946–48*, p. 46.

18. *Ibid.*

19. Stanisław Mikołajczyk, *op. cit.*, pp. 167 ff.

20. See *Articles and Speeches, 1946–48*, p. 94.

21. In an appeal published in his Polish Peasant Party (PSL) daily newspaper *Gazeta Ludowa* on 30 May 1946.

22. See Stanisław Mikołajezyk, *op. cit.*, p. 181.

23. In an interview published in *Głos Ludu* on 30 June 1946, and in *Articles and Speeches, 1946–48*, p. 154.

24. *Ibid.*

25. Also in the book of United States Ambassador Arthur Bliss Lane, *I Saw Poland Betrayed*. See also the broadcast by Józef Światło on 20 October 1954, a Radio Free Europe transcript. For a modern Polish interpretation of the elections, often surprisingly frank in its admissions, see Henryk Rechowicz, *Pierwsze Wybory* (*The First Elections*), 'Śląsk', Katowice, 1963.

26. See Stanisław Mikołajczyk, *op. cit.*, p. 218.

27. See *The Times* of London, 20 January 1947.

28. See *Articles and Speeches, 1946–48*, p. 342.

29. See the January 1947 edition of *Nowe Drogi*, p. 25.

30. See *Articles and Speeches, 1946–48*, p. 383.

31. *Ibid.*, p. 238.

32. See *Outline of the History of the Polish Workers' Movement, 1944–47* (*op. cit.*), p. 193.

33. See *Articles and Speeches, 1946–48*, p. 435.

34. In his book *Avec Jacques Duclos à la banc des accusés à la réunion constitutive du Kominform à Szklarska Poręba* (22–27 September 1947).

35. *Ibid.*, p. 27.

36. Djilas describes it in *Conversations with Stalin*.

37. See *Nowe Drogi*, January 1947, p. 12.

38. See *Nowe Drogi*, September–October 1948, pp. 40 ff.

39. *Ibid.*, page 55.

CHAPTER IX: HERESY

1. See *Nowe Drogi*, September–October 1948, p. 18.

2. *Ibid.*

3. *Ibid.*, p. 151.

4. See *Articles and Speeches, 1946–48*, p. 550.

5. Transcripts of all the speeches delivered at the Plenum, including those of Gomułka, are contained in the September–October 1948 number of *Nowe Drogi*. The quotations from the speeches in this chapter are all taken from this number.

6. For details of fluctuations in PPR membership, see Richard F. Staar, *op. cit.*, p. 167.

7. See *Trybuna Ludu* 18 December 1948.

8. See Alicja Zawadska-Wetz, *Refleksje pewnego życia* (*Reflections on a Certain Life*), p. 89.

9. See Aleksander Zawadski's speech to the November 1949 Plenum, as published in *Nowe Drogi* (special edition), p. 157.

10. Account as printed in *Trybuna Ludu*, 19 December 1948.

11. *Ibid.*

12. See the *Nowe Drogi* account of the November 1949 Plenum, *op. cit.*, p. 120.

CHAPTER X: STALINISM

1. For Bierut's speech see special issue of *Nowe Drogi op. cit.*, p. 6.

2. For Spychalski's speech see *ibid.*

3. See *Trybuna Ludu*, 21 February 1956.

4. See *Nowe Drogi, op. cit.*, p. 91.
5. For Gomułka's speech see *ibid.*, p. 111.
6. For Minc's speech see *ibid.*, p. 116.

CHAPTER XI: ARREST

1. See *Nowe Drogi*, No. 10 (October), 1956, p. 93.
2. *Ibid.*, p. 86.
3. See *Nowe Drogi*, No. 10 (October), 1956, p. 62.
4. This date was revealed by Jakub Berman in *Nowe Drogi*, No. 10 (October), 1956, p. 85.
5. A 'Radio Free Europe' transcript, broadcast on 25 October 1954.
6. See *Trybuna Ludu*, 31 July 1951.
7. An RFE transcript, broadcast on 28 October 1954.
8. See Alicja Zawadzka-Wetz, *Refleksje pewnego życia* (*Reflections on a Certain Life*), Instytut Literacki, Paris, p. 44.

CHAPTER XII: DISAPPEARANCE

1. See Bolesław Bierut, *O Partii* (*About the Party*), Warsaw, Ksiązka i Wiedza, p. 127.
2. See Józef Kowalczyk, *Bolesław Bierut, Życie i działalność*, Warsaw, Książka i Wiedza.
3. *Ibid.*, p. 110.
4. See Franciszek Jóźwiak-Witold, *PPR w walce o wyzwolenie narodowe i społeczne* (*The PPR in the Struggle for National and Social Liberation*), Warsaw, Książka i Wiedza, p. 259.
5. *Ibid.*, p. 260.
6. *Ibid.*, p. 263.
7. See report in *The Times*, 28 November 1952.
8. See *Rude Pravo* (Prague), 28 November 1952.

CHAPTER XIII: THE POINT OF RETURN

1. *Po Prostu* (Straightforward), 25 March 1956.
2. See *Przegląd Kulturalny* (Cultural Review), 5 April 1956.
3. *Po Prostu*, 24 June 1956.
4. In *Nowe Drogi*, March 1956, p. 36.

5. See for example the speech by Dworakowski on the 20th anniversary of the death of Marceli Nowotko, as reported in *Trybuna Ludu*, 28 November 1952.

6. See *Trybuna Ludu*, 7 April 1956.

7. In his speech to the Eighth Plenum delivered on 20 October 1956.

8. An interesting account of the Poznań riots is given by Flora Lewis in her book *The Polish Volcano*.

9. See the Soviet ideological monthly *Kommunist*, September 1956.

10. The November 1957 number. See also Lucjan Blit's Fabian tract *Gomułka's Poland* (March 1959).

CHAPTER XIV: OCTOBER

1. In an article in *Przegląd Kulturalny*, 25 October 1956.

2. A transcript of his speech was published in 1962 in Paris by the *émigré Kultura* under the title *Sześć Lat Temu . . . (Six years ago . . .)*, p. 61.

3. For a full transcript of the proceedings of the Eighth Plenum see *Nowe Drogi*, October 1956. This fact appears in Edward Ochab's speech, p. 112.

4. This important speech also appears in *Nowe Drogi*, October 1956. It was later published as a booklet in Polish and in many foreign languages.

5. For the text of the speech see *Trybuna Ludu*, 25 October 1956.

6. The text was published in *Trybuna Ludu* the following day.

7. It was published in Moscow's *Pravda*, 31 October 1956.

8. The sermon was published on 5 November in the Catholic *Słowo Powszechne* (The Universal Word). Excerpts from it also appear in English in *The Tablet*, 17 November 1956.

CHAPTER XV: POWER

1. According to a despatch by the *Polish Press Agency*, 19 November 1956.

2. See Zilliacus' book, *A New Birth of Freedom*, p. 201.

3. Published in *Trybuna Ludu* on 20 January.

4. A table illustrating the fluctuations in Polish agricultural collectivisation appears in *Poland 1944–62*, by Richard F. Staar, p. 91.

5. See his *Speeches, 1961*, p. 115.

6. See his *Speeches, 1956–57*, p. 84.

7. *Ibid.*, p. 393. These figures are much lower than those quoted by Western sources.

8. Quoted by Konni Zilliacus, *op. cit.*, p. 170.

9. See *Przegląd Kulturalny*, 21 September 1961.

10. Published in *Speeches, 1957–58*, p. 36.

11. Writing in *Communist Affairs*, November–December 1965, p. 22.

12. In a Radio Free Europe pamphlet called *Colonel Tykociński's Revelations*, p. 24.

13. Writing in his book *The Independent Satellite*, p. 22.

14. It appeared on 18 February 1958.

CHAPTER XVI: HIS DARKEST YEAR

1. Tadeusz Walichnowski, *Organizacje i działacze syjonistyczni*, 'Śląsk', Katowice, 1968, p. 11.

2. Tadeusz Walichnowski, *Mechanizm propagandy syjonistycznej*, 'Śląsk', Katowice, 1968, p. 18.

3. Jan Dziedzic and Tadeusz Walichnowski, *Wokół agresji Israela*, Książka i Wiedza, Warsaw, 1968, p. 78.

4. This is the figure announced by Gomułka. See his *O naszej partii* (*About our Party*), p. 653. His 19 March speech was also published the following day in *Trybuna Ludu* and the other main newspapers.

BIBLIOGRAPHY

ANDERS, W. *Bez ostatniego rozdziału* (Without a Final Chapter). *Wspomnienia z lat 1939–46.* London, 'Veritas', 1949.

BIAŁA KSIĘGA (White Book). Paris, Instytut Literacki, 1964.

BIERUT, BOLESŁAW. *O Partii* (About the Party). Warsaw, Książka i Wiedza, 1952.

Bolshaya sovyetskaya entsiklopediya (Large Soviet Encyclopaedia). 53 vols. Moscow, 1949–58.

CHURCHILL, WINSTON S. *The Second World War.* Volume Five: *Closing the Ring.* Volume Six: *Triumph and Tragedy.* London, Cassell, 1954.

DJILAS, MILOVAN. *Conversations with Stalin.* London, Rupert Hart Davis, 1962.

DZIEWANOWSKI, M. K. *The Communist Party of Poland.* Harvard University Press, Cambridge, Mass., 1959.

GOMUŁKA, WŁADYSŁAW. *Artykuły i Przemówienia* (Articles and Speeches). Vol. I: 1943–45. Vol. II: 1946–48. Vol. III: 1956–57. Vol. IV: 1957–58. Vol. V: 1959. Vol. VI: 1960. Vol. VII: 1961. Vol. VIII: 1962. Warsaw, Książka i Wiedza.

— *W walce o demokrację ludową* (Struggle for a People's Democracy). Warsaw, Książka i Wiedza, 1947.

— *O naszej partii* (About our Party). Warsaw, Ksiąka i Wiedza, 1968.

GÓRA, WŁADYSŁAW. *P.P.R. w walce o Niepodległość i Władzę Ludu* (The Polish Workers' Party in the Struggle for Independence and People's Power). Warsaw, Książka i Wiedza, 1963.

GÓRA, WŁADYSŁAW *et al. Zarys Historii Polskiego Ruchu Robotniczego.* (Outline History of the Polish Workers' Movement.) Warsaw, Książka i Wiedza, 1962.

HISCOCKS, RICHARD. *Poland, Bridge for the Abyss?* London, Oxford University Press, 1963.

Istoriya Polshi (History of Poland). Vol. III. Moscow, 1958.

JÓŹWIAK, F. *Polska Partia Robotnicza w walce o wyzwolenie narodowe i społeczne* (The Polish Workers' Party in the Struggle for National and Social Liberation), Warsaw, Książka i Wiedza, 1952.

KLISZKO, ZENON. *Z problemów historii PPR* (Problems in the History of the Polish Workers' Party). Warsaw, Książka i Wiedza, 1959.

KOŁOMEJCZYK, NORBERT. *P.P.R. 1944–45* (The Polish Workers' Party, 1944–45). Warsaw, Książka i Wiedza, 1965.

KOMOROWSKI, TADEUSZ BÓR. *Armia podziemna* (The Underground Army). London, Katolicki Ośrodek Wydawniczy, 'Veritas', 1951.

KORBOŃSKI, STEFAN. *Warsaw in Chains.* London, Allen and Unwin, 1959.

KOT, S. *Listy z Rosji do Gen. Sikorskiego* (Letters from Russia to General Sikorski). London, 1955.

KOWALSKI, JÓZEF. *Trudne Lata* (Difficult Years). Warsaw, Książka i Wiedza, 1966.

KOWALSKI, WŁODZIMIERZ T. *Walka dyplomatyczna o Miejsce Polski w Europie 1939–45* (The Diplomatic Struggle for the Place of Poland in Europe 1939–45). Warsaw, Książka i Wiedza, 1967.

KWIATKOWSKI, JAN KRZYSZTOF. *Komuniści w Polsce* (Communists in Poland). Brussels, Polski Instytut Wydawniczy, 1946.

LANE, ARTHUR BLISS. *I Saw Poland Betrayed.* Indianapolis, Bobbs-Merrill Co., 1948.

LEWIS, FLORA. *The Polish Volcano.* London, Secker and Warburg, 1959.

Malaya sovetskaya entsiklopediya (Small Soviet Encyclopaedia). 2nd edn. II vols. Moscow, Sovetskaya Entsiklopediya, 1937–47.

MALINOWSKI, MARIAN. *Z dziejów powstania PPR* (Events in the Establishment of the Polish Workers' Party). Warsaw, Książka i Wiedza, 1958.

MALINOWSKI, MARIAN *et al*. *Polski Ruch Robotniczy w Okresie Wojny i Okupacji Hitlerowskiej* (The Polish Workers' Movement during the War and the Nazi Occupation). Warsaw, Książka i Wiedza. 1964.

MIKOŁAJCZYK, STANISŁAW. *The Pattern of Soviet Domination.* London, Sampson Low, Marston, 1948.

MOCZAR, M. *et al*. *Ludzie, fakty, refleksje* (People, Facts, Reflexions). Warsaw, Ministry of Defence Publishing House, 1961.

OSÓBKA-MORAWSKI, E., and GOMUŁKA, WŁADYSŁAW. *Walka o jedność narodu* (Struggle for Unity of the Nation). Łódź, Spółdzielnia Wydawnicza "Książka", 1946.

POBÓG-MALINOWSKI, W. *Najnowsza historia polityczna Polski 1864–1945.* Vol. III, *1939–45.* London, 1960.

Publicystyka Konspiracyjna P.P.R. 1942–45 (Conspiratorial Journalism of the Polish Workers' Party). 3 vols. Warsaw, Książka i Wiedza, 1964.

P.P.S. Lewica, 1926–31 (The Polish Socialist Party. 'Left', 1926–31). Warsaw, Książka i Wiedza, 1963.

RACZYŃSKI, E. *Polska polityka zagraniczna w czasie Drugiej Wojny Światowej* (Polish foreign policy during the Second World War). London, 1953.

REALE, E. *Avec Jacques Duclos à la banc des accusés à la réunion constitutive du Kominform à Szklarska Poręba (22–27 Septembre, 1947).* Paris, Plon, 1958.

RECHOWICZ, HENRYK. *Ludzie P.P.R.* (Men of the Polish Workers' Party). Katowice, 'Śląsk', 1967.

REGUŁA, JAN ALFRED (PSEUD.). *Historia Komunistycznej Partii Polski w świetle faktów i dokumentów* (History of the Polish Communist Party in the Light of Facts and Documents). 2nd edition. Warsaw, Drukarnia 'Drukprasa', 1934.

ROOS, HANS. *A History of Modern Poland*. London, Eyre and Spottiswoode, 1966.

RÓŻEK, EDWARD J. *Allied Wartime Diplomacy: A Pattern in Poland*. New York, John Wiley & Sons, 1958.

SETON-WATSON, HUGH. *The East European Revolution*. London, Methuen, 1952.

STAAR, RICHARD F. *Poland, 1944-62*. Louisiana State University Press, 1962.

STEHLE, HANSJAKOB. *The Independent Satellite*. London, Pall Mall, 1965.

SYROP, KONRAD. *Spring in October: The Polish Revolution of 1956*. London, Weidenfeld and Nicolson, 1957.

TURLEJSKA, M. *Rok przed klęską* (The year before the disaster. September 1938–September 1939). Warsaw, Książka i Wiedza, 1962.

ULAM, ADAM B. *Titoism and the Cominform*. Harvard University Press. 1952.

W dziesiątą rocznicę powstania Polskiej Partii Robotniczej (The Tenth Anniversary of the Foundation of the Polish Workers' Party). Warsaw, Książka i Wiedza, 1952.

WETZ, ALICJA. *Refleksje pewnego życia* (Reflections of a certain life). Paris, Instytut Literacki, 1967.

INDEX